EARNINGS MANAGEMENT AND EARNINGS QUALITY
Evidence from Japan

Masumi Nakashima, Ph.D.

Hakuto Shobo Publishing

Earnings Management and Earnings Quality
: Evidence from Japan

ISBN 978-4-561-36210-6

Published by Hakuto-Shobo Publishing Company, Japan
5-1-15, Sotokanda, Chiyoda-ku, Tokyo, Japan
Zip 101-0021
www.hakutou.co.jp

First Published in 2015

© Masumi Nakashima, 2015
All rights reserved
Printed in Japan

No part of this book may be reproduced, scanned, stored in, or distributed in any printed, electronic form or by any means without prior written permission of both copyright owner and the publisher of this book. Please do not participate in or encourage piracy of copyrighted materials in violation of the author's rights. Purchase only authorized editions.

The greatest care has been taken in this book. However, no responsibility can be accepted by the publishers or author for the accuracy of the information presented.

Foreword

Our society is characterized by authority relations, relations of trust, norms, sanctions, and distribution of power. We exchange resources and events, which are the object of our attention in order to satisfy our interests. Previously, the necessary condition for these exchanges to take place was that each person must have been willing to sacrifice his or her resources or experiences for the resources or experiences of another. However, circulation of money negated this condition, and resulted in increases in the probability of succeeding in such transactions; it also brought the development of markets. A person who participates in exchanges through markets tries to make a decision that maximizes his or her own utility. This rationale of utilitarianism not only controls markets but also is the basis of social systems.

The players, who compose a market, are natural persons and corporate organizations including firms. Since the quality of a market depends on how they behave, it is vital to analyze it focusing on the players and the relationship of the interests, which exist among the players. The quality of the market is determined by whether the value of the resources and the events, which trade in at the market, reflect their prices properly. When there are no authority relations that influence the price among the participants, a mutual trust relationship regarding payments and the quality of the resources or events, and laws, norms, and sanctions that guarantee a safe transaction, there is a greater probability that a high quality market will appear.

The objects of an exchange are securities in a capital (stock) market. It can be said that a market is of higher quality when there is a greater degree of accuracy in the representation of corporate value per share. A fundamental analysis is required in order to presume the enterprise value. A fundamental analysis predicts a firm's ability to generate future cash flow by combining the trends of macroeconomics and industry, competitive advantage, corporate strategy and a firm's financial information. Therefore, when financial information is inaccurate, it is not possible to presume the proper corporate value, which results in a lower quality market. The quality of the financial information is an important element, which also influences the quality of a market. Because a central indicator of financial information is "earnings", this book discusses the quality of financial information using the concept of "earnings quality."

The concept of earnings quality is polysemous. When a firm acquires finance from many unidentified people by issuing securities, or when a firm lists in a stock exchange and circulates widely, a report of financial information is requested by the national law. The goal for local accounting standards is to become convergent with International Accounting Standards and International Financial Reporting Standards (IFRSs). However, local accounting standards (Generally Accepted Accounting Principles, GAAP), which prescribe financial information are different in each nation respectively, the differences in earnings quality in each country is the object of research. Recently, the differences in earnings quality, which is measured by IFRSs, SEC standards under the U.S. GAAP and Japan GAAP, is an issue in accounting standard setting bodies. Accounting standards are social choices that treat a country as a unit. Earnings quality that treats a country as a unit is impacted by the social environment including such factors as societal and cultural values, legal systems and customs, and business environment such as labor markets, capital markets, and product markets.

In chapters three through five of this book, the author focuses on the Japanese firms that prepare consolidated financial statements following the SEC standards. Although the firms whose parent firm is located in Japan, they have prepared consolidated financial statements following the SEC standards, since they received financial resources in the U.S. while stock markets in Japan were immature. These firms are the representative Japanese multinational firms as the third place of economic nation. Therefore, the reader needs to pay attention to the results from these chapters as they are the results regarding internal controls of consolidated financial information that combined many overseas subsidiaries.

I make a distinction between an individual choice and a social choice. The individual choices are choices of accounting policies, estimation methods and disclosure methods by individual firms. An individual choice is affected by many factors including but not limited to the firm's operating characteristics, governance and incentive systems, managerial backgrounds at the firm, corporate norms, sanctions on managers, auditor backgrounds and cultures, and the relationship between tax accounting and financial accounting. Therefore, the empirical studies are performed based on the hypothesis that these factors impact earnings quality, namely financial reporting quality. The objective of this book is to clarify the real condition of earnings management by managers and accountants who have an individual choice. This book analyzes earnings management by distinguishing between accruals management that managers affect and real management that impacts cash flow in order to control earnings. Also, the author documents what kind of changes in earnings management the firms generated focusing on the factors that impact earnings management in chapters three through five.

According to the COSO (Committee of Sponsoring Organizations of the Treadway Commission) Framework, control environment, risk assessment, control activities, information and communication, and monitoring are the standards to evaluate the effectiveness of internal controls. Because internal controls are the means for a manager to watch and supervise the business operations in which an employee is engaged. Managers also are regulated by the board of directors utilizing a structure of internal controls. The internal controls are also the means by which corporate governance becomes useful. The internal controls' impact on earnings management is through the discretional behavior of managers and accountants respectively, because players of a private choice in a financial report are a manager and an accountant. A difference in characteristics between accruals and real management raises the hypothesis that there is a different player for each earnings management.

Internal control is a process that is performed by a board of directors, managers and others that intends to provide reasonable assurance regarding the achievement of objectives concerning the effectiveness and efficiency of operations, reliability of financial reporting, and compliance with laws, and promotion of property preservation. Therefore, the implementation of internal controls is a basis of the reliability of a firm and an internal control report is one source of information for a person who is interested in a given firm.

According to the theory of "bureaucracy organization" by Max Weber, the organization and the members consists of a hierarchy of authority level. The objectives of internal controls are achieved by fulfilling given responsibilities that are defined at each authority level. However, as you can see from examples of employee fraud, ultimately, it is an issue of ethics for each individual within the organization. This means that maintenance of an internal control system is not full proof for measuring the reliability of the organization. Also, although earnings quality is regarded as an issue of financial reporting information within a firm, or organization, earnings management is an ethical issue involving the person who possess the authority over those earning, which means it is mainly discretional behavior. Therefore, it is interesting to resolve the research question of earnings quality through a sociological approach that includes the individual player.

In addition, it is of interest to implement a case-study approach, since there is a possibility that real management is a result as a business strategy such as tax avoidance measures or restructuring. The research questions of internal controls and earnings quality have been of interest and studied by accounting researchers previously. However, if considered from the above-mentioned point of view, it is also a problem of sociology and business management. Additionally, when we are reminded of the spirit of fair play in competition that Adam Smith emphasizes in *The Theory of Moral Sentiments*, we could see earnings quality as information that indicates the level of the social responsibility execution and the level of the manger's moral as an individual.

Professor Nakashima has contributed to literature of accounting in Japan for some time. She is one of the top researchers regarding earnings quality and internal controls. She has analyzed the present state of the Japanese accounting society through the approaches following to the models in the U.S. literature and communicates evidence from Japan to the world through the publication of her articles and the presentations at academic conferences overseas. This book is not only the fruit of her research regarding financial information, but also a result of research regarding internal morality of a firm, the director and its managers.

                        Yukiharu Kurokawa, Ph.D.
                        Professor of Accountancy
                        Faculty of Business and Commerce
                        Keio University
                        Tokyo, Japan

Foreword

It was a number of years ago that I first met the author of this book, Masumi Nakashima. It was at a Southeast Regional Meeting of the American Accounting Association and Masumi was working on her doctorate. We started a conversation regarding our mutual interest in accounting research and I was quickly struck by her curiosity to understand how accounting works in the real world (particularly in her home country of Japan). Since then, I have learned much from my friend, colleague, and coauthor. And, I have also learned more of her deep interest in understanding the accountancy and auditing profession in Japan. At the time of our initial meeting, I was concerned that her interest was going to be constrained to replicating prior academic accounting studies using Japanese data with little regard to considering Japanese culture, legal environment, and business institutions. Since that meeting, my concerns have been dispelled as Masumi has taken research questions of importance to our scholarly community and studied them in Japan.

Masumi brings an understanding of Japanese culture and business to the table as she conducts her research on important issues such as financial reporting quality and earnings management. Masumi Nakashima combines her insights into the Japanese business environment and provides insights from an international perspective of her home country that few others can accomplish. This makes her portfolio of studies an important contribution to our literature on international accounting issues. As you, the reader, work through her chapters, I believe you will realize the importance of a set of analyses on a number of important topics, conducted by the same researcher, and providing a deeper understanding of accountancy, auditing, and corporate governance within a Japanese environment. As a reader, work through the chapters as if they are parts of a common story – financial reporting quality in Japan. Ultimately, you will have learned from the insights her research provides the academic community as well as to regulators of our profession.

Masumi asked me to write this foreword and I was deeply honored to be asked. However, I have struggled to prepare a foreword that does justice to Masumi's work. Her passion for research combined with her relentless drive to produce research that is rigorous and addresses important issues is hard to describe. Probably the best way is just to encourage you, the reader, to be engaged as you read this book and learn for yourself. Enjoy!

> David A. Ziebart, Ph. D.
> PwC Professor of Accountancy
> Von Allmen School of Accountancy
> Gatton College of Business and Economics
> University of Kentucky
> Lexington, KY
> USA

Preface

Following a series of incidents of accounting fraud, the internal controls reporting system was introduced to restore the reliability of financial reporting. But what changes has it brought about in the quality of financial reporting by Japanese firms? Has the internal controls reporting system effectively accomplished its objective of improving the quality of financial reporting?

This book examines whether the Sarbanes-Oxley Act of 2002 (US-SOX) and the Financial Instruments and Exchange Act of 2006 (J-SOX) have an impact on earnings quality and the earnings management factor by focusing on the Japanese public firms. This book is divided into two parts: part one covers earnings quality of Securities and Exchange Commission (SEC)-registered Japanese firms, including Chapters three through five, and part two covers earnings quality and earnings management of public firms in Japan, including Chapter six and seven.

In the first half of this book, an empirical analysis using data on SEC-registered Japanese firms is carried out to investigate whether the internal controls reporting system has changed managers' discretionary accruals (earnings management); accuracy of forecasts of cash flows; the quality of accruals, which are indicators of the quality of earnings as financial reporting quality. Following Francis et al. (2008), earnings quality is influenced by two factors; the factor which reflects innate characteristics and the earnings management factor which reflects the financial reporting process. Also, the determining factors behind these changes are investigated.

In its second half, data on firms listed in Japan is used and the deficiencies of Japanese firms' internal controls is examined. Also, the quality of earnings and managers' earnings management are focused on and clarified in terms of the differences between Japanese firms that have disclosed material weaknesses in internal controls and control firms. Also, I examine whether earnings management of sample firms is accomplished through accruals management and discusses whether earnings management of sample firms is related to managerial opportunism. Finally, I compled the survey about managers, attitudes toward internal controls in the post-J-SOX period for the Japanese firms.

Chapters one, three, four, and five are based on chapters one, five, six, and seven of my book published in Japanese, *Earnig Quality and Corporate Goverance – Theory and Empirical Research* by Hakuto Shobo Publishing. The portion of chapter two is based on the Earnings Management from *Keiei Bunseki Jiten,* by Dobunkan Publishing. The condensed versions of chapter four, and seven are shown in *the Journal of Business Analysis,* Vol. 26, pp.62-73 and Vol. 28, pp. 21–36 in Japanese respectively. The condensed versions of chapter five is shown in *Accounting* Vol.177, No.6, pp.44-59 in Japanese. Chapter six is the reprinted version of the earnings quality and internal controls: Evidence from Japan, *An Analysis of Japanese Management Style, Business Researchers,* pp. 183-212, by Maruzen Planet Publishing.

Acknowledgements

I was able to complete this book through the guidance, comments and suggestions of many researchers. The research for chapter three through five came out on my dissertation in Japanese. I am grateful for the comments and suggestions I received from the members of my dissertation committee: Chair Hiyoyasu Akakabe, Co-Vice-Chair Katsushige Sawaki, Co-Vice-Chair Toshihiko Shiraki, Kazuo Yoshida, and Koichi Saito. Those chapters were further developed in writing papers in English for my following presentations. Chapter three is based on the paper that I presented at the 2009 Annual Meeting of the American Accounting Association (AAA) in New York City and the third Conference of Japanese Association for Research in Disclosure (JARDIS) in Nagoya International Center. Chapter four and five are based on the papers that I presented at the 2010 Southeast Region American Accounting Association (SEAAA) in Mobile, Alabama and the 2011 Annual Meeting of the AAA in Denver.

Chapter six is based on the paper that I presented at the 13th Asian Academic Accounting Association at Kyoto University in 2012. Chapter seven rested on the paper that I presented at the 2011 Annual Meeting of the AAA in Denver. Chapter eight is based on the portion of the paper that I presented at the 2013 Japanese Accounting Association (JAA) at Chubu University and the 10th Asia-Pacific Management Accounting Association (APMAA) in Bangkok.

Chapter eight analyzed the results of a 2012 survey with Shin'ya Okuda. The survey has the origin in the 2007 Kaken Project regarding Internal Controls and Governance with the representative, the deceased Kazuyuki Suda, Takashi Sasaki, Shin'ya Okuda, and Ryosuke Nakamura. The 2012 survey was carried out to realize the last wish of Professor Suda. The original members allowed me to use the data for the 2012 survey. I really appreciate their thoughtfulness. Specially, I would like to thank David A. Ziebart and Shin'ya Okuda who are my co-authors of other papers, and gave me precious comments for this book. Also, I am grateful to Yukiharu Kurokawa and David A. Ziebart for accepting the task of writing the foreword.

Chapter six is the reprinted version of the earnings quality and internal controls: Evidence from Japan, *An Analysis of Japanese Management Style, Business Researchers,* pp. 183-212, Maruzen Planet. I am grateful to Tsuneo Sakamoto, Editorial Chair and Hisashi Mori, the President of the Business Analysis Association (BAA) for approving the reprinting for me. In addition, I would like to thank Richard H. Fern, Douglas K. Barney, Natalie T. Churyk, Fumihiko Kimura, Kenji Shiba, Shigeo Aoki, Koji Oyanagi, Maria da Conceição da Costa Marques, Fouad K. AlNajjar, Masayuki Aobuch, Tadashi Ishizaki, Hidefuku Hiraoka, Susumu Ueno, Takashi Asano, Michimasa Sato, Shiro Ichinomiya, Tatsuo Inoue, Normah Hj Omar and anonymous reviewers and discussants of the AAA, the SEAAA, the JARDIS, the BAA, the JAA, and the APMAA for their helpful comments and precious suggestions. They helped improve all the aforementioned papers.

I appreciate the many valuable comments I received form the followingresearchers: Masaaki Aoki, Jeffrey H. Barker, Warren R. Elliott, Masahiro Enomoto, Takashi Hashimoto, Shinji Hatta, Joseph Heilman, Kazuo Hiramatsu, Noriyuki Konishi, Keiichi Kubota, Emily Harbin, Ichiro Mukai, Yoshio Matsushita, Ryoichi Miyazaki, Motoshiko Nakamura, Makoto Nakano, Yasuhiro Ohta, Takayoshi Okabe, Haruo Okamoto, Masashi Okumura, Saburo Ota, Kazuhiro Otogawa, Shota Otomasa, Ann M. Pletcher, Hisahiko Saito, Masao Sato, Manabu Sakaue, Akinobu Shuto, Satoshi Taguchi, Toshifumi Takada, Masako Takahashi, Fumiko Takeda, Hiromitsu Takemi, Terumi Takita, Yoshihiro Tokuga, Noriyuki Tsunogaya,Wade Woodward, Makoto Yada, Takashi Yaekura, Hidetoshi Yamaji, Noriaki Yamaji, JihwangYoon, Hiroshi Yoshida, and Madelyn V. Young.

I also thank Wendi A. Arms, Rebecca G. Dalton, Dell Morgan, and BeckyS. Poole at Converse College for their help for library services, and Tohru Furuyama,

Junich Ishibashi, and Kenji Murakami at Nikkei Marketing and Kenichi Oguchi at Pronexus for their professional data services.

This research including chapter three through five and this book are supported by a grant-in-aid for scientific research (C) of the fiscal year 2009-2011 (No.21530472) and a grant-in-aid for scientific research (C) of the fiscal year 2012-2014 (No.24530593) by the Ministry of Education, Culture, Sports, Science and Technology respectively.

I am grateful to Eiichiro Oya, President of Hakuto Shobo Publishing, who kindly accepted this publication in English although it is under difficult publishing parameters.

Finally, I want to thank my family and mother for their support and patience.

Contents

Foreword
Foreword
Preface
Acknowledgements

PART 1: Evidence on SEC-Registered Japanese Firms

Chapter 1   Introduction
Chapter 2   Literature Review
Chapter 3   Impacts on Accruals and Real Management
Chapter 4   Accuracy of Cash Flow Predictions
Chapter 5   Accruals Quality

PART 2: Evidence on Public Firms in Japan

Chapter 6   Internal Control Deficiencies
Chapter 7   Intention of Earnings Management
Chapter 8   Survey on Internal Controls
Chapter 9   Summary and Discussion

References
About the Author

Table of Contents

Foreword   i
Foreword   vii
Preface   ix
Acknowledgements   xi

PART 1: Evidence on SEC-Registered Japanese Firms

Chapter 1   Introduction —————————————————— 3
    1.1   Introduction   3
    1.2   The Relationship between Earnings Management and Earnings Quality   5
    1.3   The Internal Controls Reporting System in Japan   7
    1.4   A Comparison of the Internal Controls Reporting in Japan and the United States   9
    1.5   The Characteristics of This Book   10
        1.5.1   The Significance of an Analysis of Earnings Quality Impacted by Internal Controls Regulations
        1.5.2   The Importance of Analyzing the Influence of the Adoption of Sarbanes-Oxley Act on Earnings Management
        1.5.3   Grounds for Analizing SEC-registered Japanese Firms
    1.6   Outline of This Book   15

Chapter 2   Literature Review —————————————————— 24
    2.1   Framework of Earnings Management Study   24
    2.2   Quantitative changes in Earnings Management by Internal Control Reporting Regulation   25
    2.3   Intention of Earnings Management   26
    2.4   Trade-off between Accruals and Real Management   26
    2.5   The Effects of Real Management   30

Chapter 3   Impacts on Accruals and Real Management—————————— 32
    3.1   Introduction   32
    3.2   Previous Studies   34
    3.3   Determinants of Accruals and Real Management   36
        3.3.1   Accruals Management and Real Management
        3.3.2   Incentives for Accruals and Real Management

  3.3.3 Restraints for Accruals and Real Management
 3.4 Hypothesis Developments 41
 3.5 Data and Research Design 47
  3.5.1 Data and Sample
  3.5.2 Accruals Management Measures and Real Management Measures
  3.5.3 Determinants as Incentives or Restraints
 3.6 Empirical Results 52
  3.6.1 Descriptive Statistics for Earnings Management Measures
  3.6.2 The Time-Series Plots of Earnings Management
  3.6.3 Test of Hypothesis 1
  3.6.4 Test of Hypothesis 2
  3.6.5 Test of Hypothesis 3
 3.7 Implication 58
 3.8 Conclusion 61

Chapter 4 Accuracy of Cash Flow Predictions — 65
 4.1 Introduction 65
 4.2 Hypothesis Development 67
 4.3 Research Design 70
  4.3.1 Cash Flow Prediction Models
  4.3.2 Accruals Quality Measures
  4.3.3 Earning Management Measures
  4.3.4 Testing Hypotheses
  4.3.5 Sample Selection and Data
 4.4 Empirical Results 76
  4.4.1 Descriptive Statistics and Time-Series Plot of MAPEs
  4.4.2 Tests of Hypothesis 1
  4.4.3 Tests of Hypothesis 2
 4.5 Conclusion 82

Chapter 5 Accruals Quality — 84
 5.1 Introduction 84
 5.2 Accruals Quality 85
  5.2.1 Accruals Quality Definition
  5.2.2 Accruals Quality Measures
 5.3 Previous Studies 87
 5.4 Hypothesis Development 87
 5.5 Data and Research Design 92

            5.5.1   Data and Sample
            5.5.2   Estimation of Accruals Quality
            5.5.3   Testing Hypotheses
      5.6   Empirical Results   95
            5.6.1   Descriptive Statistics and Correlation Results
            5.6.2   Tests of H1
            5.6.3   Tests of H2
      5.7   Conclusion   101

PART 2: Evidence on Public Firms in Japan

Chapter 6   Internal Control Deficiencies ——————— 105
      6.1   Introduction   105
      6.2   Features of Material Weaknesses   107
      6.3   Hypothesis Development   113
      6.4   Research Design   118
            6.4.1   Determinants of Material Weaknesses
            6.4.2   Accruals Quality Measures
            6.4.3   Earnings Management Measures
            6.4.4   Testing Hypotheses
      6.5   Empirical Results   122
            6.5.1   Paired t-test
            6.5.2   Correlation
            6.5.3   Logistic Regression Analysis
            6.5.4   Earnings Quality between Material Weakness Reporting Firms and Control Firms
      6.6   Conclusion   127

Chapter 7   Intention of Earnings Manegement ——————— 134
      7.1   Introduction   134
      7.2   Hypothesis Development   135
      7.3   Research Design   143
            7.3.1   Accruals Quality Measures
            7.3.2   Cash Flow Prediction Models Specification
            7.3.3   Earnings Management Measures
            7.3.4   Testing Hypotheses
      7.4   Descriptive Statistics   147
      7.5   Empirical Results   149
            7.5.1   Empirical Results 1: Evidence from Japan

        7.5.2   Empirical Results 2: Material Weaknesses and Predictive Errors

        7.5.3   Empirical Results 3: Intention of Earnings Management

   7.6   Conclusion   156

Chapter 8   Survey on Internal Controls ——————————————————— 158

   8.1   Introduction   158

   8.2   Survey Content and Responses   159

   8.3   Survey on Internal Controls   160

        8.3.1   Management Attitudes

        8.3.2   Internal Controls and Strengthening Governance

        8.3.3   Audit Quality

   8.4   Conclusion   165

Chapter 9   Summary and Discussion————————————————————— 170

   9.1   Summary   170

   9.2   Contribution   173

        9.2.1   Comprehensive Empirical Studies on Earnings Management and Earnings Quality

        9.2.2   Meanings of Internal Controls System in Japan

        9.2.3   Significance of the Intention of Earnings Management

   9.3   Future Research   174

        9.3.1   The Impacts of Internal Controls Regulation on Corporate Value

        9.3.2   Development of Earnings Management Studies

        9.3.3   Models for Accruals Quality and Discretionary Accruals

   9.4   Implications and Suggestions   176

References

About the Author

PART 1
EVIDENCE ON SEC-REGISTERED JAPANESE FIRMS

CHAPTER 1

INTRODUCTION

1.1 Introduction

The present form of institutional accounting is accrual accounting and in order to carry out periodical calculation of accounting earnings, managers select one accounting procedure from among the generally accepted accounting principles (GAAP). That is to say, accruals accounting includes judgments and estimates by managers. Suda (2000, p. 217) discusses the meaning behind setting accounting standards with flexibility from the following two points.

The first is an information-provision meaning, that, "As managers flexibly select accounting procedures from within the GAAP framework, it becomes possible to provide useful information related to enterprise value that is not reflected in non-discretionary elements." The second meaning is a profit and loss meaning reflecting actual conditions; "As GAAP are guidelines for the accounting behavior of firms in every business category, when processing one accounting fact, a number of different types of procedures and methods are accepted as being appropriate. Firms refer to their business category, scale, and other characteristics, and they value accounting judgments that can be selected and applied based on any of these characteristics. This is the principle of economic freedom. The periodical calculation of accounting earnings that shows the firms' actual situation is possible only by managers, and it is necessary to entrust them with carrying out periodical calculation of accounting earnings that reflects actual situations" (Suda 2007, pp. 17-19).

The framework for the calculation of accounting earnings that is based on accrual accounting with these two types of meanings was published in 2010 in the United States. In Financial Accounting Standards Board (FASB) Conceptual Framework for Financial Reporting No. 8 (SFAC8), Chapter 1, The Objective of General Purpose Financial Reporting, and Chapter 3, Qualitative Characteristics of Useful Financial Information (FASB 2010)[1], a central concept in financial reporting remained unchanged. FASB consistently locates accounting earnings at the center of financial reporting. In SFAC8, it indicates the following and this assertion has remained unchanged:

> A longstanding assertion by many constituents is that a reporting entity's financial performance as represented by comprehensive income and its components is the most important information (FASB 2010, p. 13, BC1. 31: The Significance of Information about Financial Performance).

> Accrual accounting depicts the effects of transactions, and other events and circumstances on a reporting entity's economic resources and claims in the periods in which those effects occur, even if the resulting cash receipts and payments occur in a different period. This is important because information about a reporting entity's economic resources and claims and changes in its economic resources and claims during a period provides a better basis for assessing the entity's past and future performance than information solely about cash receipts and payments during that period. (FASB 2010, p.4, OB17: Financial Performance Reflected by Accrual Accounting)

In clarifying both theoretically and empirically the superiority of accounting earnings information, coincidentally, in 1998 Securities and Exchange Commission (SEC) Chairman A. Levitt expressed his concerns for a financial environment in which the quality of earnings was trending downward due to managers excessively carrying out earnings management, and warned the related parties, such as managers, auditors, and analysts, to focus their energies into constructing a financial reporting system with high levels of transparency and reliability. (Levitt 1998) In accrual accounting with the meanings indicated above, it is acceptable for managers to conduct earnings management, but if they misuse this acceptance it can result in violations of GAAP in the form of accounting fraud, also known as window-dressing accounting. Despite the warning of Levitt, the consequences of misusing earnings management were the accounting frauds perpetuated by Enron and WorldCom.

The quality of earnings was a topic developed from the perspective of financial analysts from the second half of the 1980s to around 2000. However, due to a sequence of historical events–namely, following the series of incidents of accounting fraud around the start of the 2000s and then because of them, the enforcement of an internal controls reporting system–the effects were felt not only by those involved in accounting, but also by the regulatory authorities, the business world, and research societies as a whole, and it is no exaggeration to say that accounting earnings came to be seen from a qualitative viewpoint.

So to realize high-quality earnings, "The setting of accounting standards without room for selections is not to prevent the selection of opportunistic accounting procedures, and has left unchanged the selection of efficient accounting procedures (Suda 2000)", and the control of opportunistic earnings management by managers was expected. In other words, Suda (2007, p. 20) argued that, "What is necessary to prevent a window-dressing accounting is not comformed accounting standards, but appropriate corporate governance and well-organized internal controls system." This is to say, what is necessary to secure reliability for the quality of earnings is corporate governance and an internal controls system. Thus, an internal controls reporting system was actually introduced as a way for controlling opportunistic accounting procedures while maintaining informative accounting procedures and efficient accounting procedures that can mitigate asymmetry of information between firms and investors through accrual accounting.

1.2 The Relationship between Earnings Management and Earnings Quality

From a perspective of the structural components of accounting society, which are the accounting information supply process and the influencing factors, a concept of earnings quality are affected by social choice, which is the judgment by the institution that sets accounting standards that exist in each country and individual choice phase, in which a company's managers and the accountants controlled by them are able to choose from among several difference accounting options (Kurokawa 2008, pp.202-205). In particular, judgments and estimates carried out by managers who implement accounting policy influence the quality of earnings. "Earnings quality can be improved when accruals smooth out value-irrelevant changes in cash flows, but earnings quality is reduced when accruals are used to hide value-relevant changes in cash flows (Dechow and Schrand 2004, p. 7)

From this rathinale, if the quality of earnings is focusing on measured managers' intentions, earnings manipulation which is the form of earnings management that deviates from GAAP and opportunistic earnings management by managers will decrease the quality of earnings, as they do not accomplish their signaling objective. Thus, when market participants discover that managers are manipulating earnings, the quality of earnings is deemed to be low and thoritical valuation adjusted down wsrds (Kurokawa 2008, p.213). Within the research on the quality of earnings, research in which earnings management was set as the proxy variable as been conducted. (Lobo and Zhou 2006; Cohen et al. 2008; Epps and Guthrie 2010; Nakashima 2011).

In the definition of earnings management, disclosure management in the sense of a purposeful intervention in the external financial reporting process, with the extent of obtaining some private gain, as opposed to merely facilitating the neutral operation of process (Schipper 1989, p. 92) and "the active manipulation of earnings toward a predetermined target, which may be set by management, a forecast made by analyst, or an amount that is consistent with a smoother, more sustainable earnings stream" (Mulford and Comiskey 2002, p.3). "In the GAAP framework, reporting of earnings from the selection of accounting procedures by managers is a discretionary measurement process" (Suda 2007, p. 22). In this book, managers' earnings management is defined as "managers having the intention of changing the amount of earnings within the range of GAAP."

According to Francis et al. (2008), the quality of earnings is influenced by two factors; "the firm's attributes factor, which reflects the firm's business model and business environment," and the "financial reporting process factor, which reflects the financial reporting process (discretionary factor)". The firm's attribute factor is based on the business model and the business environment, but in contrast the discretionary factor is related to (1) managers' decision-making for financial reporting, including their judgments and estimates; (2) the quality of the information systems used to support the financial reporting; (3) monitoring, including internal audits and external audits; (4) governance, including the board of directors, compensation agreements, and the share ownership structure; (5) due diligence by the regulatory authorities (SEC regulations and compulsory enforcement by the SEC); and (6) financial reporting process of accounting standards, such as GAAP. A discretionary factor that influences the quality of earnings is managers' selections of accounting procedures. Earnings manipulation[2] that deviates from GAAP naturally influences quality, and even in the event of earnings management within the GAAP framework, quality is still influenced by whether accounting procedures are implemented through managers' opportunistic discretion or through information-provision-type discretion. Also, in earnings management, there is "accruals management" of accounting accruals and "real management" that influence cash flow, and so it is also possible that quality is changed by accruals management and real management.

In such ways, we can expect the quality of earnings to be influenced by earnings-management factors. Therefore, in this paper, changes to the quality of earnings that are influenced by earnings-management factors, and to earnings management itself, are analyzed. That is to say, the focus is placed upon verifying how the quality of earnings, as the quality of financial reporting due to the internal controls reporting system, and managers' earnings management, have changed.

1.3 The Internal Controls Reporting System in Japan

Starting with the United States' Sarbanes-Oxley Act of 2002 (US-SOX), regulations relating to internal controls have been introduced in every country in the world and have been given the generic name of the internal controls reporting system.

Since 1996, Japan has been reforming its financial system, and as one of this series of reforms it has progressed reforms of its accounting systems. But, in 2004, following a number of cases of accounting fraud such as Kanebo, the Financial Services Agency (FSA) implemented disclosure-related reforms with the objectives of securing and recovering the reliability of the markets. In November 2004, the

FSA published "Regarding Responses toward Securing the Reliability of the Disclosure System,"[3] and for a system for reviewing securities reports, which was one of the policies it deemed should be promoted, it issued guidance that all firms should independently check the information they disclosed, such as their shareholder conditions, and if necessary, submit a corrected securities report. One month later in December of the same year, the FSA published "Regarding Responses toward Securing the Reliability of the Disclosure System" based on the feedback it had received with regards to the independent checks by all firms, and it promoted the construction of an internal controls system to prevent and discover irregularities.

After it promoted the use of a system of confirmation reports by managers that it introduced as a voluntary system,[4] and from the fiscal period ending March 2005, it required disclosure of corporate governance-related information. This includes the status of the internal audit, the independence of outside directors and outside auditors, the system of audits by accounting auditors, and the number of years of continuous auditing, and also in the event that the disclosing entity has a parent company, the disclosing entity is required to disclose information on two items relating to the parent company, as it is considered important information in order to understand the management of the relevant disclosing entity and its corporate governance situation. In November 2005, the FSA implemented a priority review of the disclosure conditions of the relevant two items for all firms and requested corrections from firms when it recognized that the information disclosed was incorrect. As a result, 167 firms submitted corrected securities reports. Looking at this result, it seems that differences exist between firms in terms of the steps they are taking for corporate governance.

From 2004 to 2005, there were a series of accounting Fraud. In order to secure the reliability of the disclosure system, the FSA enacted the Financial Instruments and Exchanges Act of 2006 (J-SOX)[5] (Financial Service Agency 2007) in June 2006. Further, the Business Accounting Council (BAC), after first preparing it as an exposure draft in July 2005, in December of the same year published the "Standards for Management Assessment and Audit concerning Internal Control over Financial Reporting (draft)." Moreover, on November 21, 2006, the BAC Working Group published the exposure draft of the "Practice Standards for Management Assessment and Audit concerning Internal Control over Financial Reporting," and up to December 20, collected public comments. Following careful deliberation based on these public comments, on February 15, 2007, the BAC published "On the Setting of the Standards and Practice Standards for Management Assessment and Audit concerning Internal Control Over Financial Reporting (Council Opinions) (Business Accounting Counsil 2007). Following its publication, from the start of the next fiscal year, April 1, 2008, listed firms became legally required to carry out assessments by managers of their internal controls for financial reporting and to have them audited by a certified public accountant. Japanese listed firms began to work to put in place an internal-controls environment toward the enforcement of the J-SOX in April 2008.[6] The details of the process until the internal controls reporting system was introduced in Japan are similar to those of the U.S.

1.4 A Comparison of the Internal Controls Reporting in Japan and the United States

US-SOX and J-SOX were prescribed with the objectives of strengthening corporate governance, improving the quality of financial reporting, restoring the reliability of the capital markets in both Japan and the United States, and contributing to their development through having domestic firms and firms that are developing their businesses internationally in both the United States and Japan comply with the relevant laws and regulations.

In the J-SOX, the definition of an "internal controls audit" is "an audit by auditors of the results of the assessment of internal controls for financial reporting by managers" (Business Accounting Council 2006, p. 16). In the U.S. also, in AS2, an "internal controls audit" is defined as "an audit by auditors of the results of the assessment of internal controls for financial reporting by managers". In the United States, prior to the publication of the revised audit standards in December 2006, to comply with AS2 auditors were required to carry out the audit "of the results of the assessment by managers on the effectiveness of internal controls" and in addition an audit "to directly assess themselves the effectiveness of the internal controls". This was criticized for the burden it placed on auditors, who had to carry out multiple tasks. So in the Revised Audit Standards No. 5 (AS5) (PCAOB, 2007), the expression of opinion by the auditors on the "assessment by managers of the effectiveness of internal controls" was abolished, and instead they were required to carry out direct reporting; or in other words, only to directly provide an expression of opinion on internal controls. In Japan the "internal controls audit" (Business Accounting Council 2006, Article 1. 16) is defined as an audit by auditors who audit the financial statements on "the results of the assessment by managers of the effectiveness of internal controls relating to financial reporting." Therefore, the "internal controls audit" is implemented in Japan based on its own definition, and so in Japan direct reporting was not adopted.

1.5 The Characteristics of This Book

1.5.1 The Significance of an Analysis of Earnings Quality Impacted by Internal Controls Regulations

In Japan in April 2008, the internal controls reporting system was enforced and from the start of the following fiscal year, April 1, 2008, listed firms became legally required to have managers assess their internal controls relating to financial reporting and to have an audit carried out by a certified public accountant. In this research, data on firms applying SEC standards is used to verify the effects of the internal controls reporting system on the quality of financial reporting. Currently, with regards to US-SOX, a problem that has been pointed out is that the costs to prepare the documents to conform to the Act are excessive compared to the benefits of constructing the internal controls system.

In this book, changes to the quality of accounting accruals, the accuracy of cash flow predictions, and earnings management from before and after the adoption of US-SOX are clarified. Therefore, it is thought that it will provide one clue as to the costs and benefits of adopting US-SOX. In this research, data on Japanese firms whose stocks are listed in the U.S. markets based on SEC standards (SEC-registered Japanese firms) is used, and as evaluation scales for profits, the effects of the internal controls reporting system on "discretionary accruals," "the quality of accruals," and "the accuracy of cash flow predictions" are clarified, and the results of this verification for Japan are communicated. First, in this research, as an assumption for the verification of the effects of the internal controls reporting system on the quality of earnings, from results of the analysis using data on Japanese firms applying SEC standards and the results of previous research in the U.S., the accruals management of Japanese firms applying SEC standards in chapter three are shown to have been controlled since the adoption of US-SOX, which can be presented as evidence consistent with the findings of Cohen et al. (2008).

Second, with regards to the quality of accruals, this research is different to previous result on the point that in addition to the model of Dechow and Dichev (2002), the quality of accounting accruals is calculated from the model of Francis et al. (2008). In accounting accruals, managers select accounting procedures, but this process reflects elements such as non-intentional mistakes by managers and also their intentional management of earnings and the attributes of firms, and these elements cannot be ascertained by Dechow and Dichev (2002). But the quality of accounting accruals can be clarified using the model of Francis et al. (2008).

Third, in chapter three, the following are clarified and presented as new findings; changes to accruals management and operating cash flows, abnormal manufacturing costs, and the real management scale for abnormal discretionary spending before and after the introduction of the internal controls reporting system; whether these changes were due to governance regulations on debt or were due to managers' stock-market motivations of avoiding decreases in earnings and losses; and the factors determining the changes to earnings management. Fourth, there is a trade-off relationship between accruals management and real management, and it can be shown that following the adoption of US-SOX, accruals management has been controlled, and real management, particularly in the form of abnormal manufacturing costs, has increased for SEC-registered Japanese firm sample. Moreover, previous research had not shown that these changes to earnings management have affected the accuracy of cash flow predictions and the quality of accruals.

1.5.2 The Importance of Analyzing the Influence of the Adoption of Sarbanes-Oxley Act on Earnings Management

If I adopt the viewpoint of Francis et al. (2008), the factors determining the quality of earnings are the firm's attributes factor and the earnings-management factor. That is to say, the firm's attribute factor that reflects the business model and the business environment, and the earnings management factor that reflects the financial reporting process, affect earnings quality. Therefore, via the quality of earnings, these two factors have a direct effect on market outcomes. The firm's attributes factor is based on the business model and the business environment, while the earnings management factor is based on managers' decision-making, the quality of information systems, monitoring activities, governance activities, due diligence through GAAP.

As is shown in Figure 1.1, the internal control system is ascertained to be positioned upon the firm's innate characteristics and the earnings management factor, which are the factors determining the quality of earnings, and the focus is placed on verifying the quality of financial reporting and whether or not the internal controls reporting system influences the earnings-management factor. Or in other words, as the effects of the internal control regulations on the earnings management factor cannot be directly observed, as the outcome in this research, it is assessed whether the quality of financial reporting–that is to say, the quality of earnings–has been changed.

US-SOX stipulates that both a firm's CEO (Chief Executive Officer) and CFO (Chief Financial Officer) certify the accuracy and completeness of its financial statements and also prescribes criminal punishments for violations. This is a controlling factor to avoid earnings management in which the CEO and CFO report an excessive amount of profits. In particular, Article 906 provides for criminal punishments and liability for lawsuits in cases of window-dressing accounting (Lobo and Zhou, 2006), which can be expected to be a factor controlling managers' earnings management. In Section 3, whether there were changes to adoption behavior between before and after the adoption of the internal controls reporting system is analyzed. Also, Krishnan (2005) showed that the quality of internal controls has a significant relationship with the management quality.[7] If the adoption of US-SOX effectively establishes an internal controls system and results in the separation of authorities, managers' earnings management will itself be controlled, and at the same time, it will become easier to discover. Due diligence by external auditors and regulatory authorities due to the adoption of US-SOX may be a factor that controls earnings management. On the other hand, even after the adoption of US-SOX, managers' stock-market incentives (avoiding losses and decreased profits) and restrictive financial covenant means it is possible that earnings management will not be controlled and that instead, there will be a shift from accruals management to real management. Also, it is unclear whether governance through debt will become a control or an incentive for earnings management.

Also, through the effective implementation of the internal controls system and monitoring via this system, managers' earnings management will be controlled, and through an effective internal controls system itself, errors in estimates in the financial reporting process can be reduced, and the risk associated with operating activities and strategies that influence the quality of reported information can be mitigated (Browna et al. 2014, p.1). In this way, an internal controls reporting system influences discretionary factors and as a result, it can be expected to improve the quality of earnings of SEC-registered Japanese firms.

In chapter three, first of all data on SEC-registered Japanese firms is used and changes to accruals management and real management from before and after the adoption of US-SOX are verified, and then whether it has been a promoting incentive or a controlling factor for accruals management and real management is analyzed. In particular, whether motivation with regards to the securities markets, such as avoiding decreased profit and losses, or governance rules on debt, have had an effect on earnings management after the adoption of US-SOX is analyzed.

Changes to earnings management due to the internal controls reporting system can also be expected to influence the accuracy of cash flow prediction. Due diligence by external auditors and regulatory authorities based on the internal controls reporting system will control earnings management, and the establishment of an internal controls system will reduce errors in estimates. As a result, it is anticipated that the accuracy of predictions of cash flow and the quality of accounting accruals will also increase.

On the other hand, the internal controls reporting system has controlled managers' accounting discretions and increased real management. This can be expected to lower the accuracy of cash flow predictions and the quality of accruals. Therefore, in Capter four, assuming that earnings management has been changed, the changes in earnings management are considered to be one discretionary factor and the analysis is carried out, focusing on the accuracy of cash flow predictions as a proxy of earnings quality. Also, the changes in earnings management because of the internal controls reporting system can be expected to have an impact on the quality of accruals. Therefore, in Chapter five, the changes in earnings management are considered to be an evaluation scale for earnings quality, and the effects on the quality of accruals are verified.

1.5.3 Grounds for Analizing SEC-registered Japanese Firms

The subjects of analysis in this research are Japanese firms applying SEC standards. There are a number of grounds for doing this in this research. As some of the foreign companies registering for the standards at an early stage, Japanese firms listed on U.S. stock markets applied the standards from the fiscal year ended July 15, 2006 (COSO 2005)[8]. First, in this research, SEC-registered Japanese firms were set as the sample, and upon positioning them as Japanese and U.S. intermediate firms, it can be considered that this research has a certain level of significance as a pilot study for an empirical analysis of the Japanese version of the internal controls reporting system.

Second, it is possible to present this research as one grounds for research into changes in the quality of accounting information in ADR firms due to their adoption of US-SOX. In previous research in the United States, grounds have been presented in the form of the internal controls reporting system's effects in improving the quality of financial reporting, but what about the quality of financial reporting by SEC-registered Japanese firms? Japan has an independent corporate environment and there are likely to be international differences between Japanese firms and U.S. listed firms and other U.S. ADR firms. Through the application of SEC standards, the analysis will be carried out based on the premise that the environment that surrounds the firms is the same, such as complying with the same U.S. accounting standards and existing in the same U.S. regulatory environment, and this makes it possible to discover behavior unique to Japan with regards to internal controls and governance.

Third, according to the international classifications of Leuz et al. (2003), the characteristics of Japan are an economy marked by the intentions of interested parties with an undeveloped securities market, an owner-intensive-type economy, weak investor protection, strong enforcement of laws, and low risk of lawsuits. Following their listing on a U.S. stock market, Japanese firms with these characteristics–namely the characteristics of Japan, of weak investor protection and low risk of lawsuits–become subject to the regulations of the SEC and due diligence by investors, the legal environment of the United States, compliance with a litigious society, and a high level of disclosure to be compliant with U.S. accounting standards (Coffee 1999). In other words, they are required to provide information with a high level of transparency, and so listing in the United States may in itself function as a corporate governance mechanism (Machuga and Teitel 2007 p. 40). Listing on the U.S. stock markets signifies having to comply with the more severe U.S. accounting standards, and may also lead to a high level of transparency for disclosed information and having to meet the higher needs of investors (Coffee 1999, p. 24). Therefore, it may be possible to discover whether or not applying SEC standards is, in itself, a governance function. Going forward, in the event of a comparison of the effects of internal controls on the accounting information of firms listed in Japan, SEC standards can be examined as a governance variable.

Fourth, the Japanese Institute of Certified Public Accountants (Kansanin・Kansa hoshu Mondai Kenkyuusha 2008, p.4) has suggested that, as the amount of audit free paid by SEC-registered Japanese firms is extremely high, they should be analyzed separately from other firms listed in Japan. Also, it is highly likely that SEC-registered Japanese firms have different characteristics than firms listed in Japan as they have to comply with SEC standards, or have different governance structures, share ownership structures, and capital structures as a consequence of complying with SEC standards. So for these reasons also, they should be analyzed separately from firms listed in Japan. The subjects of the analysis in this research are SEC-registered that have experience of an internal controls reporting system through the adoption of US-SOX in advance of firms listed in Japan. It is considered that it might be possible to clarify their characteristics as Japanese firms that are also foreign firms, and also their characteristics as SEC-registered Japanese firms that are different from the characteristics of public firms in Japan. Toward this, an empirical analysis is carried out from chapters three through five.

1.6   Outline of This Book

The objective of US-SOX is to restore creditability which had declined due to a series of accounting frauds. Section 302 of SOX requires managers to certify all material accuracy and completeness. Section 404 of SOX requires managers to disclose internal controls reporting. Section 906 of SOX imposes penalties on managers for knowingly certifying financial statements that do not meet the requirements of US-SOX. Suda et al. (2011a; 2011b) suggest that Japanese managers have more positive attitudes for internal controls through the comparison in the survey results. Thus, an improvement in financial reporting quality is predicted since managers' estimation errors decreased and earnings management declined under effective internal controls systems after the application of US-SOX.

On the other hand, Graham et al. (2005) and Suda and Hanaeda (2008) give the implication that there is a possibility that managers might shift from accruals management to real management after the passage of SOX. Cohen et al. (2008) document that accruals management increased until the passage of US-SOX and real management declined prior to US-SOX and increased after the passage of US-SOX. It is predicted that decreases in accruals management will improve the accuracy of cash flow predictions but the increases in real management will reduce the accuracy and the accruals quality. Previous studies which focus on the effect of SOX regulations on financial reporting quality (Lobo and Zhou 2006; Cohen et al. 2008) suggest that US-SOX improves financial reporting quality. Therefore, this study examines whether financial reporting quality has been changed in pre-and post-US-SOX periods through analyzing various financial reporting measures.

The purpose of this Book is to analyze the effect of internal controls regulation on earnings quality (financial reporting quality)[9] and earnings management. In chapter one, I describe why academics, practitioners, and the public have focused on the qualitative aspect of earnings and I discuss various perspectives from which to analyze earnings quality and focus on accounting-based measures following the financial analyses perspective. This book follows Francis et al.'s (2008)[10] financial analysis perspective and focuses on accounting-based earnings quality measures. In chapter two, I review numerous studies regarding the financial reporting quality measurers and earnings management, and the effect of internal controls regulation.

On the basis of those theoretical discussions, I investigate whether earnings quality and earnings management have been improved in pre- and post-US-SOX periods. I take discretionary accruals, accuracy of cash flows predictions, and accruals quality as measures for financial reporting quality in this book. Also, I examine what determines earnings management, predictive accuracy of future cash flows, and accruals quality.

There is no consensus regarding definitions for earnings quality and there are different perspectives from which to analyze earnings quality. This book tests the changes in earnings quality in pre-and post-US-SOX periods comprehensively by testing three earnings quality attributes: discretionary accruals, accuracy of cash flow predictions, and accruals quality following one perspective. This book also provides evidence regarding the changes in financial reporting quality after the passage of US-SOX.

Evidence from the empirical tests regarding whether US-SOX regulations have an impact on earnings quality in the pubic firms in the U.S. by employing SEC-registered Japanese firm data gives a clue to the current controversy regarding the cost-benefits of US-SOX regulations. Results from the U.S. Stock Exchanges provide evidence for Japanese managers' behavior as a foreign firm in the U.S. market. This book is evidence from Japan for the effect of internal control regulations on earnings quality.

The first half of this book cross-tests the association between the changes in accruals management and real management in pre-and post-US-SOX periods and determinants of earnings management, such as capital market motivation and leverage regulation. I provides new insights into earnings management research. I find that after the passage of US-SOX, only opportunistic accruals management declined and accruals management which conveys private information remains through the association with predictive errors and accruals quality. Also I finds that real management reflects opportunistic management through the association with predictive errors and accruals quality. Also, I finds that increases in real management for production costs provide negative impacts on the accuracy of cash flow prediction and accruals quality. By finding that real management has a significant association with operating cash flow (OCF) volatility, opportunistic earnings management reflects real management through the association between OCF volatility and accruals quality.

Chapter three investigates whether accruals management and real management have been changed in the pre-and post-US-SOX periods. Discretionary accruals are estimated by the firm-specific time-series DeAngelo (1986) model and the cross-sectional Jones' (1991) model as accruals management measures. Abnormal operating cash flows, abnormal production costs and abnormal discretionary expenses are employed as real management measures following Roychowdhury (2006). Also, I examine whether the changes in incentive factors and restraint factors of such earnings management impact on the changes in accruals and real management in chapter five by setting up the following two hypotheses: (1) the association between earnings management and stock market motivation remains unchanged in the pre-and post of US-SOX periods and (2) the association between earnings management measures and leverage remains unchanged in the pre-and post of US-SOX periods.

I document that real management increases after the passage of US-SOX and that capital stock motivations and debt contracts restraint affect the decline of earnings management. I also document that operating characteristics and current performance affect accruals management and that operating cash flows affect real management. I examine how the increases in real management affect the predictive accuracy of future cash flows and accruals quality in chapter six and chapter seven.

Chapter four investigates whether the ability of earnings to predict future cash flows[11] has been improved in the pre- and post-US-SOX periods. Also, I examine what are the determinants of the accuracy of cash flow predictions by setting up the following hypotheses: (1) whether accruals quality impacts on the accuracy of cash flow predictions, (2) whether managers communicate their private information for future cash flows through accruals, and (3) whether real earnings management affects the accuracy of cash flows prediction. The results reveal that the accuracy of cash flow predictions by the earnings model has been improved slightly but the accuracy of cash flow predictions by the accruals component model has remained unchanged in the pre-and post-US-SOX periods. Also I investigate whether the associations between predictive errors and accruals quality, discretionary accruals and earnings management have been changed in the pre-and post-US-SOX periods.

I find that predictive errors are not associated with accruals quality in the pre-US-SOX period but predictive errors are associated with accruals quality in the post-US-SOX period. Following Bissessur (2008), who asserts that if predictive errors are affected by accruals quality, accounting information reflects earnings management, this suggests that information reflects estimation errors and opportunistic earnings management due to weak internal controls in the pre-US-SOX period, but information does not reflect opportunistic earnings management under the well-organized internal controls in the post-US-SOX period.

I also find that predictive errors are not associated with discretionary accruals and accruals in the pre-and post-US-SOX periods, suggesting that discretionary accruals and accruals do not reflect opportunistic earnings management but reflect managers' private information. This result reveals that predictive errors are not associated with neutral accrual management in the post-US-SOX period and that they are not associated with discretionary accruals in the pre-and post-US-SOX periods, but are significantly associated with abnormal production costs, suggesting that neutral accruals management in the pre-US-SOX period and discretionary accruals in the pre-and post-US-SOX periods do not reflect opportunistic earnings management but abnormal production costs reflect opportunistic earnings management.

It should be noted that there is a significant positive correlation between accruals quality and prediction errors and that both accruals quality are associated with predictive errors, suggesting that accruals quality has been affected by managers' estimation errors and earnings management. Also, accruals management has a significant explanatory power for prediction errors. On the other hand, real management, abnormal production costs, makes prediction errors larger in the post-US-SOX period. Managers of SEC-registered Japanese firms decreased opportunistic accruals management and increased real management, such as abnormal production costs, in general. In summary, there is no change in the ability of earnings to predict future cash flows in the pre-and post-US-SOX periods.

Chapter five investigates whether accruals quality has been improved in the pre- and post-US-SOX periods. I examine whether the increases in real management in the post-US-SOX periods and no change in the accuracy of cash flow predictions have an impact on accruals quality. I document that accruals quality from the Dechow and Dichev (2002) model improved but accruals quality from the Francis et al.'s (2008) model has remained unchanged through the time-series plot and the mean differences analyses. Also, I examine what determines the changes in accruals quality by setting up the following hypotheses: (1) Operating characteristics impact on accruals quality, (2) Investment in internal controls influences accruals quality, (3) Business fundamentals affect accruals quality, (4) Auditor quality impacts on accruals quality, (5) Operating characteristics such as volatility and operating cycle impact on accruals quality.

I find that operating characteristics, such as operating cycles and return on assets (ROA) and business fundaments, such as growth has a positive significant association with accruals quality, and that investment in internal controls has a negative significant association with accruals quality. Also, I find that production costs have a positive significant association with accruals quality. I document that determinants of accrual quality are operating characteristics such as operating cycles and ROA, business fundamental such as growth, investment in internal controls, and real management.

Also, I find that real management affects operating volatility and results in lower accruals quality. This suggests that managers smooth OCF through accruals management in order to reduce irrelevant volatility and results in no association with OCF volatility. On the other hand, managers smooth OCF through real management to hide value relevant volatility and results in association with OCF volatility. This is consistent with Dechow and Schrand (2004, p.7), suggesting that the significant associations between OCF volatility and accruals quality imply opportunistic earnings management.

Chapter six examines the type of material weaknesses for the firms that disclosed material weaknesses in the internal control statements (material weakness reporting firms), and the determinants of material weaknesses through a comparison between material weakness reporting firm and their pair sample (control firms). Also, I examines whether there are differences in accruals quality and earnings management between material weakness reporting firms and control firms. The analyses indicate the following: (1) The most frequent material weaknesses are involved with Period End/Accounting Policies, and this is particular to Japanese public firms. The reason is likely because Japan should set up the internal control system and have a requirement to disclose material weaknesses for public firms simultaneously. (2) Material weaknesses are significantly associated with segment, loss portion, and audit. The more complicated the transactions the firms have, the more loss portion the firms have, and non-BIG 4 auditors they have, the more material weaknesses they disclose. These results are consistent with the results of previous studies in the U.S. (3) While accruals quality for material weakness reporting firms does not improve, accruals quality for control firms improves. There are differences in accruals management and real management between material weakness reporting firms and control firm.

Chapter seven examines whether earnings management of sample firms is accomplished through accruals management and discusses whether earnings management of sample firms is related to managerial opportunism. This chapter

FIGURE 1.1 Framework of This Book

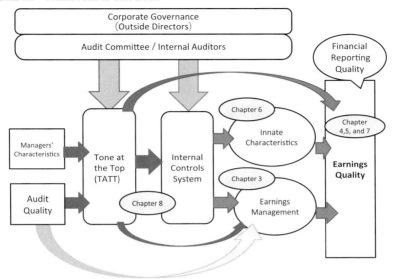

finds the following: Based on the results that predictive errors are significantly associated with accruals quality and that accruals quality is associated with discretionary accruals, it is likely that earnings management focuses on accruals management and that earnings management reflects managerial opportunism. Thus, managers of material weakness reporting firms have opportunism through accruals. They have not reached to move to real management as a method of earnings management by J-SOX.

Chapter eight explore of their attitudes toward the internal control in the post-J-SOX period through a survey research for managers in the public firms in Japan. Some implications can be shown as a result of survey analysis: First, although the managers are quite positive for setting up internal controls system and a target for earnings, it seems that they evaluate the manager's decision-making as low objective. Next, they do not expect highly about a direct reporting, suggests that the public firms in Japan seem to give a fixed evaluation to J-SOX which has not adopted a direct reporting. Moreover, many firms seem that they accept J-SOX positively by answering that it is effective for strengthening the internal controls system and governance. Furthermore, since they evaluate the quality of auditing for the financial statements and internal controls as high, it is said that Japanese firms realize that it is affirmative to the present condition of auditing. The following figure shows the framework of this book.

Notes:
1 FASB (2010) A replacement of FASB Concepts Statements No. 1 and No. 3.
2 Suda (2000) and Dechow and Skinner (2000) called the accounting procedures within the scope of GAAP "earnings management" and distinguished it from "earnings manipulation" that deviates from the scope of GAAP. In this book, a distinction is made between "earnings manipulation" as discretionary management that deviates from the scope of GAAP and "earnings management" as management by managers within the scope of GAAP as well.
3 In order to secure the reliability of the disclosure system, the FSA is promoting the following four elements: 1. A review system for securities reports, etc., 2. Supervision of certified public accounts, etc., 3. Maintenance of a disclosure system, 4. Requirements with regards to market makers.
4 In the fiscal year ended March 2005, more than 200 confirmation reports were submitted, including by the main financial institutions.
5 The law generally known as J-SOX refers to the part within the Financial Instruments and Exchanges Law promulgated in June 2006. It became generally known by this terminology in the media and elsewhere.
6 Suda and Sasaki (2005) and Suda et al. (2011a; 2011b) carried out a survey to ask managers of Japanese listed firms about internal controls. In the 2012 survey, basically the same questionnaire as the 2007 survey was sent to Japanese listed firms, and they surveyed the respondents on changes to their awareness about their firms' internal controls following the Kanebo window dressing accounting incident, and also before and after the promulgation of the J-SOX Act. The results showed that by the time of the 2007 survey, their awareness of internal controls had increased.
7 Krishnan (2005) assumed that the internal controls problem is related to the management quality and set each of the following as variables: whether or not the managers possessed CPA qualifications (managers' professionalism); even if senior managers had not undertaken formal training, whether or not they had experience of supervising accounting and financial work (managers' work experience); and whether or not they had come into contact with compulsory legal enforcement by the SEC (managers' ethics). Then, he verified whether or not these variables had a significant relationship with material incompleteness and showed that they had significantly negative relationships.
8 The Committee of Sponsoring Organizations of the Treadway Commission (COSO) published "Guidance on Internal Controls for SMEs" in October 2005. According to this Guidance, an internal controls reporting system was to be adopted by firms of every scale, but the timing of its adoption was to be considered. The adoption of the internal controls reporting system was to conform to the scale of the firm. The time periods of the adoption were to be the fiscal year that ends on November 5, 2004, the fiscal year that ends on July 15, 2006, and the fiscal year that ends of July 15, 2007, for domestic firms registering at an

early stage, foreign firms registering at an early stage, and domestic and foreign firms not registering at an early stage, respectively.

9 I define earnings quality as a summary indicator of financial reporting, following Francis et al. (2008).

10 Earnings quality has some perspectives to be evaluated; (1) financial analysis perspective which is supported by Dechow and Schrand (2004) and extended by Francis et al. (2008), (2) roles of contract and decision usefulness perspective, (3) decision usefulness perspective from Financial Accounting Standard Board's (FASB) Conceptual Framework, which is advocated by Schipper and Vincent (2003), and (4) comparative usefulness of cash flows v.s. earnings information perspective. Since measures are different depending on the perspectives, which perspective should be determined in order to discussing earnings quality. My perspective follows Dechow and Schrand (2004) and Francis et al. (2008). Although Francis et al. (2008) identify as accounting-based earnings quality; accruals quality, abnormal accruals, persistence, predictability, and smoothness, this study focuses on accruals quality as one of earnings quality measures.

11 I take predictability as earnings quality measure. This attribute also follows Dechow and Schrand's (2004, p.12) assertion that earnings are judged to be of high quality when they are more strongly associated with future cash flow realizations.

CHAPTER 2
LITERATURE REVIEW

2.1 Framework of Earnings Management Study

This book analyzes the effect of internal controls regulation on earnings quality and earnings management. Chapter three through five focus on changes in eanings quality and I review exsiting literature on quantitative changes in earnings quality in each chatper respectively. Therefore, I discuss earnings management study this chapter.

In earnings management research, the study which clarifies the current situation of a manager's accruals management before internal control report system introduction, and the research which solves the motive of a manager's accruals management have been conducted. Moreover, many studies which analyze the relevance of governance as a constraint factor of earnings management were also completed.

After internal control reporting system introduction, the research which verifies a quantitative changes in earnings management in the pre- and post-internal controls system, and the studies which make not only accruals management but also real management analysis increased. The studies that a trade-off between accruals management and real management has generated more attention paid after internal control report system introduction. It can be said that the internal control reporting system changed an actual corporate activity as a result, and also changed development in earnings management research itself, although the internal controls system was a primary aim to improve the reliability of financial information.

Chapter two focuses on whether earnings management research is how far documented currently. The actual condition of earnings management study, the motive of earnings management, the quantitative changes in earnings management by internal control reporting system introduction, the intention of earnings management, the trade-off between accruals management and real management.

2.2 Quantitative Changes in Earnings Management by Internal Control Reporting Regulation

Since US-SOX enacted in the world, the studies on whether earnings management has changed have been conducted in the pre-and post- US-SOX period (Lobo and Zhou 2006; Cohen et al. 2008; Epps and Guthrie 2010; Li et al. 2008; Nakashima 2011). Lobo and Zhou (2006) indicate that public firms report lower discretionary accruals after the US-SOX.

Epps and Guthrie (2010) investigated discretionary accruals using the firms that disclosed a material weakness and the control firms in the post-US-SOX periods. They suggested that discretionary accruals increased among firms that disclose a material weakness. Also, from a sample of firms that disclosed a material weakness, Epps and Guthrie (2010) analyzed the relationship between discretionary accruals and material weaknesses for three groups of firms; those with high negative discretionary accruals, those with high positive discretionary accruals, and those with low discretionary accruals. From the results of the analysis, they observed that firms with high negative discretionary accruals had a large, significantly negative relationship with material weaknesses, while firms with high positive discretionary accruals had a large, significantly positive relationship with material weaknesses. This indicated that firms with a material weakness and with positive accruals management carried out the task of upwardly revising earnings.

Li et al. (2008) analyzed the reaction of the stock markets to events that aimed to decrease uncertainty about the regulations in US-SOX and events that aimed to make the enforcement of US-SOX effective, and clarified that stock returns have a positive relationship with earnings management, but a negative relationship with auditing committee members' non-independence and non-auditing services by external auditors. That is to say, the findings of Li et al. (2008) show that through US-SOX, earnings management is controlled and governance is improved, and that investors expect positive results from US-SOX in the form of improvements to the accuracy and reliability of financial information.

2.3 Intention of Earnings Management

When selecting accounting procedures, managers have the viewpoint of choosing efficient procedures that result in the maximization of corporate value. But, in addition, they can have the viewpoint of choosing opportunistic accounting procedures in order to improve the financial situations of the managers themselves (Suda, 2000, p.358), and also the viewpoint of selecting accounting procedures to communicate information in order to improve investors' ability to predict financial statement (Suda 2000, pp.361-362). Through managers flexibly selecting accounting procedures, it becomes possible for them to provide useful information related to corporate value reflecting non-discretionary elements, which improves communication between managers and investors (Suda 2000, p.417).

The intention of earnings management, informativeness or opportunism has not much conducted. Nakashima (2012) defined informative earnings management as earnings management that is an appropriate indicator for investors to predict financial statement data and that improves accruals quality, and opportunistic earnings management as earnings management that is not an appropriate indicator for investors to predict financial statement data and that lowers accruals quality. She discussed the intentions of earnings management. Nakashima (2012) examined whether the earnings management intentions of firms that disclose a material weakness were opportunistim or informativeness, and showed that in the earnings management of firms disclosing a material weakness, it is highly possible there will be an opportunistic intention in accruals management that uses discretionary accruals.

2.4 Trade-off between Accruals and Real Managemnet

Since the enforcement of internal controls reporting regulations, there has been an increase in research investigating the trade-off relationship between accruals management and real management. Accruals management is more susceptible to due diligence by auditors and regulatory agencies than actual decision making on prices and production (Roychowdhury 2006; Gunny 2010) and it has been suggested that accruals management is controlled by due diligence. On the other hand, real management is not easily detected though it imposes costs (Cohen et al. 2008, p.759; Graham et al. 2005). In particular, following the introduction of US-SOX, managers had to guarantee to interested parties that they were not conducting accruals management and, for example, even if they selected appropriate accounting procedures, there are concerns about the risk that the regulatory authorities would conclude that the accounting procedure is an outcome for earnings management (Graham et al. 2005), and so naturally accruals management can be expected to be constrained.

Section 302 of US-SOX requires that public firms' CEOs and CFOs certify the accuracy and the completeness of the financial statements. In addition, Section 906 imposes criminal penalties on those who certify to the above while knowing that their financial statements do not satisfy US-SOX regulations. Due to the strengthened criminal penalties, the CEO and the CFO can be expected to constrain accruals management. Cohen et al. (2008) indicated that positive discretionary accruals with regards to unexercised options increased during the period of accounting fraud, but decreased significantly following the introduction of US-SOX, and that this decrease in accruals management after the introduction of US-SOX was in part due to the criminal penalties imposed on violations involving stock options.

Section 404 stipulates that the CEO and CFO must submit an internal controls report that assesses the effectiveness of their firm's internal controls. As indicated by the PCAOB, that "the objective of the internal controls system is to prevent and (or) detect errors and irregularities that would become misrepresentations on the financial statements" (PCAOB 2004), the internal controls reporting regulation requires that firms maintain an internal controls system to prevent errors and irregularities that can result in misrepresentations or "window dressing" of financial statements that violate GAAP, and it imposes on managers the obligation of ensuring that the internal controls system is working effectively.

Through an effective internal controls system, it can be expected that the problems of insufficient recognition standard and an incomplete seglegation of duties will be resolved and that managers' earnings management will be prevented. When there are weaknesses in internal controls system, the risk that weaknesses cause estimate errors and intentional earnings management by managers, increases. For example, overlooking intentional earnings management can lead to false disclosure (Ge and McVay 2005). Therefore, it can be expected that establishing an internal controls reporting system will constrain accruals management.

But, what about real management after the introduction of US-SOX? According to Graham et al. (2005), the reasons why managers came to prefer real management is that the accounting procedures of firms came to be examined closely by auditors, but in real management, it is not possible to easily see them all because they are normally considered to be a series of economic activities, that it is necessary to guarantee to interested parties that there is no accruals management in the books.

Managers conduct earnings management with the objectives of avoiding losses and impairment (Burgstahler and Dichev 1997; Suda and Shuto 2008). Public firms have the markets-related motivation of avoiding losses and decreases in earnings. Even if US-SOX is introduced, it can be expected to sustain these motivations as long as they continue to be listed. Therefore, after the introduction of US-SOX, it can be expected that managers will change their method of earnings management from accruals management to real management.

The results of the surveys in Graham et al. (2005) and Suda and Hanaeda (2008) suggest the possibility that managers shifted to real management in the U.S. and in Japan respectively after accounting scandals and the introduction of internal controls reporting systems. Based on the implications of these surveys, Cohen et al. (2008) investigated whether managers changed their earnings management method after the introduction of an internal controls reporting system. Cohen et al. (2008) analyzed whether managers had the trade-off between accruals management and real management from before and after accounting scandals and before and after the introduction of US-SOX, and found that accruals management increased prior to the adoption of US-SOX and then significantly decreased after its introduction, and that real management decreased before the introduction of US-SOX and significantly increased after its introduction. Cohen et al. (2008) indicated that the decrease in accruals management after the introduction of US-SOX was mainly due to a decline in profits-increase-type earnings management; or in other words, due to an increase in due diligence by investors, auditors, and regulatory authorities and the imposition of criminal penalties for violations related to incentive remuneration, there was a decrease in discretionary accruals after the introduction of US-SOX.

Badertscher (2011) investigated how overvaluations of stock prices had an impact on earnings management, and found that the managers of firms with overvalued stock prices, when there were stock options and bonuses linked to their firm's performance, they possessed a strong incentive to sustain the overvalued equity; that the longer the overvaluation was maintained, the more the volume of earnings management increased; and that in order to maintain the overvalued price, managers conducted accruals management at an early stage of the overvaluation. That is to say, it was shown that an overvalued stock price and the period of the overvaluation are determinants of managers' selection of earnings management.

Chi et al. (2011) and Burnett et al. (2012) investigated the relationship between high-quality audits and real management. Chi et al. (2011) particularly focused on firms with incentives to achieve earnings target and documented that there was a significant association between high-quality audits and real management. Burnett et al. (2012) also showed that when a high-quality audit consrains accruals management, firms tend to carry out real management in the form of purchasing their own shares in order to meet the forecasts of analysts.

Cohen and Zarowin (2010) investigated whether managers' preference for earnings management changes, depending on the capabilities of firms using accruals management (net operating assets) and costs (due diligence by the capital markets and the detection of potential penalties, and the difficulty in achieving profit targets), and found there to be a significant relationship between the quality of the audit, industries with a lot of lawsuits, the level of net operating assets, the Sarbanes-Oxley Act, and an increase in real management when there was a capital increase through public offering. Mangers use real management in the event of a capital increase through a public offering, and because of US-SOX, accruals management came to incur more costs. So after the introduction of the Act, it was found that firms shifted from accruals management to real management.

Zang (2012) examined whether managers' preference can be changed by a firm's ability to use accruals management which refers to net operating assets, and costs which refer to scrutiny by market, detecting potential penalty, and difficulty of reaching earnings targets. She showed that audit quality, the industry with more lawsuits, levels of net oprating assets, and US-SOX are significantly associated with increases in real management when public offering. She suggested that when public offering, managers had real management, and that since accruals management imposed costs to the firms in the post-US-SOX period, managers tended to change from accruals management to real management.

Chen et al. (2014) analyze the real condition of family firms by using family firm data and non-family firm data and documented that family firm has a tendency to carry out earnings management which sustain their reputation, and which can reduce costs. As a result of this analysis, it was found that accruals management of family firms was higher than that of non-family, but that the real management of family firms was lower.

2.5 The Effects of Real Management

Real management does not violate GAAP as long as the accounting for the transaction is correct, and therefore real managemnet does not result in a qualified audit opinion, or compulsory enforcement by SEC. But, it does have a material effect on earnings quality and also a significant impact on firms' future performance (Dechow and Schrand 2004, p.39).

Roychowdhury (2006) focused on three proxies of real management; sales manipulation, a reduction in discretionary expenditures, and over productions, and analyzed the effects they had on the level of OCF accompanying earnings management. Sales manipulation is when the managers generate additional sales through cutting prices and postponing payments, and in the relevant fiscal period, sales are made to temporarily increase. The cash revenue generated from the additional sales due to the price cuts cancels out the decline because of the lower prices, but decrease as gross income declines. Positive gross income is assumed and additional sales are recorded and so total profits in the relevant period increase. But production costs increase abnormally due to the low gross income from the price cuts. Also, the postponement of payments results in low cash revenues as long as the buyers don't indicate the discount to firms. This sort of sales manipulation decreases cash revenues in the relevant fiscal period and leads to high production costs compared to those from a normal sales level (Roychowdhury 2006).

Firms that reduce discretionary expenditures, such as R&D costs and advertising costs, can lower reported costs and increase profits. Actual cash revenues decline due to the reduction in discretionary expenditures and OCF in the relevant fiscal period increases. But on the other hand, the risk that future cash flows will decline is incurred. To increase profits, managers can produce products more than the level necessary for the expected demand. The fixed cost of each unit is lowered by the higher level of production. This lowers sales cost and firms can report a high gross income. However, firms will incur extra production and storage costs due to the overproduction, and as a result, cash revenues from operating activities are reduced to a level beneath that from usual sales. In such ways, excessive price cuts and over-production have the effect of abnormally raising production costs and reducing OCF. However, a reduction in discretionary expenditures increases OCF (Roychowdhury 2006, pp.340-341).

   Gunny (2010) and Yamaguchi (2009) documented the negative effects of real management. Gunny (2010) examined whether the four aspects of real management; the reduction of R&D costs in order to reduce costs and the reduction of sales costs and SG&A costs; the sale of fixed assets in order to report profits, sales manipulation through cutting prices and changing credit conditions, and excessive production in order to reduce sales costs, are related to satisfying two profit benchmarks (break-even point and year-on-year profits), and whether real management that satisfied profit benchmarks was related to future performance. The results indicated that real management is significantly associated to satisfying profit benchmarks, and that real management to satisfy profit benchmarks has a significant association with future performance, compared to firms that do not carry out real management and firms that do not satisfy the benchmarks. Yamaguchi (2009) analyzed whether profit-increase-type real management had a negative effect on future performance in the form of rate of return on net assets. As a result of this analysis, it was shown that firms that opportunistically increased profits through real management have significantly lower future performance than firms that do not carry out real management and firms that carried out real management but without opportunistic intentions. This finding is consistent with the basis of the argument of Roychowdhury (2006).

CHAPTER 3

IMPACTS ON ACCRUALS AND REAL MANAGEMENT

3.1 Introduction

Since internal control disclosure regulation was introduced in the world, several studies have been conducted on the impact of the regulation on financial information (Lobo and Zhou 2006; Bedard 2006; Leggett 2008; Cohen et al. 2008). This study examines whether the Japanese managers change earnings management preferences, that is whether accruals management and real management change in the pre- and post-US-SOX periods and investigates whether the determinants of changes in each earnings management are stock market motivation or leverage governance.

A survey by Graham et al. (2005) implies that the aftermath of accounting scandals at Enron and WorldCom and the certification requirements imposed by US-SOX may have changed managers' preferences for the mix between taking accounting versus real actions to manage earnings. Suda and Hanaeda (2008) also interpret that public firms in Japan might take a shift from accruals management to real management by the effect of accounting scandals and J-SOX regulation.[1] Cohen et al. (2008) investigate whether the prevalence of both accruals management and real management in the period of pre-and post-US-SOX periods and document that accruals management increases prior to US-SOX and real management increased after US-SOX. Based on the implication from the survey research and the empirical study, I examine whether managers have changed the way for earnings management in the pre- and post-US-SOX periods.

Previous studies on motivation of earnings management research find Japanese managers are willing to manage earnings to avoid loss (Suda and Shuto 2008), the motivation of the earnings management for avoiding loss is managers' compensation, manager's change, and finance contracting regulation (Shuto 2010). Suda and Sasaki (2008) conducts empirical studies regarding the impact on internal control system based on the survey results and documents that one of the determinants of a good internal control system is leverage regulation. Therefore, I investigate, given the impact of US-SOX's application on accruals management and real management, whether the changes in earnings management is through capital market motivations or through bank-oriented governance.

Capter three contributes to the literature as follows: First, since I document how the internal control compliance impacts on managers' earnings management as a whole, this result is one clue of considering cost-benefits of internal controls regulation for financial statement users. Second, I discuss accruals management and real management through focusing on six measures; conservative accounting management (C_AM), neutral accounting management (N_AM),[2] and aggressive accounting management (A_AM) as accrual management proxies, and abnormal OCF ($AbnOCF$), abnormal production costs ($AbnPROD$), and the sum of the standardized $AbnOCF$ and $AbnPROD$, Z_RM as real management proxies.[3] Third, I document that internal control regulation affects the association between earnings management and stock market motives and the association between earnings management and governance. While there are studies which focus on incentives for earnings management, this study focuses not only on motives but also restraints for earnings management. In addition, I employ a model which includes interaction terms between POST, and indicator variable equal to one if the year is the year when US-SOX is applied by the firm and zero otherwise, and control variables.

The rest of the paper proceeds as follows: Section two reviews the previous studies that examine the impact of the internal control regulation on financial information. Section three discusses the incentives and the restraints for earnings management. Section four provides hypothesis development. Section five describes data and research design. Section six discusses the tests and results. Section seven gives implications and Section eight summarizes and concludes.

3.2 Previous Studies

Accounting scandals such as Enron and Worldcom and a series of corporate failure lead to a decline in financial statement credibility for investors. In order to restore creditability to investors, US-SOX was passed in 2002. The main objective of US-SOX is to protect investors by improving accuracy and creditability of corporate disclosure following the SEC (U.S. House of Representatives 2002, p.1). While the US-SOX is not intended to change financial reporting system, prior studies document that the US-SOX has impact and changes to the financial information.

Cohen et al. (2008) investigate whether mangers change their earnings management in the pre-and the post-of US-SOX periods, focusing on accruals management and real management. They find that while accruals management increased prior US-SOX and decreased after the passage of SOX significantly, real management decreased in the pre-SOX but increased significantly after the passage of US-SOX. They suggest that the period after US-SOX was characterized by lower accrual-based earnings management and this decrease primarily resulted from a decrease in income-increasing earnings management. The contribution to decrease earnings management activities after passage of US-SOX includes the increased vigilance of investors, auditors and regulators, and greater care taken by mangers in financial reporting after the adverse publicity caused by the scandals.

Lobo and Zhou(2006) investigate the change in managers' earning management in the pre-and post-of US-SOX periods. First, they document that firms report lower discretionary accruals after US-SOX. Second, they find that firms incorporate losses more quickly than gains when they report income in the post-US-SOX period, based on the Basu's (1997) model measure. Through these results, they document an increase in conservatism in financial reporting following US-SOX. Lobo and Zhou (2006) predict that firms have incentives to use discretionary accruals to report an increase in income to avoid decrease and loss in income before discretionary accruals. They include these two dummies as independent variables and they provide that firms reporting small decreases in earnings before discretionary accruals employ income-increasing discretionary accruals.

Bedard (2006) finds that the absolute level of unexpected accruals increases in the year internal control weaknesses are disclosed. This result is consistent with an increase in the earnings quality and suggests that managers reverse voluntarily or at the auditor's request prior accruals that were too large in the internal control weaknesses disclosure year. She finds a decreasing the magnitude of unexpected accruals in the year of their firms report. Her result suggests that because of Section 404 formal internal control assessment process, firms improve their internal controls and auditors increase their audit effort and that US-SOX internal control requirements result in an improved earning quality.

Machuga and Teitel (2007) investigate whether Mexican internal control regulations improve earnings quality using a sample of Mexican firms listed on the Mexican Bolsa and Mexican firms listed on the U.S. stock exchange. They document improvement in income smoothing and timely loss recognition for Mexican firms listed on the U.S. stock exchange.

Leggett (2008) measures persistence as a proxy of earnings quality in the pre- and post-US-SOX periods. She predicts that earnings from real management cannot be sustained indefinitely without negative consequences. She considers that earnings persistence should increase. Also, she mentions that US-SOX has the potential to improve earnings persistence by reducing errors and inaccurate accruals estimations that would reverse in future periods. Also, the new auditing standards which make auditors monitor their clients more closely. The new auditor independence rules improve earnings persistence by reducing financial reporting errors and excessive accrual that reverse over a short time horizon. Also, new corporate responsibility rules hold CEOs and CFOs personally liable for financial reporting accuracy. The internal control rule mitigates financial reporting errors and excessive accruals that reverse in future periods. The increase in real earnings management and the timing differential between the recognition of gains and losses support a prediction that earning persistence will decrease after US-SOX. The reduction in discretionary accruals and the increased auditor independence will increase persistency. Although there are conflicting predictions, she documents that while persistence of total accrual and cash flow increase, persistence of operating cash flows remains unchanged.

These previous studies provide evidence that US-SOX regulation improves financial information quality. I consider that there must be a change in earnings management in pre-and post-US-SOX of periods behind the improved accounting information quality. Therefore, earnings management is discussed through their incentives and restraints in the next section.

3.3 Determinants of Accruals and Real Management

3.3.1 Accruals Management and Real Management

Schipper (1989, p.92) defines earnings management as a purposeful intervention in the external financial reporting process, with the intent of obtaining some private gain.

Dechow et al. (1996) assert that while earnings management is generally restricted to reporting practices that are within the bounds of GAAP, earning manipulation can occur both within and outside the bounds of GAAP. Mulford and Comiskey (2002, p.3) define earnings management as the active manipulation of earnings toward a predetermined target, which may be set by management, a forecast made by analysis, or an amount that is consistent with a smoother, more sustainable earnings stream[2]. Scott (2006, p.344) asserts that given that managers can choose accounting policies from a set of policies, it is natural to expect that they will choose policies so as to help achieve their objectives. These choices can be motivated either by efficient markets and contracts or by opportunism and rejection of market efficiency. And he defines earnings management as "the choice by a manger of accounting policies so as to achieve some specific objective. Therefore, I define earnings management as "earnings management is generally restricted to accounting choices and real cash flow choices that are within the bounds of GAAP which includes conservative accounting, neutral earnings, and aggressive accounting, following Dechow and Skinner's (2000) distinction.

Earnings divide into accruals and cash flows. This means that earnings managements are classified into accruals management, which means that managers produce managers' profound earnings by choosing accounting methods or estimating accruals, affect accruals, and real management, which means that managers take economic actions to impact on cash flows.[3] Accruals management includes "overly aggressive recognition of provisions or reserve," "overvaluation of acquired in-process R&D in purchase acquisitions," and "overstatement of restructuring charges and asset write-offs" as *conservative management*, "earnings that result from a neutral operation of the process" as *neutral management*, and "understatement of the provision for bad debts" and "drawing down provisions of reserves in on overly aggressive manner" as *aggressive management* (Dechow and Skinner, 2000). On the other hand, real management includes "delaying sales," "accelerating R&D or advertising expenditures" as conservative management and "postponing R&D or advertising expenditures" and "accelerating sales" as aggressive management" (Dechow and Skinner 2000).

Real management is earnings management in which a manager can take real economic actions that affect cash flows (Dechow and Schrand 2004, p.39). Roychowdhury (2006) defines real activities manipulation as departures from normal operational practices, motivated by managers' desire to mislead at least some stakeholders into believing certain financial reporting goals have been met in the normal course of operations. Real management includes decreasing R&D expenses and increasing sales by discounting products. Dechow and Schrand (2004) assert that real management is also not a GAAP violation and does not result in a qualified audit opinion or enforcement actions by the SEC. However, they assert that real management affects earnings quality.

Compared to accruals management research, there are a few which discuss real management. Both survey results of Graham et al. (2005) and Suda and Hanaeda (2008) show that managers state that earnings are the most important financial

TABLE 3.1 Accounting Fraud, Accruals and Real Management

	Accruals Management Within GAAP	Real Management
Conservative Accounting	Overly aggressive recognition of provisions or reserves Overvaluation of acquired in-process R&D in purchase acquisitions Overstatement of restructuring charges and asset write-offs	Delays sales Accelerating R&D or advertising expenditures
Neutral Accounting	Earnings that result from a neutral operation of the process	
Aggressive Accounting	Understatement of provision for bad debts Drawing down provisions or reserves in an overly aggressive manner	Postponing R&D or advertising expenditures Accelerating Sales
	Violates GAAP	
Fraudulent Accounting	Recording sales before they are realizable	
	Recording fictitious sales Backdating sales invoices Overstating inventory by recording fictitious inventory	

Souce: Dechow and Skinner (2000, p.239, Figure 1).

metric to external constituents and most of them report that they take real economic actions to meet earnings benchmarks. Barber et al. (1991) investigate whether concerns about reporting net income or increased income affect managerial decisions to invest in R&D and find that R&D expenditures is significantly decreasing when they cannot report net income or increase income. Thomas and Zhang (2002) document that inventory change is most strongly related to next year's abnormal returns and that firms with inventory increases (decreases) have experience higher (lower) levels of profitability, growth and abnormal returns over the prior five years, and those trends reverse immediately after the inventory change. They explain that the reason why the impact of the profitability shift is masked in contemporaneous reported profitability is because it is related to earnings management, potentially by misstating inventory balances, and also is related to variation in production levels altering cost of goods sold (COGS) by affecting the amount of fixed manufacturing overhead absorbed in to each unit produced.

Bartov (1993) documents that managers manipulate earnings through the timing of income recognition from disposal of long-lived assets and investments.

3.3.2 Incentives for Accruals and Real Management

I discuss the incentives for each earnings management.

Stock Market Motivation-To Avoid Decreases in Earnings or Losses

Burgstahler and Dichev (1997) and Suda and Shuto (2008) document that managers report earnings to avoid decreases in earnings and losses. Shuto (2010) documents that determinants of earnings management to avoid losses are contract incentives, such as managers compensation, management changes, and debt-covenant. Lobo and Zhou (2006) find that managers use discretionary accruals to avoid decreases in earnings and losses before US-SOX but decrease using discretionary accruals after US-SOX.

Management Compensation such as Options

Cohen et al. (2008) document that the increase in accrual accounting in the scandal period was associated with a contemporaneous increase in option based compensation but option based compensation decreased after US-SOX. They suggest that option compensation increases managers' incentives to manipulate earnings upward and explain that the reason why accrual management decreased significantly in the post-US-SOX period is because US-SOX introduced penalties on incentive compensation. They find that after US-SOX, provided stock and options increases incentives to manage earnings using real methods.

Incentive for Earnings Management though Debt Contract

Roychowdhury (2006) considers that debt contracts routinely have minimum tangible net worth requirements that increase annual earnings, but are not adjusted when the firm reports losses. At the very least, losses would make the covenants more binding. It follows that suspect firm years with debt covenants that make losses undesirable have a greater incentive to engage in real management. She documents that the presence of debt are positively associated with real management.

3.3.3 Restraints for Accruals and Real Manegement

I examine restraints for accruals and real manegement as follows.

Scrutiny by Auditors and Regulators

Accruals management is more likely to draw auditor and regulators scrutiny than real management (Roychowdlhury 2006, p.338). Graham et al. (2005, p.36) mention that auditors cannot readily challenge real economic actions to meet earnings targets that are taken in the ordinary course of business. Also, executives have a pressure that firms go out of their way to assure stake holders that there is no accounting based earnings management in their books and that they express a corporate fear that even an appropriate accounting choice runs the risk of an overzealous regulator concluding that accounting treatment was driven by an attempt to manage earnings. Cohen et al. (2008, p.759) assert that real management is more costly to shareholders, and harder to detect.

The Decline of Earnings Management by Penalty

Section 906 of SOX imposes severe criminal penalties for false certifications made knowingly or willfully (Geiger and Taylor 2003). Cohen et al. (2008) assert that for unexercised options this effect increased significantly in the SCA period for positive discretionary accruals and decreased significantly in the post-US-SOX period. The decline after US-SOX could be due to the penalties on incentive compensation introduced by US-SOX.

Lobo and Zhou (2006, p.58) assert that the increase in fines and regulatory scrutiny imply that the expected penalty for aggressive financial reporting are greater after US-SOX and they imply that this asymmetrical penalty function is that CEOs/CFOs have greater incentives to avoid using their discretion to overstate earnings and to be more conservative when faced with uncertainty and increased legal liability. (should not have a one paragraph sentence –make into two sentences)

Earnings Management Prevention through Effective Internal Controls System

The major objective of US-SOX is to protect investors by improving the accuracy and reliability of corporate disclosure and to restore investors' confidence the integrity of firms' financial reporting (U.S. House of Representatives 2002). To meet this objective, Section 302 of SOX directed SEC to require CEOs/CFOs to certify the material accuracy and completeness of the financial statements. Section 404 of SOX requires CEOs/CFOs report the assessment of internal control over financial reporting in the form of an internal control report with each annual report (Geiger and Taylor 2003).

Since PCAOB (2007, para.2) states "Effective internal control over financial reporting provides reasonable assurance regarding the reliability of financial reporting and the preparation of financial statements for external purposes," That means that US-SOX requires public firms set up effective internal controls system to prevent errors and opportunistic discretions which lead misstatements and violation of GAAP and CEOs/CFOs responsible for the internal control system's working well. Suda (2000, p.218) asserts that while tighter accounting standard constrains opportunistic accounting choices, at the same time also inhibit efficient accounting choices. Suda (2007) states that what is needed to prevent earnings management is not strict accounting standards, but appropriate governance and well-organized internal controls system. Bedard (2006, p.9) states that internal control weakness may increase the risk of error or managerial opportunism. Financial statements may be misstated because of unintentional errors caused by deficient control activities or through intentional misstatement in accruals from earnings management because of Internal Controls deficiencies such as inadequate monitoring of controls, ineffective accounting, internal audit or information technology staff and ineffective accounting and information system.

Ashbaugh-Skife et al. (2008, p.218) assert that if a firm has weak internal control, managers are less able to determine reliable accrual amounts, and a consequence of these unintentional misrepresentation is that financial information is noisy and less reliable, in addition, manager of firms with weak internal control can more readily override the control and intentionally prepare biased accrual estimates that facilitate meeting their opportunistic financial reporting objectives. Thus, under weak internal control systems, it is harder to stop intentional earnings management and unintentional errors for accruals choices.

Earning Management Mitigation through Governance

Osano (2005) asserts that leverage by capital structure works as monitoring as well as governance by ownership. Ofek (1993) finds that highly-leveraged firms react faster to a decline in performance than do less-leveraged companies, suggesting that a choice of high leveraged during normal operations subject the firms to the discipline that debt provides. High leverage appears to induce a firm to respond operationally and financially to adversity after a short period of poor performance, helping to avoid lengthy periods of losses with no response. Bushee (1998) documents that managers are less likely to cut R&D to reverse an earnings decline when institutional ownership is high, implying that institutions are sophisticated investors who typically serve a monitoring role in reducing pressure for earning management.

Earning Management Mitigation through Audit Quality

Becker et al. (1998) suggest that the discretionary accruals of the firm which is not audited by a BIG 5 auditor is larger than the discretionary accruals of the firm which is audited by a BIG 5 and that BIG 5 works as a restraints for earnings management, suggesting that auditor quality affect on earnings management.

3.4 Hypothesis Developments

There are several studies which document that US-SOX improves accounting information. Lobo and Zhou (2005) investigate the change in managerial discretion in pre- and post-US-SOX periods. They find a significant reduction in discretionary accruals in the post-US-SOX period relative to the pre-US-SOX period and a significant increase in Basu's (1997) measure, conservatism in the post-SOX period. They suggest that US-SOX have altered managers' discretionary behavior to make it more conservative.

Cohen et al. (2008) investigate whether both accrual-based and real earning management change between the pre-US-SOX period and the post-US-SOX period. They document that accrual-based earning management increased until the passage of SOX but the level of real earnings management activities declined prior to US-SOX and increased significantly after the passage of US-SOX. Based on the results, they suggest that firms switched from accrual-based activities to real earning management activities after the passage of US-SOX.

Altamuro and Beatty (2006) investigate whether the Federal Deposit Insurance Corporation Improvement Act of 1991 (FDICIA), internal control regulation has an impact on earnings persistence, earnings smoothing, earnings predictability, and the earnings response coefficient. They suggest that the FDICIA reforms lead to improvements in the characteristics associated with high quality earnings.

Based on the results, Graham et al. (2005, p.36) suggest that in the aftermath of accounting scandals at Enron and WorldCom and the certification requirements imposed by the US-SOX may have changed managers' preferences for the mix between taking accounting versus real actions to manage earnings. Also, Suda and Hanaeda (2008, p.61) suggests that public firms in Japan may take a shift from accruals management to a real action after the Kanebo scandal and the release of J-SOX. They point out that accounting regulation urges public firms in Japan to manage earnings through a real action and this would be a disadvantage to the Japanese economy.

Roychowdhury (2006) posits that there are two reasons for their willingness to take real activities as earnings management: (1) accrual management draws auditor and regulatory scrutiny more than real decisions about pricing and production, and (2) concentration on accrual management alone is too risky. That is, he asserts that if the realized year-end shortfalls between unmanipulated earnings and the desired threshold can exceed the amount by which it is possible to manipulate accruals, and when reported income falls below the threshold, real activities cannot be managed at year-end.

Lobo and Zhou (2006, p.64) assert that given and increased legal liability perceived by CEOs/CFOs following US-SOX and the asymmetrical implications of aggressive financial reporting versus conservative financial reporting, CEOs/CFOs are more likely to delay the recognition of good news in earnings in the post-US-SOX period. Cohen et al. (2008, p.789) finds that those individual with more stock and un-exercisable options were less likely to use accrual-based means to manage earnings. These results support the conjecture that after US-SOX, stock and options prices increased incentive to manage earning using real management. If managers expect earnings management using real management to be harder to detect, the passage of US-SOX is like to result in a substitution of real earnings management for accrual management. Zang (2012)[4] examines whether a trade-off between accruals management and real management, and finds that managers treat the two as substitute[5]. Also, she finds that real manipulation and accruals management are negatively related with their own cost determinants and positively correlated with earning management incentives.

Based on implications from the survey results (Graham et al. 2005; Suda and Hanaeda 2008) and these empirical studies regarding the effects of US-SOX, I predict that managers take a shift from accruals management to real management as a substitute after US-SOX. Thus, this leads to the following hypothesis:

H1: There is no trade-off between accruals management and real management after the passage of US-SOX.

As Suda (2007, p.34) mentioned, "Since stock market can see through managers' earning management, managers cannot impact on corporate value through earnings management," and determinants of earnings management has been considered focusing on debt contract, compensation contract, and government contract (Suda 2000). However, recently, Burgstahler and Dichev (1997) and Suda and Shuto (2008) provide evidence that managers manage earnings in order to avoid losses or decrease in earnings and to meet earnings target. Shuto (2010) finds that earnings management to avoid losses is related to contract incentives such as management compensations, management relief, debt-covenants, and earnings management to avoid decreases in earnings to meet target is associated with stock market motivation, such as equity incentives, earning value relevance, growth, and direct financing.

Graham et al. (2005) and Suda and Hanaeda (2008) suggest that the reasons of earnings management are (1) to build credibility with the capital market, (2) to maintain or increase our stock price, (3) the external reputation of our management team, (4) to convey our future growth prospects to investors, (5) to maintain or reduce stock price volatility, (6) to assure customers and suppliers that our business is stable, (7) our employees achieve bonuses, (8) to achieve or preserve a desired credit rating, and (9) to avoid violating debt-covenants. The reasons which have more answers, (1), (2), (4), (5) are related to stock market motivation. The reasons which have relatively less answers (7), (8) and (9) are related to contract incentives. Based on the survey results, as Suda and Haneda (2008) point this out, managers both in the U.S. and Japan manage earnings not only by considering the contracts but also by stock market.

The result of Graham et al.'s (2005) survey shows that 80% of CFOs manage earnings by reducing discretionary expenses such as R&D, advertising, and maintenance and 55.3% by delaying the start of a new project to meet an earning target. Suda and Hanaeda (2008) suggest that 67% of public firms manage earnings by decreasing discretionary expenses such as advertising. This means that managers manage earning through real management when the firm might come in below the desired earnings target. Graham et al. (2005) suggest that the reasons why managers have a willingness to take real managements are auditors can second-guess the firm's accounting policies, but they cannot readily see through real managements to are taken in ordinary course of business.

Thus, I predict that scrutiny does not allow managers to have accruals management and that manager's concerns for penalty and legal liability which has been introduced by US-SOX make aggressive management decrease as restraints. Therefore, is stock market motivation, such as to avoid losses or decreases in earnings related to accruals management or real management specifically? If the accruals management and real management has changed in the pre-and post-US-SOX periods, on what incentives or restraints of US-SOX impact for earnings management? Then, I post the hypotheses and test this:

H2: The association between earnings management and stock market motivation remains unchanged in the pre-and post of US-SOX periods.

Former chairman of SEC, A. Levitt (1999) states that corporate governance is important to report quality information as follows:

Information is the lifeblood of markets. But unless investors trust this information, investor confidence dies. Liquidity disappears. Capital dries up. Fair and orderly markets cease to exist. As the volume of information increases exponentially, the quality of information for investors and the market they comprise must be our signal concern. The promise of a global marketplace, like never before, depends on it. As more countries move to an equity culture, high-quality financial information becomes the currency that drives the marketplace. And nothing honors that currency more than a strong and effective corporate governance mandate. A mandate that is both a dynamic system and a code of standards. A mandate that is measured by the quality of relationships: the relationship between companies and directors; between directors and auditors; between auditors and financial management: and ultimately, between information and investors.

There is the Japanese original relationship between a firm and the big lender in Japan which is called "Main bank system" (Patrick 1994 pp.358-361). Aoki et al. (1994, p.41) assert that debt financing from the bank as the main lender works also monitoring for management. A main bank has a limited intervention as the corporate governance in normal operating situation, but the main bank turns to manage the firm when they go into liquidation. Osano (2005, pp.160-162) assert that the pressure of the main bank as a big lender does not always mean the corporate governance but works as a discipline. Kimura et al. (2007, p.127) assert that the treatments for bad debts by monetary facilities made headway in 1990's and when they have "no willingness to lend" or "take away to lend," they monitor the financing position of the firms through systematic treatment following to "inspection manual" Therefore, as Kimura et al. (2007, p.128) point out that the characteristics of the relationship between a firm and the main lender may change, since the monitoring itself by the bank has been changed since the beginning of 1990's.

Arikawa and Miyajima (2007) suggest that one third of Japanese public firms depend on capital markets for their financial resources, and institutional investors are playing a major role in corporate governance for the firms. The rest of the firms fell into two categories; high growth firms and low growth firms. For the firms with low growth opportunities, the main bank was potentially expected to serve a disciplinary role to prevent them from over-investment or to encourage corporate restructuring. For the firms with high growth opportunities, the main bank was supposed to play a facilitating role in corporate finance. Thus, even after the banking crisis in Japan in the late 1990s, their monitoring capabilities was restored.

Also, as Osano (2005, p.136) asserts that firms with high leverage and bad performance are afraid of liquidation by the lenders, they strive for refined management; the pressure to the firms by the big lenders works as a leverage restraint. Suda (2000) examines the hypotheses that firms with high leverage have a willingness to build an effective internal control system and suggests that the leverage affects the firm's attitude for building the internal control system.

On the other hand, Lobo and Zhou (2006) predict that managers use discretionary accrual to satisfy debt covenant requirement, since more highly leveraged firms have greater incentive to increase earnings, and suggest that the coefficient on leverage is positive for earnings management. Suda (2000) and Shuto (2010) provide evidence that the managers who have nearly violated debt covenants have an incentive to manage earnings. Kimura (2004) examines the association between earnings management and leverage by dividing borrowing and bond issuing and suggests that while leverage for the firms with more borrowing works as monitoring, leverage for the firms with more bond issuing is associated with earnings management.[6] Thus, I predict that leverage affects on a manager's earnings management as governance or incentives. This prediction leads the following hypothesis:

H3: The association between earnings management measures and leverage remains unchanged in the pre-and post-of US-SOX periods.

3.5 Data and Research Design

3.5.1 Data and Sample

This study employs data of the U. S. listed Japanese firms from 1990 through 2006[7 8]. Data are hand-collected from LexisNexis at Converse College, from the web-site of each firm, and from the Japan Securities Dealers Association. Although NEC and Pioneer have already withdrawn from the U.S. stock market, I include them in the sample since data from 1989 through 2006 is employed.[9 10] The SEC extended the compliance date for US-SOX and the public firms in the U.S. begin to comply with US-SOX for their first fiscal year ending on or after November 15, 2004[11]. The SEC extended the compliance period for foreign private issuers and U.S. listed Japanese firms started to comply with US-SOX for their first fiscal year ending on or after July 15, 2006[12]. Hitachi, Kubota, and NEC disclosed material weaknesses in the company's internal control over financial reporting in their 2006 annual reports (Nihon Keizai Shinbun 2006, Dec 15). Variables are from the statements of cash flows for accruals variables for comparability with prior studies.

3.5.2 Accruals Management Measures and Real Management Measures

I use three proxies as accruals management measures and three proxies as real management measures to capture different dimensions regarding managers' discretionary behaviors.

Conservative Management Measure (C_AM)
Following to Leuz et al. (2003),[13] I develop the medial ratio of the firm-level volatility of reported earnings divided by the firm-level volatility of cash flow from operations (OCF) as the first proxy for earnings management, especially for income smoothing. My first earnings management measure captures the degree to which managers smooth the variability of reported earnings by managing accruals. Low values of this measure of accrual management indicate that managers exercise discretion to smooth reported earnings.

Neutral Management Measure (N_AM)

Managers sometimes may use their discretionary accruals to produce the desired level of earnings. Dechow and Schrand (2004) point out that a high level of accruals in absolute magnitude is a potential "opportunistically earnings management." Dechow et al. (1996) document that according to accounting enforcement actions by SEC, accruals increase at the year of the manipulation and have a sharp decline compared to the control sample. Richardson et al. (2002) show that the restatement firms have larger total accruals than non-restatement firms do.

Dechow and Schrand (2004, pp.42-43) show the accounts that the SEC most frequently alleged were manipulated in Accounting and Auditing Enforcement Release (AAER) No 1.-through No.1745. The overstatement of revenues and accounts receivable/ understated bad-debt allowance is the most frequent form of earnings management (70% of the cases), understated expense (other than cost of goods sold) (30%), overstated inventory/ understated cost of goods sold (10%) and understated accounts receivable discounts/ allowances other than bad debts (3%). This result shows that most of earnings manipulations are related to the accounts related to accruals. Richardson et al. (2005) show that total accruals are positively associated with the likelihood of observing an earnings restatement. Thus, my third earnings management measure is the absolute value of firms' accruals scaled by the absolute value of firms' cash flows, following Leuz et al. (2003) as a proxy for the extent to which managers exercise discretion in reporting earnings. As Leuz et al. (2003) mention, managers use their discretion not only in order to misstate their firms' performance, but also to convey their inside information to increase imformativeness (Subramanyam 1996).

Aggressive Management Measure (A_AM)

We use the average of the absolute value of discretionary accruals from Jones' (1991) and the absolute value of *NI* (*A_AM*) as managers' discretionary activities (Balsam1998; Suda et al. 2007)[14]. Balsam (1998) documents that discretionary accruals are associated with CEO's cash compensation. Suda et al. (2007) estimate discretionary accruals for 2,110 public firms in Japan and summarize the extent to which discretionary accruals affect accounting earnings through the Jones' (1991) model, the modified Jones model (Dechow et al. 1995), the CFO Jones model and the CFO modified Jones model (Kasznik 1999).

While the results of Balsam (1998) report that ratios of absolute value of discretionary accruals to absolute value of current income are 108% and 370% (median, mean) respectively, those of Suda et al. (2007) report that that ratios of absolute value of discretionary accruals to absolute value of current income are range from 108% to 147% (median), range 575% to 752% (mean) respectively.

Balsam (1998) uses the absolute value of discretionary accruals calculated under the Jones' (1991) model as a percentage of the absolute value of income as a proxy for manager's discretionary manipulation. Following Balsam (1988), I use this measure as the fourth earnings management measure (A_AM), especially for managers' discretionary activities.

AbnOCF and AbnPROD

Managers can take real actions which affect cash flows by delaying or accelerating sales and accelerating or postponing R&D expenses in order to mask economic shock to the operating cash flows. Leuz et al. (2003) assert that accruals buffer cash flow shocks and result in a negative correlation between changes in accruals and operating cash flows. Although Dechow (1994) documents that there is a negative correlation between changes in accruals and operating cash flows theoretically, Luez et al. (2003) indicate that larger amounts of negative correlation do not reflect a firm's underlying economic performance and capture the extent of a firm's income smoothing. This is my second earning management measure, especially for real earnings management.

Dechow and Schrand (2004) assert that it's difficult to document the extent to which firms engage in real management to manipulate earnings. Merely observing that a firm enters into a transaction that receives favorable accounting treatment is not evidence that the firm entered into the transaction just because of its accounting consequence. Therefore, I develop two proxies, abnormal OCF (*AbnOCF*) and abnormal PROD (*AbnPROD*) for real management, following Roychowdhury (2006) and Cohen et al. (2008). Roychowdhury(2006) and Cohen et al.(2008) focus on three earnings management techniques: sales manipulation, reduction of discretionary expenditure, and production manipulation and how these affect OCF, discretionary expenses, such as R&D, and production costs.[15] Examples of sales manipulation include accelerating sales or delaying sales. Examples of production cost manipulation include reporting lower *COGS* to increase production:

$AbnOCF_t = a_0 + a_1 SALES_t + a_2 \Delta SALES_t + \varepsilon$.
$AbnPROD_t = COG_t + \Delta INV_t$,
$= a_0 + a_1 SALES_t + a_2 \Delta SALES_t + a_3 \Delta SALES_{t-1}$.

Following Cohen et al. (2008), I generate the normal OCF and the normal production cost by using the above equations. I compute normal OCF as a linear function of sales and change in sales. I compute abnormal OCF by subtracting the normal level of OCF calculated using the estimated coefficient from the equation from actual OCF.[16] I compute abnormal production costs by subtracting the normal level of the sum of COGS and change in inventory from actual production cost. I estimate the normal level of production costs as the above equation:

$OCF_t = SALES_t + \Delta SALES_t + \varepsilon_t$.
$COG_t = SALES_t + \varepsilon_t$.
$\Delta INV_t = \Delta SALES_t + \Delta SALES_{t-1} + \varepsilon_t$.
$PROD_t = SALES_t + \Delta SALES_t + \Delta SALES_{t-1} + \varepsilon_t$.

3.5.3 Determinants as Incentives or Restraints

Suda and Shuto (2008) find that Japanese firms manage reported earnings to avoid decreases in earnings and losses by examining distribution. I include an indicator equal to 1 if the observation has a small decrease in income before discretionary accruals in income. Also, I include an indicator variable for small loss that equals 1 if the observation has a small loss before discretionary accruals. Therefore, since the firms have incentives to increase discretionary accrual to report an increase in earnings or no loss before US-SOX but it is harder to use discretionary accruals to report an increase in earnings or no loss after US-SOX and managers shift to manage earnings through real activities, I predict that there is a positive coefficient on *DECAVOID* and *LOSSAVOID* for accruals management in the pre-US-SOX and that there is a positive coefficient on *DECAVOID* and *LOSSAVOID* for real accounting in the post-SOX.

Suda (2000, pp.224-225) suggests that leverage is one of determinants for R&D and that debt covenants affect a manager's accounting choices. On the other hand,

Lobo and Zhou (2006) suggest that since firms with high leverage need to satisfy debt covenant requirement, they have a greater incentive to increase earnings. Therefore, there is a mixed evidence regarding whether leverage works as incentives or constraints for earnings management.

SOX is 1 for all firm-year observation in 2006, 2007, and 2008, and 0 for observation in 2005 and earlier. While Japanese listed firms as ADR firms in the U.S. stock market were supposed to apply US-SOX regulation from 2006, only Canon applied US-SOX in 2006. Most of Japanese listed firms in the U.S. did not report Internal Control Report in 2006. I predict that they had already set up their internal control system in 2006 but they are not ready for reporting that in 2006. I include control variables to avoid the effect by other factors except US-SOX for regression analyses. To adjust the difference between the current year and previous years, I used each variable which deduct mean in the year for leverage and OCF following Yoshida's (2005) model.

Becker et al. (1998) suggest that the discretionary accruals of the firm which is not audited by a BIG 5 auditor is larger than the discretionary accruals of the firm which is audited by a BIG 5 and that BIG 5 works as a restraint for earnings management. This suggests that auditor quality affects on earnings management as a restraint. Therefore, I include the variable *AUDIT* to control for the effect of auditor quality. *AUDIT*, is 1 if the firm is audited by a BIG N, and 0 otherwise[17]. I predict its coefficient to be negative as auditor works constraints for earnings management.

Lobo and Zhou (2006) assert that larger firms may have more opportunities to overstate earnings because of the complexity of their operations and their difficulties for external users to detect such overstatement. On the other hand, Lobo and Zhou (2006) suggest that larger firms are subject to more scrutiny from financial analysis and investors because larger firms have more influence on the stock market due to their larger market capitalization. Thus, I include *SIZE* to control for the potential effects.

Lobo and Zhou (2006) suggest that firms with strong operating cash flow performance have no incentive to manage earnings through discretionary accruals. I also predict that firms with larger operating cash flows do not need to manage earnings to report increases in earnings or income, but I might consider that firms with larger operating cash flows might have an incentive to manage earnings through real management using *OCF*. Therefore, I predict the coefficient of *OCF* to be negative before US-SOX, but the coefficient of *OCF* to be positive after US-SOX.

3.6 Empirical Results

3.6.1 Descriptive Statistics for Earnings Management Measures

Table 3.2 presents descriptive statistics for cross-sectional data from the sample firms. Mean (S.D) of *DA1*, *OCF1*, *PROD2*, *Z_RM2* are 0.000 (-0.032), 0.001 (0.031), -0.007 (0.130), 0.000(1.500) respectively. I have median test to make sure whether the distribution has no problems before the mean analyses. The result of the median test is shown in the Table 3.3. I use *ABS_DA* and *ABS_DA_B* as accruals management proxies and *OCF_B*, *PROD_B*, *Z_RM* as real management proxies.

Table 3.4 presents the correlation. Consistent with the results of Cohen et al. (2008)[18], there is a significant negative correlation between *Z_RM1* and *N_AM* (-0.264 Pearson; -0.241 Spearman), a significant negative correlation between OCF1 and *PROD1*, and *C_AM* (-0.162, -0.170 Pearson ; -0.230, -0.139 Spearman). Thus, there is a trade-off relationship between real management proxies and accruals management proxies. This supports the implication from Graham et al.'s (2005) survey results. Table 3.4 also indicates that there is a significant negative correlation between *C_AM* and *N_AM* and between *C_AM* and *ABS_DA_B*.

Table 3.5 presents the time period analyzed in this study and also shows important events which incurred in the U.S. and Japan, such as accounting fraud and internal control regulation. Kanebo Window Dressing occurred in 2004. US-SOX was issued in 2002 in the U.S. and US-SOX was applied to ADR firms in the U.S. in 2006, when J-SOX was released in Japan. However, the Japanese firms in the U.S. have applied in 2007.

3.6.2 The Time-Series Plots of Earnings Management

Figure 3.1 illustrates the time-series trend of earnings management proxies. *ABS_DA_B* has been increasing with the climb of the so-called "Babble Economy" which

Chapter 3 Impacts on Accruals and Real Management

TABLE 3.2   Descriptive Statistice (n=418)

	Mean	Median	Standard Deviation	Minimum	Maximum	25th Percent	75th Percent
ΔWC	0.003	0.004	0.025	-0.221	0.085	-0.010	0.017
$\Delta SALES$	0.030	0.031	0.115	-0.505	0.611	-0.011	0.076
Total Accruals	-0.038	-0.038	0.030	-0.123	0.050	-0.059	-0.017
SALES	1.053	0.896	0.485	0.211	2.785	0.745	1.106
SIZE	6.291	6.271	0.591	4.923	7.328	5.864	6.838
LDEBT	0.000	-0.009	0.109	-0.157	0.356	-0.087	0.046
OCF	0.000	-0.003	0.037	-0.102	0.126	-0.024	0.022
DA1	0.000	0.000	0.032	-0.238	0.213	-0.016	0.015
TA1	0.000	0.000	0.032	-0.112	0.131	-0.020	0.018
OCF1	0.001	-0.001	0.031	-0.111	0.118	-0.015	0.017
PROD1	-0.007	0.001	0.130	-1.601	0.461	-0.024	0.029
ABS_DA1	0.022	0.016	0.024	0.000	0.238	0.008	0.031
ABS_TA1	0.024	0.019	0.021	0.000	0.131	0.008	0.033
ABS_OCF1	0.023	0.016	0.021	0.000	0.118	0.007	0.031
ABS_PROD1	0.054	0.026	0.119	0.000	1.601	0.011	0.047
DA1_B	3.420	0.760	10.062	0.003	105.238	0.324	2.021
TA1_B	3.627	0.847	10.984	0.005	120.878	0.357	2.332
OCF1_B	3.398	0.735	10.333	0.001	105.942	0.275	2.501
PROD1_B	9.724	1.221	31.646	0.005	321.280	0.379	3.945
C_AM	0.651	0.691	0.353	0.001	1.672	0.304	1.000
N_AM	0.350	0.219	0.319	0.000	1.001	0.105	0.509
Z_RM1	0.000	0.009	1.500	-12.134	7.368	-0.616	0.683
LOSSAOID_DA	0.187	0.000	0.390	0.000	1.000	0.000	0.000
LOSAVOID_TA	0.163	0.000	0.370	0.000	1.000	0.000	0.000
DECAVOID_DA	0.168	0.000	0.374	0.000	1.000	0.000	0.000
DECAVOID_TA	0.146	0.000	0.354	0.000	1.000	0.000	0.000
ABS_DA1_B	3.420	0.760	10.062	0.003	105.238	0.324	2.021
decavoid_DA1	0.002	0.004	0.041	-0.243	0.191	-0.019	0.025
decavoid_TA1	0.002	0.002	0.045	-0.224	0.222	-0.020	0.026
lossavoid_DA1	0.025	0.024	0.046	-0.208	0.223	-0.004	0.050
lossavoid_TA1	0.025	0.023	0.048	-0.116	0.246	-0.004	0.051
DA2	0.000	-0.001	0.021	-0.184	0.059	-0.012	0.012
TA2	0.000	-0.002	0.025	-0.069	0.076	-0.016	0.015
OCF2	0.000	-0.003	0.036	-0.156	0.156	-0.021	0.017
PROD2	0.000	0.006	0.283	-1.395	3.644	-0.073	0.074
ABS_DA2	0.015	0.012	0.014	0.000	0.184	0.006	0.020
ABS_TA2	0.019	0.015	0.016	0.000	0.076	0.007	0.029
ABS_OCF2	0.026	0.020	0.024	0.001	0.156	0.008	0.035
ABS_PROD2	0.136	0.074	0.248	0.000	3.644	0.041	0.134
DA2_B	1.946	0.561	4.301	0.005	42.932	0.218	1.490
TA2_B	2.742	0.687	9.636	0.000	171.769	0.295	2.023
OCF2_B	3.668	0.954	14.296	0.018	259.769	0.352	2.719
PROD2_B	22.466	3.724	82.206	0.004	1012.189	1.245	14.314
Z_RM2	0.000	-0.055	1.437	-6.371	14.831	-0.572	0.577
decavoid_DA2_2	0.002	0.001	0.030	-0.189	0.125	-0.011	0.018
decavoid_TA2	0.002	0.002	0.035	-0.118	0.169	-0.017	0.019
lossavoid_DA2_2	0.025	0.022	0.038	-0.154	0.169	0.002	0.046
lossavoid_TA2	0.025	0.022	0.042	-0.120	0.206	-0.001	0.048
DECAVOID_DA2	0.268	0.000	0.443	0.000	1.000	0.000	1.000
LOSSAVOID_DA2	0.179	0.000	0.384	0.000	1.000	0.000	1.000

Variable Definitions: all varibales are deflated by average assets.

ΔWC	changes in working capitals $= \Delta AR + \Delta INV - \Delta AP - \Delta TAX$ Payable $+ \Delta$other assets (net)
$\Delta SALES$	changes in SALES
Total Accruals	net income minus operating cash flows
SALES	sales
SIZE	the log of SALES
LDEBT	long debt
OCF	cash flows from operations
DA1	discretionary working capital accruals by estimated DeAngelo model
TA1	deAngelo all accruals by estimated DeAngelo model
OCF1	abnormal OCF, residulas by estimated $OCF_t = SALES_t + \Delta SALES_t$
PROD1	abnormal production costs, resisuals by estimated $COG + \Delta INV = \alpha_1 + \alpha_2 SALES_t + \alpha_3 SALES_t + \alpha_4 SALES_{t-1}$
ABS_DA1	aBS of DA1
ABS_TA1	abs of TA1
ABS_OCF1	abs of OCF
ABS_PROD1	abs of PROD1
DA1_B	discretionary working capital accruals by estimated DeAngelo model/ABS of NI
TA1_B	all accruals by estimated DeAngelo model/ABS of NI
OCF1_B	abnormal OCF, residulas by estimated $OCF_t = SALES + \Delta SALES / ABS$ of NI
PROD1_B	abnormal Production Costs, resisuals by estimated $COG + \Delta INV$, $\alpha_1 + \alpha_2 = SALES_t + \alpha_3 SALES_t + \alpha 4 SALES_{t-1}$
C_AM	conservative Accountingt $= NI$ volatility $/ OCF$ volatility
N_AM	neutral Accountingt $=$ The average of the absolute value of working capitals /the average of the absolute value of OCF
Z_RM1	sum of standardize Abnormal OCF and Standardez Abnormal Production Cost
LOSSAVOID_DA	1 if [(current year's income before discretionary working capital accruals by estimated by DeAngelo models- last years' incomel/average assets) js between (-0.015, 0) and 0 otherwise.
LOSAVOID_TA	1 if [(current year's income before discretionary total accruals by estimated by DeAngelo models $-$last years' incomel/average assets] is between (-0.015, 0) and 0 otherwise.
DECAVOID_DA	1 if [(current year's income before discretionary working capital accruals by estimated by DeAngelo models) $-$average assets] is between (-0.03, 0) and 0 otherwise
DECAVOID_TA	1 if (current year's income before discretionary total accruals by estimated by DeAngelo models) is betwee (-0.03, 0) and 0 otherwise.
ABS_DA1_B	The average of the absolute value of discretionary accruals from Jones/ the average of the absolute value of NI
decavoid_DA1	current year's income before discretionary working capital accruals by estimated by DeAngelo models- last years' income/average assets.DeAngelo
decavoid_TA1	current year's income before discretionary total accruals by estimated by DeAngelo models- last years' incomel/average assets.
lossavoid_DA1	current year's income before discretionary working capital accruals by estimated by DeAngelo model/average assets.
lossavoid_TA1	current year's income before discretionary total accruals by estimated by DeAngelo model/average assets.

TABLE 3.3 Median Test for Earnings Management Measures

Panel A	n	Median	Chi-Square	df	Asymp. Sig.	Yates' Continuity Correction		
						Chi-Square	df	Asymp. Sig.
DA1	418	0.000	0.623	1.000	0.430	0.398	1.000	0.528
TA1	418	0.000	0.025	1.000	0.875	0.000	1.000	1.000
OCF1	418	-0.001	0.224	1.000	0.636	0.100	1.000	0.752
PROD1	418	0.001	3.013	1.000	0.083	2.490	1.000	0.115
ABS_DA1	418	0.016	4.209	1.000	0.040 **	3.586	1.000	0.058 *
ABS_TA1	418	0.019	1.220	1.000	0.269	0.897	1.000	0.344
ABS_OCF1	418	0.016	3.013	1.000	0.083 *	2.490	1.000	0.115
ABS_PROD1	418	0.026	0.623	1.000	0.430	0.398	1.000	0.528
DA1_B	418	0.760	15.564	1.000	0.000 ***	14.344	1.000	0.000 ***
TA1_B	418	0.847	13.174	1.000	0.000 ***	12.053	1.000	0.001 ***
OCF1_B	418	0.735	13.174	1.000	0.000 ***	12.053	1.000	0.001 ***
PROD1_B	418	1.221	7.197	1.000	0.007 ***	6.375	1.000	0.012 **
Z_RM1	418	0.009	0.623	1.000	0.430	0.398	1.000	0.528
ABS_DA1_B	418	0.760	15.564	1.000	0.000 ***	14.344	1.000	0.000 ***
Panel B:								
DA2	418	-0.001	0.623	1.000	0.430	0.398	1.000	0.528
TA2	418	-0.002	0.025	1.000	0.875	0.000	1.000	1.000
OCF2	418	-0.003	0.025	1.000	0.875	0.000	1.000	1.000
PROD2	418	0.006	0.224	1.000	0.636	0.100	1.000	0.752
ABS_DA2	418	0.012	0.025	1.000	0.875	0.000	1.000	1.000
ABS_TA2	418	0.015	0.224	1.000	0.636	0.100	1.000	0.752
ABS_OCF2	418	0.020	0.025	1.000	0.875	0.000	1.000	1.000
ABS_PROD2	418	0.074	0.623	1.000	0.430	0.398	1.000	0.528
DA2_B	418	0.561	8.990	1.000	0.003 ***	8.069	1.000	0.005 ***
TA2_B	418	0.687	8.990	1.000	0.003 ***	8.069	1.000	0.005 ***
OCF2_B	418	0.954	8.990	1.000	0.003 ***	8.069	1.000	0.005 ***
PROD2_B	418	3.724	3.013	1.000	0.083 **	2.490	1.000	0.115
Z_RM2	418	-0.055	1.220	1.000	0.269	0.897	1.000	0.344
ABS_DA2_B	418	0.561	8.990	1.000	0.003 ***	8.069	1.000	0.005 ***

TABLE 3.4 Correlation between Earnings Management Proxies, 1990-2008 (n=418)

	Real Management Proxies			Accruals Management Proxies		
	OCF1_B	PROD1_B	Z_RM1	ABS_DA1_B	C_AM	N_AM
OCF1_B	1.000	0.455	0.042	0.763	-0.162	0.197
	.	0.000	0.395	0.000	0.001	0.000
		***		***	***	***
PROD1_B	0.530	1.000	-0.277	0.381	-0.170	0.142
	0.000	.	0.000	0.000	0.000	0.004
	***		***	***	***	***
Z_RM1	0.014	0.052	1.000	0.039	0.093	-0.263
	0.782	0.293	.	0.432	0.058	0.000
					*	***
ABS_DA1_B	0.711	0.579	0.012	1.000	-0.112	0.229
	0.000	0.000	0.802	.	0.022	0.000
	***	***			**	***
C_AM	-0.230	-0.139	0.044	-0.177	1.000	-0.232
	0.000	0.004	0.365	0.000	.	0.000
	***	***		***		***
N_AM	0.219	0.213	-0.241	0.258	-0.181	1.000
	0.000	0.000	0.000	0.000	0.000	.
	***	***	***	***	***	

Notes: Pearson correlation is shown at the top and Spearman correlation is show at the bottom.
See Table 3.2 fir variable definition. *, ** and *** indicate that significant at 0.1 level, 0.5 level and 0.01 level 10 % respectively.

TABLE 3.5 Period Analyzed, Accounting Scandals and Regulations in Japan and the U.S.

年	89	90	91	92	93	94	95	96	97	98	99	2000	2001	2002	2003	2004	2005	2006
U.S.												Enron, WorldCom Accounting Scandals		US-SOX Released.		US-SOX Applied to U.S. Public Firms.		U.S. Listed Japanese Firms Applied US-SOX.
JAPAN												Cash Flow Statement Standards Introduced.				Kanebo, SeibuTetsudo Accounting Scandals		J-SOX Released.

FIGURE 3.1   Absolute Value of Discretionary Accruals over Time

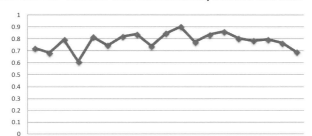

FIGURE 3.2   Real Management Proxy over Time

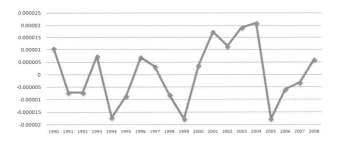

started in late 1980 in Japan. *ABS_DA_B* was the highest in the Bubble Economy's collapse in1993. *ABS_DA_B* has been decreasing during the "Lost Decade" after the Bubble Economy's collapse (Ito et al. 2005).[19] The introduction of cash flow statement standards decrease *ABS_DA_B* for a short period. However, *ABS_DA_B* has been increasing as the economy improved until the accounting scandals, such as the misstatements of Kanebo occurred. *ABS_DA_B* peaked in 2004 when the Kanebo scandal occurred and decreased after the Kanebo scandals. *ABS_DA* has been decreasing by the effect of US-SOX after the accounting scandals and continued to increase following US-SOX application and J-SOX's release in Japan.

Figure 3.2 presents time-series trends of real management proxies. Generally, Figure 3.2 shows that real management proxies are not stable. Real management decreased during the introduction of cash flows statement standard in Japan. After that, real management kept increasing until the Kanebo scandals in 2004 but decreased after the scandal occurred and US-SOX was released in the U.S. The plot after US-SOX is similar to the graphical illustration of the absolute value of

TABLE 3.6 Descriptive Statistics for Accruals and Real Management Measures

	Pre-US-SOX			Post-US-SOX				
	N	Mean	Standard Deviation	N	Mean	Standard Deviation	Significance	
DA1_B	352	3.934	10.853	66	0.578	0.740	-5.745	***
TA1_B	352	4.141	11.853	66	0.786	0.949	-5.230	***
OCF1_B	352	3.875	11.155	66	0.759	1.087	-5.123	***
PROD1_B	352	11.137	34.163	66	1.910	3.750	-4.919	***
Z_RM1	352	-0.067	1.523	66	0.373	1.281	2.171	**
ABS_DA1_B	352	3.934	10.853	66	0.578	0.740	-5.745	***
C_AM	352	0.622	0.357	66	0.811	0.288	4.641	***
N_AM	352	0.367	0.322	66	0.258	0.285	-2.753	***

Notes: See table 3.2 for variable definition. *, ** and *** indicate that significant at 0.1 level, 0.5 level and 0.01 level 10 % respectively.

discretionary accruals from Cohen et al. (2008, p.772, Figure 3.2). Cohen et al. (2008) show that the absolute value of discretionary accruals management peaked in 2000 during the scandal period in the U.S. Accruals management proxy in this study peaked in 2004 when accounting scandal in Japan occurred. This figure also indicates that U.S. listed Japanese firms decreased accruals management after the accounting scandals in Japan occurred and US-SOX was applied to them.

The plot of Figure 3.2 shows that the level of real management increased until the accounting scandals in Japan. Real management proxy shows a drop when US-SOX was applied to all public firms in 2004 in the U.S. The U.S. listed Japanese firms have increased real management since 2005. This means that they decreased discretionary activities and accruals management after US-SOX's release and J-SOX's introduction, but there might be a surrogate between accruals management and real management.

3.6.3 Test of Hypothesis 1

Table 3.6 presents descriptive statistics for the variable in the pre- and post-US-SOX periods. The means of N_AM and ABS_DA1_B in the pre-US-SOX and the means of N_AM and ABS_DA1_B in the post-US-SOX are 0.367, 3.932, 0.258, 0.578 respectively. The means of accruals management in the post-US-SOX are significantly smaller than the means of accruals management in the pre-SOX. On the other hand, the means of Z_RM in the pre-US-SOX and the means of Z_RM in the post-US-SOX are -0.067, 0.373 respectively. The means of real management in the post-US-SOX are significantly larger than the means of real management in the pre-US-SOX.

I conducted the mean difference test for the differences in the pre-US-SOX (1998-2005) and in the post-US-SOX periods (2006-2008). Table 3.6 shows the results of the mean difference. Table 3.6 indicates that a significant mean difference in *DA_B*, *TA_B*, *ABS_DA_B*, *OCF_B*, *PROD_B*, and *Z_RM* in pre-US-SOX and in post-US-SOX periods is observable. This result is consistent with the plot. This suggests that US-SOX affected the decreases in accruals management and increases in real management.

3.6.4 Test of Hypothesis 2

Table 3.7 presents the result of determinants of changes in accruals and real management through the regression analysis using the developed Lobo and Zhou's (2006) model. To test H2, I focus on *DECAVOID* and *LOSSAVOID* variables. The sign of coefficient of US-SOX for *ABS_DA_B* is negative, suggests that US-SOX reduces aggressive management. *ABS_DA_B* is significantly negatively related to *DECAVOID*, suggesting that US-SOX decreases the association between aggressive management and *DECAVOID*, and US-SOX leads a decrease in accruals management through market motivation The sign of coefficient of US-SOX for *N_AM* is also negative, suggests that US-SOX reduces neutral management. *N_AM* is significantly negatively related to *DECAVOID* and *DECAVOID*SOX*, suggesting that US-SOX decreases the association between neutral management and *DECAVOID*. Therefore, I document that US-SOX leads a decrease in accruals management through market motivation.

As for real management (*Z_RM*), the sign of the coefficient of US-SOX is significantly positive, suggesting that US-SOX increases real management after US-SOX. *Z_RM* is significantly positively associated with *LOSSAVOID*, suggesting that US-SOX increases the association between real management and *LOSSAVOID*, and US-SOX increases real management through *LOSSAVOID* incentives.

Based on the results, "H2: The association between earnings management and stock market motivation remains unchanged in the pre-and post-of US-SOX period" is rejected. Therefore, I document that US-SOX application reduces the association between the incentive "to decrease in earnings" and accruals management, and increases the association between the incentive "to decrease in earnings" and real management.

3.6.5 Test of Hypothesis 3

How about the association between leverage and earnings management? Table 3.7 shows that aggressive management is negatively related to leverage and neutral management is significantly negatively associated with leverage after US-SOX passage. On the other hand, Z_RM is positively associated with leverage, suggesting that leverage affects on decreases in accruals management as restraints and on increases in real management as incentives. Table 3.7 also presents that *AbnPROD* is significantly positively related to *LDEBT* and significantly negatively related to *LDEBT*SOX*, suggests that leverage increases *AbnPROD* as incentives before US-SOX but leverage reduces *AbnPROD* as governance.

There is a significant negative association between OCF and accruals management but a significant positive association between OCF and real management. This suggest that firms with strong operating cash flow performance have less incentives to manage accruals management, but if they have sufficient operating cash flows which are affected by real management, they seem to have a willingness to manage earnings through real methods.

Based on the results, "H3: The association between earnings management measures and leverage remains unchanged in the pre-and post of US-SOX period" is rejected. Generally speaking, leverage decreases accruals management and increases real management, but I document that leverage increases *AbnPROD* before US-SOX but decreases *AbnPROD* as governance.

3.7 Implication

Accruals management has a feature which is called "accruals reversal". As Dechow and Schrand (2004) mention, since accruals management affects the recognition time of earnings, even if managers understate bad-debts expense in one period to increase earnings, a write-off of accounts receivable will exceed the allowance to decrease earnings in another period. Therefore, accruals management is said to be rational only if the expected benefits of the initial accruals management exceed the expected costs associated with accruals reversal and earnings in the future are sufficiently high to include the accrual reversals.

Suda (2007, p.22) asserts that although aggressive accounting management is an accounting choice within GAAP and is not an SEC violation, aggressive accounting has a significant impact on economic society. Dechow and Schrand (2004) assert that real management is also a GAAP violation as long as the firm properly accounts for the transaction and that these actions generally do not result in a qualified audit opinion or an enforcement action by SEC. Nonetheless, such actions can have a significant impact on earnings quality and devastating effects on the company's future performance. Suda and Hanaeda (2008) express their concerns that tighter accounting regulation urge real management and have a negative impact on national economy.

Ewert and Wagenhofer (2005) document that tighter accounting standard increases real management and costs. Roychowdhuly (2006, p.338) suggests that real management can reduce firm value because actions taken in the current period to increase earnings can have a negative effect on cash flows in future periods. Aggressive price discounts to increase sales volume and meet some short-term earnings target can lead customers to expect such discounts in future periods as well. This can imply lower margins on future sales overproduction generates excess inventories that have to be sold in subsequent periods and imposes greater inventory holding cost on the company. Therefore, real management potential imposes great long-term costs on the company.

Roychowdhury (2006, pp.340-341) suggests that price discount, channel stuffing, and overproduction have a negative effect on current abnormal OCF, while reduction of discretionary expenditures has a positive effect, possibly at the risk of lower cash flows in the future. Nakashima (2010) examines whether US-SOX impacts on cash flows predictive ability of the Japanese listed firms in the U.S. and she documents that determinants of lower cash flow predictive ability is the increases in real managements.

While US-SOX is intend to increase creditability of financial reporting, since it is hard for managers to give up stock market motivation, they find a way to switch from accrual management to real management. US-SOX not only contributes to improve quality of accruals, but also incur costs, such as declines of cash flow prediction, cost burden for inventory.

TABLE 3.7. Determinants of Earning Management

$EM = \beta_0 + \beta_1 SOX + \beta_2 LOSSDECAVOID + \beta_3 LOSSDECAVOID*SOX + \beta_4 LOSSAVOID + \beta_5 LOSSAVOID*SOX + \beta_6 LDEBT + \beta_7 LDEBT*SOX + \beta_8 SIZE + \beta_9 OCF + \beta_{10} AUDIT + \varepsilon$

Panel A: Determinants of Accruals Management

	Consevative_AM			Neutral_AM				ABS_DA1_B		
	B	t-value	significance	B	t-value	significance		B	t-value	significance
(Constant)	1.154	4.890	0.000 ***	0.420	2.380	0.018 **	(Constant)	-13.647	-2.075	0.039 **
SOX	0.275	4.360	0.000 ***	-0.082	-1.725	0.085 *	SOX	-2.397	-1.137	0.256
DECAVOID_DA	0.032	0.664	0.507	-0.075	-2.105	0.036 **	DECAVOID_DA	-2.654	-1.990	0.047 **
DECAVOID_DA1*SOX	-0.152	-1.279	0.202	0.029	0.330	0.742	DECAVOID_DA1*SOX	2.860	0.859	0.391
LOSSAVOID_DA	-0.016	-0.349	0.727	-0.058	-1.663	0.097 *	LOSSAVOID_DA	0.030	0.023	0.981
LOSSAVOID_DA1*SOX	-0.040	-0.243	0.808	0.102	0.821	0.412	LOSSAVOID_DA1*SOX	-0.340	-0.083	0.934
LDEBT	-0.010	-0.041	0.967	0.240	1.306	0.192	LDEBT	-4.993	-0.730	0.466
LDEBT*SOX	0.610	1.550	0.122	-0.723	-2.459	0.014 **	LDEBT*SOX	-12.839	-1.158	0.248
SIZE	-0.066	-1.779	0.076 *	-0.005	-0.172	0.863	SIZE	2.773	2.697	0.007 ***
OCF	0.353	0.578	0.564	-4.545	-9.949	0.000 ***	OCF	-60.761	-3.257	0.001 ***
AUDIT	-0.121	-1.936	0.054 *	-0.008	-0.166	0.868	AUDIT	-0.933	-0.539	0.590
Z_RM1	0.016	1.202	0.230	-0.010	-1.021	0.308	Z_RM1	1.233	3.355	0.001 ***
Z_RM1*SOX	-0.018	-0.491	0.624	0.028	1.033	0.302	Z_RM1*SOX	-0.443	-0.432	0.666
ABS_DA1_B	-0.002	-1.136	0.257	0.003	1.924	0.055 *	N_AM	4.347	2.220	0.027 **
ABS_DA1_B*SOX	-0.081	-1.195	0.233	-0.067	-1.316	0.189	N_AM3*SOX	-5.939	-1.248	0.213
R^2		0.091			0.375				0.137	
Adjusted R^2		0.059			0.353				0.107	
Fvalue (Pr>F)		2.877 (<0.0001)			17.238 (<0.0001)				4.567 (<0.0001)	

Panel B: Determinants of Real Management

	OCF1_B			PROD1_B				Z_RM1		
	B	t-value	significance	B	t-value	significance		B	t-value	significance
(Constant)	1.380	0.296	0.767	1.564	0.080	0.936	(Constant)	1.081	1.168	0.243
SOX	0.392	0.244	0.808	-3.859	-0.573	0.567	SOX	0.264	0.826	0.409
DECAVOID_DA	1.175	1.238	0.217	10.206	2.568	0.011 **	DECAVOID_DA	-0.050	-0.264	0.792
DECAVOID_DA1*SOX	-0.962	-0.410	0.682	-8.747	-0.890	0.374	DECAVOID_DA1*SOX	0.233	0.501	0.617
LOSSAVOID_DA	0.477	0.533	0.595	2.993	0.799	0.425	LOSSAVOID_DA	0.744	4.190	0.000 ***
LOSSAVOID_DA1*SOX	-0.854	-0.258	0.797	0.342	0.025	0.980	LOSSAVOID_DA1*SOX	-0.348	-0.530	0.597
LDEBT	-5.349	-1.110	0.268	79.741	3.951	0.000 ***	LDEBT	1.507	1.575	0.116
LDEBT*SOX	4.780	0.606	0.545	-76.873	-2.329	0.020 **	LDEBT*SOX	1.932	1.236	0.217
SIZE	0.024	0.033	0.974	1.264	0.413	0.680	SIZE	-0.198	-1.366	0.173
OCF	-4.812	-0.383	0.702	9.116	0.173	0.862	OCF	18.617	7.475	0.000 ***
AUDIT	-1.707	-1.391	0.165	-5.207	-1.013	0.312	AUDIT	-0.061	-0.252	0.801
Z_RM1	1.362	0.981	0.327	-0.902	-0.155	0.877	N_AM	-0.264	-0.960	0.338
Z_RM1*SOX	-2.224	-0.664	0.507	-0.039	-0.003	0.998	N_AM*SOX	0.512	0.770	0.442
ABS_DA1_B	0.780	22.377	0.000 ***	1.073	7.357	0.000 ***	ABS_DA1_B	0.023	3.370	0.001 ***
ABS_DA1_B*SOX	0.457	0.342	0.733	0.165	0.029	0.977	ABS_DA_*SOX	0.287	1.082	0.280
R^2		0.589			0.232				0.233	
Adjusted R^2		0.575			0.206				0.206	
Fvalue (Pr>F)		41.215 (<0.0001)			8.694 (<0.0001)				8.715 (<0.0001)	

Notes: Variable Definitions ; SOX= 1 in the post-SOX application period, and 0 otherwise; DECAVOID=1 if [(current year's income before discretionary accruals-last years' income/average assets] is between (-0.015,0), and 0 otherwise. LOSSAVOID= 1 if (current year's income before discretionary accruals/ average assets) is between (-0.03, 0), and 0 otherwise; DEBT=long-term debt /average assets, SIZE=log of total sales, OCF=cash flows from operating /average assets, AUDIT=1 if the firm is audited by a BIG N auditor, and 0 otherwise; *, **, and *** indicate significance at p< 10 %, p< 5%, p<1%;. t-value is based on White's (1980) standard error.

3.8 Conclusion

This study examines (1) the changes in real and accruals management, focusing on conservative management, neutral management, and aggressive management in pre-and-post of US-SOX application periods, and (2) determinants of real management and accrual managements through stock market motivation and leverage as incentives or restraints.

This result shows that there is a significant positive association between SOX and C_AM and Z_RM, and there are significant negative associations between SOX and $AbnPROD$, and between SOX and ABS_DA_B, suggests that managers decrease in aggressive management and increases in real management. The correlation and multiple regression analyses present that there is a surrogate relationship between real management and accrual management.

The results of H2 test shows that there are a significant negative association between $DECAVOID$ and neutral management and aggressive management, and a significant association between $LOSSAVOID$ and real management. The results of H3 test present that leverage decreases aggressive management as governance and increase real management as incentives. Especially, I document that leverage increases $AbnPROD$ before US-SOX application but leverage affects the decrease in $AbnPROD$ as governance.

This result is consistent with precious studies regarding the US-SOX and the changes in accounting information. While stock market motivations drive to shift from accruals management to real management, leverage is likely to impact on earnings management as governance.

While there are some differences such as direct reporting and protection of assets as one of objectives of the regulation, J-SOX is comparable regulation with US-SOX. Even if such a great burden of US-SOX compliance incurred to SEC-registered Japanese firms, unless they follow the US-SOX standard, they could not reach the goals, such as getting global reputation, financing from all over the world and increase of corporate values.

This study has limitations. First, since I use data for U.S. listed Japanese firms, the same analyses as this study should be conducted employing all public firms in Japan to make these results robust. Next, I focus on abnormal OCF and abnormal production expenses. R&D expenses and advertising costs should be obtained and discretionary expenses should be analyzed for further evidence of real management. In addition, while this study uses leverage, I need to use ownership as governance proxy. I discuss by dividing long term debt into bond financing and borrowings. I need to examine real management by adding R&D and advertising costs. Future research is required to examine whether changes in earnings management through US-SOX affect corporate value or costs.

Notes:

1. Gramham et al. (2005) and Suda and Hanaeda (2008) conducted a survey for their financial reporting strategy in the U.S. and Japan. Graham et al. (2005) emailed the survey to 3,174 CFOs and 267 CFOs responded to the internet survey (a response rate of 8.4%). They also handed the survey to CFOs at a conference in NY and 134 participants completed the survey. This gave a final response rate of 10.4%. Suda and Hanaeda (2008) mailed the survey to 3,926 public firms in September, 2007 and 620 firms responded to the survey (a response rate of 15.8%). This survey research would provide implications for archival research for long time.
2. Mulford and Comisky (2002) assert that the financial numbers game itself has many different names and takes on many different forms, such as aggressive accounting, earnings management, income smoothing, fraudulent financial reporting, and creative accounting practices. They define income smoothing as a form of earnings management designed to remove peaks and valleys form a normal earnings series, including steps to reduce and "store" profits during good years for use during lower years.
3. As regard with the terminology of real activities, Dechow and Schrand (2004) use "manipulation of real transaction" as managers can take real economic actions that affect cash flows. Roychowdhury (2006) shows the definition of real activities manipulation as management actions that deviate from normal business practices, undertaken with the primary objective of meeting certain earnings thresholds and also define as departures from normal operational practices, motivated by mangers' desire to mislead at least some stakeholders into believing certain financial reporting goals have been met in the normal course of operations.
4. Zang (2012) finds not only a trade-off between accruals management and real management but also captures the sequentiality of real and accruals management.
5. Real management can begin several months prior to the year end (Leggett 2008, p.7). The realized year-end shortfall between un-manipulated earnings and the desired threshold can exceed the amount by which it is possible to manipulate accruals (Roychowdhury 2006, p.338). Zhang (2012) finds that managers have real management before accruals management.
6. Since for most of the sample firms, long-term debt in the balance sheets in Japanese firms has additional information such as the percentage of borrowings and debt issuing

respectively. This study uses long-term debts as leverage.

7   The U.S. listed Japanese firms disclosed consolidated financial statements in accordance with the U.S. GAAP in order to get financing from the U.S. capital market through the issuance of American Depositary Receipts before the reporting system of consolidated financial statements was introduced in Japan in 1977. Although these firms and other Japanese-listed firms in Japan should have prepared consolidated financial statements in accordance with Japanese GAAP for the Ministry of Finance, the Business Accounting Deliberation Council (BADC) approved as the exception that these firms could submit just U. S. GAAP-based consolidated statements instead of submitting the Japanese GAAP statements. I use these firms as my sample. My sample firms are as follows; Nippon Ham, Wacol, Fuji Film, Komatsu, Hitachi, Toshiba, Mitsubishi Electric, NEC, Panasonic (former Matushita), Sanyo, Sony, Omron, Pioneer, Murata, Makita, Kyocera, Honda, Canon, Ricoh, Itochu, Marubeni, Mitsui. Although Yokado had been registered in NASDAQ, Yokado decided to cease the registration in 2003 and I drop Yokado from my sample.
    http://www.7andi.com/ir/pdf/fstatement/04_iy.pdf
    http://www.fsa.go.jp/news/newsj/13/kinyu/f-20020305-3.html#betu2
    http://www.fsa.go.jp/news/newsj/13/kinyu/f-20020305-3b.pdf

8   It seems that U. S. listed Japanese firms are influenced not only by accounting scandalsin the U.S. and US-SOX but also by accounting scandals in Japan such as Kanebo window dressing and J-SOX.

9   The SEC required NEC to make restatements regarding annual reports from 2001 through 2006. NEC was not able to disclose the 2006 annual report nor make restatements by the deadline of September 2007. Therefore, the SEC stopped NEC from trading on the NASDAQ from September 27, 2007. I employ data without restatement from 2001 through 2005. Since NEC has prepared annual reports following Japan GAAP from 2007, I exclude 2007 NEC data from the sample.

10 Pioneer decided to withdraw from the NY Stock Market in January 24, 2006. I included Pioneer data in my sample. http://pioneer.jp/corp/ir/pdf/press/announce_NYSE060124.pdf

11 http://www.sec.gov/rules/final/33-8392.htm

12 http://www.sec.gov/rules/final/33-8545.htm

13 Leuz et al. (2003) documents differences in earnings management across 31 countries. They conduct cluster analysis to identify groupings of countries with similar legal and institutional characteristics, that is (1) outsider economies with large stock markets, dispersed ownership, strong investor right sand strong legal enforcement (UK and US) ,(2) insider economies with less-developed stock markets, concentrated ownership, weak investor rights, but strong legal enforcement (Germany and Sweden) and (3) insider economies with weak legal enforcement (Italy and India) and create four proxies that capture the extent of earnings management, (1) smoothing reported operating earnings using accruals, (2) smoothing and the correlation between changes in accounting accruals and operating cash flows, (3)discretion in reported earnings: the magnitude of accruals, and (4) discretion in reported earnings: small loss avoidance. They provide evidence that outsider economies with relatively dispersed ownership, strong investor protection, and large stock markets exhibit lower levels of earnings management.

14 Leuz et. al (2003) use small loss avoidance as a proxy for managers' discretionary earnings measures in addition to the magnitude of accruals. I use Balsam's (1998) measure as a proxy for discretionary activities because of data limitation in time length and number of firms.
15 Although they posit three manipulation methods which affect sales, discretionary expenditure and production cost, since R&D costs are not available from all the U.S. listed Japanese firms, discretionary cost is not computed in this study.
16 All variables employed in the model which estimate *AbnOCF* and *AbnPROD* are deflated by average assets. Roychowdhury (2006) and Cohen et al. (2008) used beginning year assets as deflators for *AbnOCF* and *AbnPRO* as proxies for real management.
17 We call the Japanese auditors which are the partner with US-BIG 4, such as AZUSA (KPMG), ARATA (Pricewaterhouse) and Shinnihon yugen sekinin (Ernst &Young), and TOMATSU (Detroit Touche Tomatsu) as Japanese BIG 4 since Misuzu finished their operation and has been dissolved in July, 2007. As in previous years, the partnership relationship had been different before 2006, there might be a possibility to have a mix sample.
18 I compare my results with Cohen et al.'s (2008) *R_CFO, ABS_DA, RM_PROXY, ABS_DA*.
19 The good economy from 1980's through 1990's in Japan is called the Bubble Economy. The Bubble Economy collapsed in late 1991 to 1993. The long stagflation from 1991 through 2002 after the Bubble Economy collapse is called the Lost Decade.

CHAPTER 4

ACCURACY OF CASH FLOW PREDICTIONS

4.1 Introduction

This chapter investigates whether financial reporting quality has been improved from the pre-US-SOX period to the post-US-SOX period. Following Dechow and Schrand's (2004)[1] assertion that earnings are of high quality if they are more strongly associated with future cash flow realization, I take the accuracy for cash flow predictions as financial reporting quality in this chapter. That is, I investigate whether the ability of earnings to predict future cash flows has changed from the pre-US-SOX period to the post-US-SOX period. Also, I document what are the determinants of the accuracy for cash flow predictions by setting up the following hypotheses; (1) whether accruals quality impacts on the accuracy for cash flow predictions, (2) whether managers communicate their private information for future cash flows through accruals, and (3) whether real earnings management affects the accuracy for cash flow predictions.

The objective of US-SOX is to restore creditability which had declined due to a series of accounting fraud. Section 302 of SOX requires managers to certify all material accuracy and completeness. Section 404 of SOX requires managers to disclose internal controls reporting. Section 906 of SOX imposes penalties on managers for knowingly certifying financial statements that do not meet the requirements of US-SOX. I predict that since managers' estimation errors decreased and earnings management declined under effective internal controls system after the application of US-SOX, accruals quality would improve and the accuracy for cash flow predictions would improve.

On the other hand, Graham et al. (2005) and Suda and Hanaeda (2008) give the implication that there is a possibility that managers might shift from accruals management to real management after the passage of US-SOX, following the results of their survey. Cohen et al. (2008) document that accruals management increased until the passage of US-SOX and real management declined prior to US-SOX and increased after the passage of US-SOX. Nakashima (2011) suggests that real management increased after US-SOX application by employing data of the Japanese public firms in the U.S. market. I predict that the decreases in accruals management improve the accuracy for cash flow predictions but the increases in real management reduce the accuracy. This study estimates that the accuracy of cash flow predictions changes depending on the changes in earnings management.

Managers use accounting choices to communicate private information to investors (Subramanyam 1996; Suda 2000). I predict that managers are obliged to offset opportunistic earnings management and convey private information under well-organized internal control systems and corporate governance. Bissessur (2008) asserts that accruals quality does not affect the ability of abnormal accruals to predict future cash flows, indicating abnormal accruals may reflect private information about future cash flows rather earnings management. Abnormal accruals are not necessarily a signal of earnings management, but are also a signal of private information about future cash flows (Bissessur 2008).

This study contributes to the accounting literature in several ways. First, I document whether internal control system regulation affects the improvement of financial reporting quality by providing evidence about the changes in the accuracy for cash flow predictions in the pre-US-SOX period and the post-US-SOX period. The results of this study give a clue to the current controversy regarding cost-benefits of US-SOX regulations. Secondly, I document how changes in earnings management impact on the accuracy of cash flow predictions. The remainder of this chapter is organized as follows. Section two provides hypothesis development. Section three discusses the research design. Section four provides the empirical results and Section five concludes.

4.2 Hypothesis Development

Since the objective of internal controls systems is to prevent and detect accounting errors and fraud which leads to misstatement, a well-organized internal controls system is an effective system for credible financial reporting. Lobo and Zhou (2006) find that firms report lower discretionary accruals after US-SOX. Machuga and Teitel (2007) suggest that earnings quality improved after US-SOX, using a variety of earnings quality characteristics such as income smoothing and abnormal accruals. Bedard (2006) suggests that earnings quality improved in the post-US-SOX period, providing evidence of a decrease in the magnitude of unexpected accruals in their first internal control reports.

Leggett (2008) makes a mixed prediction that although earnings persistence could decrease by the increase in accounting conservatism (Lobo and Zhou, 2006) and by the increases in real earnings management (Cohen et al. 2008) after SOX, earnings persistence could increase in the post-US-SOX period through the decreases in discretionary accruals (Lobo and Zhou 2006; Cohen et al. 2008) and decreases in estimation errors and unclear estimations after US-SOX. But, Leggett (2008) provides evidence that earnings persistence increases after US-SOX.

Thus, previous studies suggest that there is an association between discretionary accruals and persistence, and internal controls. However, there are a few studies regarding the association between the ability of earnings to predict future cash flows and internal controls systems. I predict that since managers' estimation errors and earnings management would decrease under well-organized internal controls systems in the post-US-SOX period, earnings quality (such as the ability of earnings to predict future cash flows) would improve. On the other hand, if managers shift from accruals management to real management after the passage of US-SOX, the ability of earnings to predict future cash flows would decline. Therefore, I set up the following hypothesis:

H1: There is no difference in the ability of earnings to predict future cash flows in the pre-US-SOX period and the post-US-SOX period.

Previous studies (Lobo and Zhou 2006; Machuga and Teitel 2007; Cohen et al.

2008) suggest that regulation of internal control systems improves financial reporting quality (earnings quality). Therefore, if the ability of earnings to predict future cash flows as proxy for earnings quality improves after the passage of US-SOX, what improves the accuracy for cash flow predictions? Is it the improvement of accruals quality, the decreases in accruals management, or the informativeness of accruals? As a result, I posit the following hypotheses.

H2: There are determinants which affect the accuracy for cash flows predictions.

This hypothesis is tested in the following three ways. Since Dechow and Schrand (2004, p.12) suggest that earnings or cash flows are judged to be of higher quality if they are more strongly associated with future cash flow realizations, it seems that future cash flows predictability is related to the relationship between earnings and cash flows. Bissessur (2008, p.78) asserts that accruals quality reflects the relevance of current cash flows and accruals in predicting future cash flows. Bissessur (2008) shows that the ability of accruals to be informative in predicting future cash flows incremental to current cash flows is conditional on accruals quality. According to Bisserssur's (2008) assertion, when accruals quality is low, future cash flows are less likely to be predicted from current cash flows and accruals are incremental to current cash flows in predicting future cash flows. When accruals quality is high, current cash flows are more likely to persist and accruals are less relevant in predicting future cash flows relative to cash flows. This can be explained by the fact that when accrual quality is low, accruals are not more likely to be converted into future cash flows and therefore cash flows are shown to be less persistent. In this case, accruals are relevant incrementally to cash flows in predicting future cash flow.

Tazawa (2004) finds that accruals quality is associated with accruals' role for cash flow prediction and suggests that accruals quality is a determinant of cash flow predictions. Ebihara (2004) suggests that the predictive errors of accruals affect not only the accruals' predictive ability of future cash flows but also the earnings' predictive ability of future cash flows.

Dechow and Dichev (2002) suggest that accruals quality is associated with cash flows volatility, accruals volatility, and earnings volatility and that accruals are related to persistence. Dechow and Schrand (2004) suggest that overstatements and understatements of accruals in the current period are adjusted through accruals in future periods. The recording and subsequent reversal of accrual misstatements result in higher volatility of accruals than of cash flows. Estimation errors from accruals decrease earnings persistence. Thus, I predict that estimation errors by managers reduce accruals quality and cash flow prediction. Doyle et al. (2007a) observe that firm-level internal controls deficiency is significantly associated with accruals quality. I predict that firms organize internal controls systems well and reduce managerial estimation errors and increase accruals quality. Therefore, I set up hypothesis 2a below:

H2a: Accuracy of cash flow prediction is associated with accruals quality.

Graham et al. (2005) and Suda and Hanaeda (2008) suggest that managers conduct real management, such as cutting R&D expenses for stock markets incentives, such as loss avoidance, loss reduction, and to meet targets and that managers like real management better than accruals management. Cohen et al. (2008) and Nakashima (2011) suggest that managers shifted from accruals management to real management after the passage of US-SOX.

The shift from accruals management to real management impacts on earnings quality (Dechow and Schrand 2004). Previous studies regarding real management and cash flow prediction provide mixed results. Leggett (2008) predicts that increases in real earnings management negatively impacts on the persistence of the cash flow component of earnings, since real earnings management, such as the overproduction to lower cost of goods sold, the excessive price discounts to increase sales, and the decreasing R&D costs affect the cash flow component of earnings. However, Leggett (2008) suggests that total earnings persistence increased in the post-US-SOX period relative to the pre-US-SOX period with an increase in the persistence of the cash flow component of earnings.

On the other hand, Roychowdhury (2006) asserts that although outlays on discretionary expenditures lower cash outflows and have a positive effect on abnormal operating cash flows (OCF) in the current period, price discounts and overproduction have a negative effect on contemporaneous abnormal OCF. Thus, Roychowdhury (2006) points out that the net effect on abnormal OCF is unclear. He suggests that abnormal OCF and abnormal discretionary expenses of suspect firm-years have lower and negative effects compared to the rest of the sample.

Gunny (2010) asserts that real management such as reducing R&D costs and SG&A expenses is associated with significantly lower future earnings and cash flows, and that they negatively affect future operating performance. Thus, I predict that the changes in real management through US-SOX regulation affect the ability of earnings to predict future cash flows. Therefore, I set up hypothesis 2b to examine this:

> **H2b:** The ability of earnings to predict future cash flows is associated with earnings management.

Subramanyan (1996) and Suda (2000) suggest that earnings information is a superior measure than cash flows through the analysis of the relation between discretionary accruals and their predictive ability for future performance. They conclude that managers' choice of discretionary accruals communicates private information which improves the predictive ability to investors. Thus, managers' choices of accounting alternatives allow them to reflect value-relevant information on firm value which improves the accuracy of cash flow predictions. Consistent with Subramanyan (1996), Bissessur (2008) shows that accruals quality does not affect the ability of abnormal accruals to predict future cash flows, indicating that abnormal accruals can reflect private information about future cash flows rather than earnings management.

Yoshida (2005) analyzes the effect of accruals and cash flows on capital returns and provides evidence that the accuracy for discretionary accruals and cash flows are higher. Thus, I set up hypothesis 2c to examine this:

> **H2c:** Cash flow prediction is associated with accruals though which managers use to communicate private information.

4.3   Research Design

4.3.1   Cash Flow Prediction Models

In order to test hypothesis 1, I use the following models for cash flow predictions:

$$OCF_{t+1} = \theta_0 + \theta_1 OCF_t + \theta_2 \Delta AR_t + \theta_3 \Delta INV_t + \theta_4 \Delta AP_t + \varepsilon_t.$$

where,

OCF_{t+1} = cash flows from operations at time t+1 ;
NI_t = net operating income at time t ;
ΔAR_t = change in accounts receivable at time t ;
ΔINV_t = change in inventory at time t ;
ΔAP_t = change in accounts payable at time t ;
ε_t = current disturbance term.

I employ a multivariate time-series model (MULT) for one-year-ahead cash flow prediction to be estimated on a firm-specific basis, following Lorek and Willinger (1996). One-year-ahead cash flows predictions are generated in an ex ante fashion through the two cash flows prediction models above. Initially, the two models are estimated using data beginning with year 2000 and ending with year 2004 to generate cash flow prediction for the year 2005. Next, I use data beginning with year 2001 and ending with year 2005 to generate a cash flow prediction for the year 2006. This process is repeated and the models are sequentially re-estimated until all one-year-ahead cash flow predictions over the four year holdout period are obtained (2000-2008). I evaluate forecast accuracy for each model using one of the traditional measures of forecast accuracy measures which are used and accepted widely by academicians and practitioners.[2] The mean absolute percentage error (*MAPE*) is computed as follows:

$$MAPE = \sum_{t=1}^{n} \frac{|e_t|}{|Y_t|}$$

e_t = estimation error in period t,
Y_t = actual value at time t.

4.3.2 Accruals Quality Measures

I use two measures to capture accruals quality; (1) the standard deviation of the residuals from Dechow and Dichev's (2002) model which focuses on unintentional estimation errors or innate firm characteristics, and (2) the standard deviation of the residuals from Francis et al.'s (2008) model which focuses not only estimation errors but also on managers' intentional earnings management:

$$\Delta WC_t = \beta_0 + \beta_1 OCF_{t-1} + \beta_2 CFO_t + \beta_3 CFO_{t+1} + \varepsilon_t. \quad (1)$$
$$\Delta WC_t = \beta_0 + \beta_1 OCF_{t-1} + \beta_2 CFO_t + \beta_3 CFO_{t+1} + \beta_4 \Delta SALES_t + \beta_5 PPE_t + \varepsilon_t. \quad (2)$$

Accruals quality is based on the standard deviation of the residuals estimated from firm-specific time-series regression. The residuals from regression reflect the accruals that are unrelated to cash flow realizations, where higher standard deviation expresses lower quality (Dechow and Dichev 2002). This measure means the extent to which they map into past, current, and future cash flow. But, as Francis et al. (2008) points out that the Dechow and Dichev's (2002) model assesses accruals as a whole and does not separate effects of managers' discretions from all other effects. McNichols (2002) asserts that economic and structural factors can cause variation in the precision of accruals estimates, regardless of the presence or absence of managerial discretion and that managerial expertise also influences the precision of estimation, even if other factors are held constant. That is, the link between accruals and cash flow realization in adjacent periods is affected by economic and structural factors, managerial expertise, and intentional managerial discretions. By linking the Dechow and Dichev's (2002) model and Jones' (1991) models,[3] the Francis et al. (2008) model can capture errors associated with both unintentional estimations and intentional management estimations.

4.3.3 Earning Management Measures

There is a clear distinction between fraudulent accounting practices and those accounting practices which fall within GAAP. Earnings management which falls within GAAP can be focused on three types of earnings management; conservative accounting, neutral accounting, and aggressive accounting (Dechow and Skinner 2000). According to Dechow and Skinner (2000), conservative accounting includes overly aggressive recognition of provision or reserve, overvaluation of acquired in-process R&D in purchase acquisitions, overstatement of restructuring charges and asset write-offs for accruals management, and delaying sales, accelerating R&D or advertising expenditure for real management. Neutral accounting includes earnings that result from a neutral operation of the process, such as income smoothing accounting (Suda 2007). Aggressive accounting includes the understatement of the provisions for bad debts and drawing down provisions or reserves in an overly aggressive manner for accruals management, and postponing R&D or advertising expenditures and accelerating sales for real management.

I post three proxies for accruals management measures. In order to capture conservative accruals management, following Leuz et al. (2003) I use the absolute value of reported earnings volatility divided by the cash flows volatility as the proxy for conservative accruals management measure (C_EM). The conservative accounting management measure captures the degree to which managers smooth the variability of reported earnings by managing accruals. Low values of this measure of accrual management indicate that managers exercise discretion to smooth reported earnings. Managers sometimes may use their discretionary accruals to produce the desired level of earnings. Dechow and Schrand (2004) point out that high accruals in absolute magnitude is a potential "opportunistically earnings management."

I employ an absolute value of firm's accruals divided by absolute value of firms' operating cash flows as neutral accounting management measure (N_EM) for the extent to which managers exercise discretion in reporting earnings following Leuz et al (2003). But, as Leuz et al. (2003) mention, managers use their discretion not only in order to misstate their firms' performance, but also to convey their inside information to increase imformativeness (Subramanyam 1996). This study uses discretionary accruals estimated the by Jones' (1991) model as aggressive earnings management.

Managers can take real actions which affect cash flows by delaying or accelerating sales and accelerating or postponing R&D or advertising expenses (Dechow and Skinner 2000). I follow previous studies to use my proxies for real earnings management. However, it is difficult to document the extent to which managers engage in real management to manipulate earnings. Merely observing that a firm enters into a transaction that receives favorable accounting treatment is not evidence that the firm entered into the transaction just because of its accounting consequence (Dechow and Schrand 2004).

Graham et al. (2005) and Suda and Hanaeda (2008) find strong evidence that managers take real managements such as "decrease discretionary spending on R&D, advertising, and maintenance" to meet an earnings target much more than accounting management such as "book revenue now rather than next quarter" and "alter accounting assumptions." Baber et al. (1991) investigate whether concern about reporting earnings has an effect on decisions to invest in R&D and suggest that relative R&D spending is significantly less when spending jeopardized the ability to report positive or increasing earnings in the current period. Thomas and Zang (2002) document that firms with inventory increases (decreases) have experienced higher (lower) levels of profitability, growth and abnormal returns over the prior five years and those trends reverse immediately after the inventory change. They suggest two possible reasons. One possibility is related to earnings management, potentially by misstating inventory balances. The other is related to variation in production levels and altering *COGs* by affecting the amount of fixed manufacturing overhead absorbed into each unit produced. Inventory changes are related naturally to demand shifts and both possibilities rely on features unique to inventories.

Thus, following Roychowdhury (2006) and Cohen et al.(2008), this study focuses on three earnings management techniques: sales manipulation, reduction of discretionary expenditures, and production manipulation and how these affect *OCF*, discretionary expenses, such as R&D, and production costs. Sales manipulation includes accelerating or delaying sales. Production costs manipulation includes reporting lower *COGS* by reducing production costs per unit to increase production. I develop three proxies, abnormal *OCF* (*abnOCF*) and abnormal production costs (*abnPROD*), and abnormal discretionary expenses (*abnDE*) for real management.

I generate the normal *OCF* and the normal production costs. I compute normal *OCF* as a linear function of sales and change in sales. I compute abnormal *OCF* by subtracting the normal level of *OCF* calculated using the estimated coefficient from the equation from actual OCF^4:

$$OCF_t = \alpha_0 + \alpha_1 SALES_t + \alpha_2 \Delta SALES_t + \varepsilon_t.$$

I compute abnormal production costs by subtracting the normal level of the sum of *COGS* and change in inventory from actual production costs. I estimate the normal level of production costs as the following equation:

$$\begin{aligned} PROD_t &= COG_t + \Delta INV_t \\ &= \alpha_0 + \alpha_1 SALES_t + \alpha_2 \Delta SALES_t + \alpha_3 \Delta SALES_{t-1} + \varepsilon_t. \end{aligned}$$

I estimate abnormal discretionary expenses by subtracting the normal level of the sum of advertising expenses, R&D expenses, and administrative expenses. I estimate the normal level of discretionary expenses as the following equation.

$$Discretionary\ Expenses\ (DE)_t = \alpha_0 + \alpha_1\ SALES_{t-1} + \varepsilon_t.$$

4.3.4 Testing Hypotheses

In order to test H1, first, I conduct mean differences analyses for *MAPEs* for the earnings model and the accrual components model. Next, I use the following regression model. If a coefficient of SOX (β_1) <0, the earning's predictive ability for future cash flow is improved. I test hypothesis H2a using the following regression model:

$$\begin{aligned} MAPE = &\ \beta_0 + \beta_1\ SOX + \beta_2\ \Delta WC_t + \beta_3\ OCF_t + \beta_4\ WC_t{*}SOX \\ &+ \beta_5\ OCF_t{*}SOX + \theta_6\ LDEBT_t + \theta_7\ LDEBT_t{*}SOX \\ &+ \theta_8\ SIZE_t + \theta_9\ AUDIT_t + \theta_{10}\ DECAVOID_t + \theta_{11}\ LOSSAVOID_t \\ &+ \theta_{12}\ DECAVOID{*}SOX + \theta_{13}\ LOSSAVOID{*}SOX + \theta_{15}\ AQ_t + \theta_{16}\ AQ_t{*}SOX + \varepsilon_{t+1}, \end{aligned}$$

Where,

MAPE	= mean absolute percentage errors;
SOX	=1 in the post-SOX period, and 0 otherwise;
ΔWC_t	=changes in working capital;
OCF_t	=operating cash flows;
$LDEBT_t$	=long-term debt;
$SIZE_t$	=log of total sales;
$AUDIT_t$	=1 if the firm is audited by a big N auditor, and 0 otherwise;
$DECAVOID_t$	=1 if [(current year's income before discretionary accruals – last years' income) is between (0,-0.0032), otherwise 0.
$LOSSAVOID_t$	=1 if [(current year's income before discretionary accruals) is between (0,-0.00337), otherwise 0.
AQ	=accruals quality;
ε	=error term.

I test H2b and H2c using the following regression model. Managers may follow an overall earnings management strategy and choose earnings management with lower costs. As they can choose less costly earning management between accruals and real management, I put either earnings management into the model. I estimate discretionary accruals using the Jones' (1991) model.[5] I include the variables *LEV*, *SIZE*, and *AUDIT* as control variables:

$$\begin{aligned}MAPE = & \beta_0 + \beta_1 SOX + \beta_2 \Delta WC_t + \beta_3 OCF_t + \beta_4 \Delta WC_t{}^*SOX + \beta_5 OCF_t{}^*SOX \\ & + \beta_5 OCF_t{}^*SOX + \theta_6 LDEBT_t + \theta_7 LDEBT_t{}^*SOX + \theta_8 SIZE_t + \theta_9 AUDIT_t \\ & + \theta_{10} DECAVOID_t + \theta_{11} LOSSAVOID_t + \theta_{12} DECAVOID{}^*SOX \\ & + \theta_{13} LOSSAVOID{}^*SOX + \beta_{14} EM_t + \beta_{15} EM{}^*SOX + \varepsilon_{t+1}\end{aligned}$$

4.3.5 Sample Selection and Data

Since internal control regulation has been started in 2008 in Japan, all public firms in Japan should disclose their internal control statement for their first fiscal year ending on or after March, 2009. As accumulated data cannot be obtained at the present time, I employ data of listed Japanese firms in the U.S. market from 2000 through 2009.[6]

The sample used in this study is for the period 2000-2009 from the Nikkei Economic Electronic Databank System (NEEDS) through following the criteria: (1) SEC-registered firms, (2) the month in which the fiscal year ends is March or August, (3) not financial institutions.

4.4 Empirical Results

4.4.1 Descriptive Statistics and Time-Series Plot of MAPEs

Table 4.1 provides descriptive statistics of earnings management, accruals quality, and mean absolute percentage errors. The signs and magnitudes of each earnings management are consistent with those of Cohen et al. (2008). Since *DA2* is discretionary accruals estimated by the Jones' (1991) model, the average *DA2* is zero (Cohen et al. 2008, p.769).

Figure 4.1 illustrates the trends over time in *MAPEs* for the earnings model and *MAPEs* for the accrual components model. Figure 4.1 indicates that *MAPEs* for the earnings model decreases gradually but *MAPEs* for the accrual components model are stable over time. It should be noted that the accuracy of cash flows predictions for both models has been not improved after US-SOX.

4.4.2 Tests of Hypothesis 1

Table 4.2 provides descriptive statistics of *MAPEs* in the pre-and the post-US-SOX

TABLE 4.1   Descriptive Statistics (n=256)

	Mean	Median	Standard Deviaion	Minimum	Maximum	25th Percentile	75th Percentile
OCF	0.084	0.074	0.060	-0.035	0.306	0.041	0.105
NI	0.039	0.031	0.049	-0.102	0.229	0.010	0.058
ΔWC	0.002	0.002	0.029	-0.167	0.139	-0.010	0.014
ACCRULAS	-0.044	-0.042	0.048	-0.232	0.141	-0.066	-0.014
ΔAR	-0.004	-0.003	0.026	-0.125	0.179	-0.017	0.008
ΔINV	-0.003	-0.003	0.017	-0.080	0.072	-0.010	0.004
ΔAP	0.002	0.003	0.018	-0.085	0.104	-0.005	0.011
PPE	0.229	0.219	0.117	0.011	0.639	0.152	0.277
OCF_{t-1}	0.083	0.071	0.064	-0.035	0.313	0.037	0.107
OCF_{t+1}	0.083	0.073	0.059	-0.035	0.306	0.041	0.105
MAPEni	0.227	0.143	0.251	0.002	1.000	0.067	0.289
MAPEcomponents	0.140	0.072	0.194	0.000	1.000	0.029	0.160
DA2	0.000	0.000	0.020	-0.136	0.075	-0.009	0.009
abnOCF	0.000	0.001	0.021	-0.080	0.127	-0.009	0.009
abnPROD	0.000	0.000	0.015	-0.044	0.063	-0.007	0.006
abneDE	0.000	0.000	0.021	-0.096	0.117	-0.004	0.002
DECAVOID_DA2	0.001	0.002	0.247	-1.688	1.730	-0.013	0.023
LOSSAVOID_DA2	0.040	0.032	0.298	-2.206	2.402	0.007	0.066
adjustOCF	-0.001	-0.012	0.060	-0.119	0.222	-0.043	0.021
adjustLDEBT	0.003	-0.034	0.124	-0.116	0.370	-0.099	0.061
C_EM	0.686	0.755	0.338	0.013	1.421	0.394	1.000
N_EM	0.360	0.170	0.745	0.000	8.500	0.069	0.363
AQ_DD	0.027	0.023	0.018	0.008	0.123	0.016	0.033
AQ_MN	0.026	0.021	0.024	0.004	0.216	0.013	0.032

Variable Definitions: all variables are deflated by average assets.

OCF	cash flows from operations
NI	net income
ΔWC	changes in working capitals $= \Delta AR + \Delta INV - \Delta AP - \Delta TAX\ Payable + \Delta other\ assets(net)$
ACCRUAL	net income minus operating cash flows
ΔAR	changes in accounts receivable
ΔINV	changes in inventory
ΔAP	changes in accounts payable
PPE	property, plant, and equipment
OCFt-1	cash flows from operating at t-1
OCFt+1	cash flows from operating at t+1
MAPEni	mean absolute percentage errors estimating by earnings model
MAPEcomponents	mean absolute percentage errors estimating by accrual components model
DA2	discretionary current accruals estimating by Jones, (1991) model
abnOCF	the level of abnormal operating cash flows; estimated by the regression $OCF_t = \alpha_t SALES_t + \alpha_2 \Delta SALES_t$
abnPROD	the level of abnormal production cost, where production costs are defined as the sum of cost of goods sold and the changes in inventories; that is estimated by the regression $(COG + \Delta INV) = \alpha_t SALES_t + \alpha_2 \Delta SALES_t + \alpha_3 \Delta SALES_{t-1}$
abnDE	the level of abnormal discretionary expenses, where discretionary expenses are the sum of advertisement expenses, R&D expenses and administrative expenses; that is estimated by the regression $DE = \alpha_t + \alpha_2 SALES_{t-1}$
DECAVOID_DA2	1 if [(current year's income before discretionary working capital accruals by estimated by DeAngelo (1989) models)/average assets] is between (-0.03, 0) and 0 otherwise.
LOSSAVOID_DA2	1 if [(current year's income before discretionary working capital accruals by estimated by DeAngelo (1989) models) −last years' income/average assets] is between (-0.015, 0) and 0 otherwise.
adjustOCF	OCF-mean of OCF
adjustLDEBT	DEBT-mean DEBT
C_EM	conservative earnings management; the absolute value of earnings volatility/the absolute value of OCFvolatility
N_EM	neutral earnings management; the absolute value of changes in working capitals/ the absolute value of OC
AQ_DD	accruals quality; the standard deviation of the residuals from Dechow and Dichev's (2002) model
AQ_MN	accruals quality; the standard deviation of the residuals from Francis et al.'s (2008) model

Figure 4.1 Time-Series Plot of MAPEs (2004-2007)

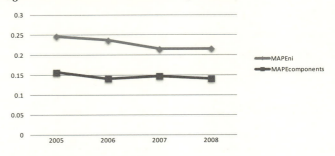

TABLE 4.2 Descriptive Statistics for MAPEs of Each Model

	Pre-US-SOX			Post-US-SOX			t-value	significance
	N	Mean	Std. Deviation		Mean	Std. Deviation		
MAPEni	159	0.237	0.267	62	0.201	0.209	-1.060	0.291
MAPEcomponents	159	0.139	0.195	62	0.142	0.197	0.110	0.913

Notes: See Table 4.1 for definitions of each variable. ** Significant at 10 percent, ** at 5 percent, and *** at 1 percent levels, respectively.

periods. Table 4.2 compares *MAPE* in the pre-US-SOX period to *MAPEs* in the post-US-SOX period. MAPEni has declined and MAPEcomponent has slightly increased in the post-US-SOX period. There are differences in the ability of earnings to predict future cash flows by both models in the pre-US-SOX period and the post-US-SOX period, but both t-values are not significant. Therefore, this result does not support H1.

4.4.3 Tests of Hypothesis 2

Test of H2a

Table 4.3 reports the correlation among accruals quality, earnings management measures and firm characteristics. Table 3 shows that the accruals quality measures, Accruals Quality_DD (*AQ_DD*) and Accruals Quality_FR (*AQ_FR*) are significantly positively correlated with MAPEs. Table 4.4 presents the results of the determinants of cash flow prediction. I find a significant positive relation between *AQ_DD* and *AQ_FR* and *MAPE*. This suggests that accruals quality has been affected by estimation errors and earnings management. Especially, this shows that estimation errors by managers and earnings management impact on accruals quality in the post-US-SOX period.

TABLE 4.3 Correlation between Accruals Quality and MAPEs (n=244)

	OCF_{t+1}	SOX	AQ_DD	AQ_FR	MAPEni	MAPEcomponents
OCF_{t+1}	1.000	0.008	0.451	0.471	-0.357	-0.326
	.	0.904	0.000	0.000	0.000	0.000
			***	***	***	***
SOX	0.050	1.000	0.011	0.051	-0.063	0.007
	0.453	.	0.866	0.412	0.347	0.920
AQ_DD	0.510	0.016	1.000	0.721	0.229	0.205
	0.000	0.804	.	0.000	0.001	0.002
	***			***	***	***
AQ_FR	0.395	0.073	0.593	1.000	0.153	0.275
	0.000	0.246	0.000	.	0.022	0.000
	***		***		***	***
MAPEni	-0.318	-0.025	0.134	0.063	1.000	0.557
	0.000	0.707	0.045	0.350	.	0.000
	***		**			***
MAPEcomponents	-0.287	-0.010	0.073	0.282	0.303	1.000
	0.000	0.876	0.279	0.000	0.000	.
	***			***	***	

Notes: Correlations above (below) the diagonal are Pearson (Spearman) correlations. The bottom number in each is a two-tail p-value. See Table 4.1 for definition of each variable. The second low is t-value following to White (1980).
** Significant at 10 percent, ** at 5 percent, and *** at 1 percent levels, respecively.

TABLE 4.4 Association between Accruals and MAPEs

Panel:MAPEni	AQ_DD			AQ_FR		
	B	t-statistic	significance	B	t-statistic	significance
(Constant)	0.101	1.598	0.112	0.085	1.269	0.206
SOX	0.036	0.410	0.682	-0.004	-0.052	0.959
ΔWC	0.723	1.125	0.262	0.551	0.846	0.399
ΔWC*SOX	-3.143	-1.818	0.071	-2.672	-1.511	0.132
OCF	-1.696	-4.439	0.000 ***	-1.632	-4.210	0.000 ***
OCF*SOX	0.230	0.278	0.781	0.377	0.465	0.642
DEBT	0.013	0.062	0.951	-0.110	-0.546	0.586
LDEBT*SOX	-0.051	-0.148	0.883	0.054	0.152	0.879
SIZE	0.014	0.397	0.692	0.032	0.873	0.384
AUDIT	-0.045	-0.790	0.430	0.013	0.225	0.822
DECAVOID_DA2	0.215	2.521	0.013 **	0.233	2.699	0.008 ***
DECAVOIDDA2* SOX	-0.014	-0.083	0.934	-0.025	-0.151	0.880
LOSSAVOID_DA2	0.001	0.033	0.974	0.009	0.204	0.839
LOSSAVOID_DA2*SOX	0.061	0.692	0.490	0.075	0.831	0.407
AQ	6.090	5.015	0.000 ***	5.276	4.207	0.000 ***
AQ*SOX	-2.946	-1.005	0.316	-1.846	-0.619	0.537
R^2	0.251			0.225		
Adjust R^2	0.194			0.166		
F-value (Pr>F)	4.401 (<0.0001)			3.822 (<0.0001)		

Notes: See Table 4.1 for definition of each variable. ** Significant at 10 percent, ** at 5 percent, and *** at 1 percent levels, respecively.

Test of H2b

Table 4.5 presents the correlation among earnings management and MAPEs. There is a positive correlation between *MAPEni* and *DA2* (Pearson 0.115), suggesting that

TABLE 4.5   Correlation between MAPEs and Earnings Management (n=256)

	SOX	OCF_{t+1}	MAPEni	MAPEcomponents	C_EM	N_EM	DA2	abnOCF	abnPROD	abnDE
SOX	1.000	0.008	-0.063	0.007	-0.081	-0.048	0.142	-0.002	0.010	-0.030
		0.904	0.347	0.920	0.196	0.451	0.023	0.971	0.877	0.634
							**			
OCF_{t+1}	0.050	1.000	-0.357	-0.326	0.060	-0.244	-0.069	0.008	0.045	0.025
	0.453		0.000	0.000	0.369	0.000	0.302	0.907	0.504	0.708
			***	***		***				
MAPEni	-0.025	-0.318	1.000	0.557	-0.030	0.204	0.115	-0.089	-0.103	-0.017
	0.707	0.000		0.000	0.658	0.002	0.088	0.186	0.125	0.801
		***		***		***	*			
MAPEcomponents	-0.010	-0.287	0.303	1.000	-0.019	0.219	0.075	-0.059	-0.003	-0.071
	0.876	0.000	0.000		0.781	0.001	0.262	0.382	0.961	0.293
		***	***			***				
C_EM	-0.074	0.137	-0.079	0.070	1.000	-0.185	0.116	-0.134	-0.005	0.077
	0.236	0.040	0.242	0.301		0.003	0.063	0.032	0.938	0.222
		**				***	*	**		
N_EM	-0.135	-0.313	0.126	0.159	-0.041	1.000	0.112	-0.162	0.010	-0.017
	0.032	0.000	0.063	0.018	0.515		0.076	0.010	0.879	0.793
	**	***	*	**			*	**		
DA2	0.117	-0.076	0.038	-0.063	0.094	0.179	1.000	-0.719	-0.214	-0.152
	0.062	0.257	0.572	0.353	0.132	0.004		0.000	0.001	0.015
	*					***		***	***	**
abnOCF	0.038	0.036	-0.074	0.049	-0.145	-0.322	-0.619	1.000	0.020	0.039
	0.549	0.594	0.271	0.463	0.020	0.000	0.000		0.751	0.534
					**	***	***			
abnPROD	-0.011	0.086	-0.090	0.018	-0.001	0.085	-0.175	-0.112	1.000	-0.098
	0.865	0.198	0.180	0.790	0.992	0.180	0.005	0.074		0.119
							***	*		
abnDE	0.029	0.013	-0.022	-0.084	0.067	0.021	-0.071	0.009	-0.102	1.000
	0.648	0.847	0.742	0.213	0.289	0.742	0.259	0.881	0.103	

Notes: Correlations above (below) the diagonal are Pearson (Spearman) correlations. The bottom number in each is a two-tail p-value. See Table 4.1 for definitions of each variable. The second low is t-value following to White (1980) . ** Significant at 10 percent, ** at 5 percent, and *** at 1 percent levels, respectively.

earnings management makes prediction error larger.

Table 4.6 shows the determinants of cash flow predictions. Table 4.6 presents that *MAPEni* is significantly negatively associated with *abnPROD* and positively associated with *abnPROD*SOX*, suggesting that real management, *abnPROD* makes the prediction errors larger.

Test of H2c

Table 4.6 shows that *MAPEni* of *abnDE* is significantly negatively associated with *ΔWC*SOX*, suggesting that working capital changes negatively affect *MAPEs*. It is noted that accruals has a role of signaling of private information.

In summary, I find that the determinants of accuracy for cash flow predictions are accruals quality, accruals management and abnormal production costs, and

TABLE 4.6   Determinants of Accruals Management

	Consevative_AM				Neutral_AM				ABS_DA1_B		
	Coefficient	t-statistic	significance		B	t-value	significance		B	t-value	significance
(Constant)	0.265	3.794	0.000 ***	(Constant)	0.185	3.346	0.001 ***	(Constant)	0.234	3.849	0.000 ***
SOX	0.009	0.093	0.926	SOX	-0.102	-2.064	0.040 **	SOX	-0.049	-1.003	0.317
ΔWC	0.049	0.076	0.940	ΔWC	-0.015	-0.023	0.981	ΔWC	-0.150	-0.156	0.876
ΔWC*SOX	-2.945	-1.575	0.117	ΔWC*SOX	-2.563	-1.335	0.183	ΔWC*SOX	-2.803	-0.951	0.343
OCF	-1.273	-3.686	0.000 ***	OCF	-1.129	-3.328	0.001 ***	OCF	-1.338	-3.135	0.002 ***
OCF*SOX	-0.195	-0.236	0.813	OCF*SOX	0.747	0.882	0.379	OCF*SOX	0.033	0.038	0.970
DEBT	-0.295	-1.528	0.128	DEBT	-0.337	-1.804	0.073 *	DEBT	-0.314	-1.536	0.126
LDEBT*SOX	-0.112	-0.302	0.763	LDEBT*SOX	0.216	0.651	0.516	LDEBT*SOX	0.150	0.422	0.674
SIZE	0.000	0.002	0.999	SIZE	0.002	0.046	0.963	SIZE	0.000	0.000	1.000
AUDIT	0.013	0.235	0.815	AUDIT	0.050	0.909	0.364	AUDIT	-0.008	-0.129	0.897
DECAVOID_DA2	0.252	2.803	0.005 ***	DECAVOID_DA2	0.216	2.402	0.017 **	DECAVOID_DA2	0.246	2.718	0.007 ***
DECAVOIDDA2*SOX	-0.043	-0.250	0.803	DECAVOIDDA2*SOX	0.016	0.092	0.927	DECAVOIDDA2*SOX	-0.028	-0.158	0.875
LOSSAVOID_DA2	-0.047	-1.105	0.270	LOSSAVOID_DA2	-0.040	-0.969	0.334	LOSSAVOID_DA2	-0.012	-0.263	0.793
LOSSAVOID_DA2*SOX	0.071	0.755	0.451	LOSSAVOID_DA2*SOX	0.120	1.315	0.190	LOSSAVOID_DA2*SOX	0.073	0.778	0.437
C_EM	-0.043	-0.745	0.457	N_EM	0.041	1.669	0.096 *	DA2	0.948	0.688	0.492
C_EM*SOX	-0.105	-0.895	0.372	N_EM*SOX	0.059	0.865	0.388	DA2*SOX	-0.298	-0.074	0.941
R^2		0.142		R^2		0.158		R^2		0.152	
Adjust R^2		0.850		Adjust R^2		0.102		Adjust R^2		0.088	
F-value (Pr>F)		2.506 (<0.002)		F-value (Pr>F)		2.833 (<0.0001)		F-value (Pr>F)		2.362 (<0.004)	
	Consevative_AM				Neutral_AM				ABS_DA1_B		
	Coefficient	t-statistic	significance		B	t-value	significance		B	t-value	significance
(Constant)	0.232	3.816	0.000 ***	(Constant)	0.244	4.079	0.000 ***	(Constant)	0.228	3.634	0.000 ***
SOX	-0.050	-1.020	0.309	SOX	-0.067	-1.390	0.166	SOX	-0.058	-0.897	0.371
ΔWC	0.185	0.217	0.828	ΔWC	-0.103	-0.146	0.884	ΔWC	0.489	0.678	0.499
ΔWC*SOX	-3.139	-1.418	0.158	ΔWC*SOX	-2.970	-1.487	0.139	ΔWC*SOX	-3.970	-1.768	0.079 *
OCF	-1.381	-3.038	0.003 ***	OCF	-1.437	-3.633	0.000 ***	OCF	-1.435	-3.454	0.001 ***
OCF*SOX	0.143	0.160	0.873	OCF*SOX	-0.538	-0.581	0.562	OCF*SOX	-0.121	-0.128	0.898
DEBT	-0.309	-1.500	0.135	DEBT	-0.298	-1.486	0.139 *	DEBT	-0.336	-1.560	0.121
LDEBT*SOX	0.158	0.450	0.653	LDEBT*SOX	0.079	0.233	0.816	LDEBT*SOX	-0.373	-0.513	0.608
SIZE	0.000	0.002	0.999	SIZE	-0.003	-0.072	0.943	SIZE	0.010	0.225	0.822
AUDIT	-0.006	-0.101	0.919	AUDIT	-0.017	-0.293	0.770	AUDIT	0.000	0.004	0.997
DECAVOID_DA2	0.245	2.700	0.008 ***	DECAVOID_DA2	0.221	2.465	0.015 **	DECAVOID_DA2	0.241	2.585	0.011 **
DECAVOIDDA2*SOX	-0.027	-0.156	0.876	DECAVOIDDA2*SOX	0.018	0.107	0.915	DECAVOIDDA2*SOX	0.375	1.309	0.192
LOSSAVOID_DA2	-0.013	-0.279	0.781	LOSSAVOID_DA2	-0.017	-0.381	0.704	LOSSAVOID_DA2	-0.016	-0.326	0.745
LOSSAVOID_DA2*SOX	0.077	0.811	0.418	LOSSAVOID_DA2*SOX	0.087	0.944	0.346	LOSSAVOID_DA2*SOX	0.019	0.154	0.878
abnOCF	-0.324	-0.260	0.795	abnPROD	-2.415	-1.884	0.061 *	abnDE	0.048	0.049	0.961
abnOCF*SOX	-0.517	-0.207	0.837	abnPPOD*SOX	6.102	2.434	0.016 **	abnDE*SOX	-0.782	-0.286	0.775
R^2		0.151		R^2		0.187		R^2		0.166	
Adjust R^2		0.087		Adjust R^2		0.125		Adjust R^2		0.096	
F-value (Pr>F)		2.340 (<0.004)		F-value (Pr>F)		2.999 (<0.000)		F-value (Pr>F)		2.381 (<0.004)	

Notes: See Table 1 for definitions of each variable. * Significant at 10 percent, ** at 5 percent, and *** at 1 percent levels, respecively.

accruals, suggesting that the results support H2a, H2b, and H2c in general. It is noted that accruals quality had been negatively affected by accruals management in the pre-US-SOX period, but accruals quality and the accuracy for cash flow predictions have been improved in the post-US-SOX period. On the other hand, the accuracy for cash flow predictions declined through real management, such as abnormal production costs. Overall, there is no change in earnings management in the pre-US-SOX and post-US-SOX periods.

4.5 Conclusion

This chapter investigates whether the ability of earnings to predict future cash flow has been changed in the pre-and post-US-SOX periods. The results show that the accuracy for cash flow predictions by the earnings model has been improved but the accuracy for cash flow predictions by the accruals component model has remained unchanged. Next, I examine the determinants of the accuracy for cash flow predictions. It should be noted that there is a significant positive correlation between accruals quality and prediction errors and that both accruals quality are associated with *MAPEs*, suggesting that accruals quality has been affected by managers' estimation errors and earnings management. Also, accruals management has a significant explanatory power for prediction errors. On the other hand, real management, abnormal production costs, makes prediction errors larger in the post-US-SOX period.

In summary, managers of SEC-registered Japanese firms decreased accruals management and increased real management, such as abnormal production costs, in general. This suggests that there is no change in the accuracy for cash flow predictions in pre-and post-US-SOX periods.

Notes:
1. Financial reporting quality has the following perspectives to be evaluated: (1) financial analysis perspective which are supported by Dechow and Schrand (2004) and Francis et al. (2008), (2) contracts and decision usefulness perspective, (3) Financial Accounting Standard Board's (FASB) conceptual framework perspective which is supported by Schipper and Vincent (2003), and (4) comparative usefulness of cash flows v.s. earnings information perspective. Since measures are different depending on the perspectives, an author should determine which perspective should be taken for discussing earnings quality. My perspective follows Dechow and Schrand (2004) and Francis et al. (2008) which extend Dechow and Schrand (2006). Earnings quality is defined as a summary indicator of financial reporting quality. Francis et al. (2008) identify as accounting-based earnings: quality; accruals quality, abnormal accruals, persistence, predictability, and smoothness.

2. There are the mean absolute error (MAE), the mean square error (MSE), the root mean square error (RMSE), and Theil's U other than MAPE. This study employs the MAPE following Loreck and Willinger's (1996) measure of forecast accuracy.
3. In Jones' (1991) model, $\Delta WC_t = \beta_0 + \beta_1(\Delta SALES) + \beta_2 PPE + \varepsilon_t$, $\beta_0 + \beta_1(\Delta SALES) + \beta_2 PPE + \varepsilon_t$ are assumed to be non-discretionary accruals, and ε_t, the residual from the equation is discretionary accruals.
4. All variables employed in the model which estimates abnormal OCF and abnormal PROD are deflated by average assets. Roychowdhury's (2006) and Cohen et al.'s (2008) models used beginning year assets as deflators for abnormal OCF and abnormal PROD as proxies for real management. Since I use average assets as deflators for all variables for the Dechow and Dichev's (2002) model, Francis et al.'s (2008) model, and Doyle et al' study (2007a), I used average assets as the same deflators for abnormal OCF and abnormal PROD as the accrual quality model.
5. I estimate Jones' (1991) model each year cross-sectionally for all sample firms, using the following regression model. $\Delta WC_t = \beta_0 + \beta_1 \Delta SALES_t + \beta_2 PPE_t + \varepsilon_t$ *Discretionary Accruals* are computed by deducting estimated non-discretionary accruals from real accruals.
6. The sample firms are as follows: Nippon Ham, Wacol, Fuji Film, Komatsu, Hitachi, Toshiba, Mitsubishi Electric, NEC, Panasonic (former Matsushita), Sanyo, Sony, Omron, Pioneer, Murata, Makita, Kyocera, Honda, Canon, Ricoh, Itochu, Marubeni, Mitsui. The SEC required NEC to make restatements regarding annual reports from 2001 through 2006. NEC was not able to disclose the 2006 annual report nor make restatements by the deadline of September 2007. Therefore, the SEC stopped NEC from trading on the NASDAQ from September 27, 2007. Pioneer decided to withdraw from the NY Stock Market in January 24, 2006. NEC and Pioneer data are excluded in my sample.

CHAPTER 5
ACCRUALS QUALITY

5.1 Introduction

This chapter investigates whether financial reporting quality has been improved from pre-US-SOX period to post-US-SOX period. Following Francis et al.'s (2008), financial analysis perspective, I take accruals quality as the financial reporting quality measurement in this chapter. Also, I document what determines accruals quality. Nakashima (2011) documents that real management increases in the post-US-SOX period and Nakashima (2010) suggests that there is no change in the ability of earnings to predict future cash flows after the passage of SOX. Therefore, I examine whether changes in the accuracy for cash flow predictions and the changes in earnings management in the pre-US-SOX and the post-US-SOX periods impact on accruals quality.

Since internal control systems were introduced in the world, studies which focus on the effect of US-SOX regulations on financial reporting quality had been conducted (Lobo and Zhou 2006; Machuga and Teitel 2007; Brown et al. 2007; Cohen et al. 2008; Leggett 2008; Ruth and Guthrie 2008; Nakashima 2010; Nakashima 2011). Although Lobo and Zhou 2006; Machuga and Teitel 2007; Brown et al. 2014; Cohen et al. 2008) suggest that US-SOX improves financial reporting quality, Nakashima (2010; 2011) suggests that it is not known that US-SOX is associated with the accuracy for cash flow predictions. Therefore, I examine what determines accruals quality in Japanese firms in this study.

This study is different from previous studies in two major ways. First, this study provides evidence regarding changes in accruals quality in the pre-US-SOX and the post-US-SOX periods, using SEC-registered Japanese firms. Second, this study suggests that real management is associated with accruals quality. Providing that the effects of SOX on earnings management and suggesting how the changes in real management through US-SOX impact on accruals quality helps us consider the cost-benefit of internal control systems.

The remainder of this chapter is organized as follows. Section two discusses the definitions and the estimation model of accrual quality. Section three shows previous studies. Section four develops the hypotheses. Section five provides research design. Section six presents the empirical results. Section seven concludes this chapter.

5.2 Accruals Quality

5.2.1 Accruals Quality Definition

Doyle et al. (2007a) find that there is a relationship between internal control deficiency and accruals quality measures used by Francis et al. (2008). I take the definition of accruals quality as the degree to which accruals map into cash flows and the residuals from firm-specific regressions of changes in working capital on past, present and future operating cash flows as developed by Dechow and Dichev (2002).

5.2.2 Accruals Quality Measures

The Dechow and Dichev's (2002) model (1) and the Francis et al.'s (2008) model (2) to estimate accruals quality are shown as follows:

$$\Delta WC_t = \beta_0 + \beta_1 OCF_{t-1} + \beta_2 CFO_t + \beta_3 CFO_{t+1} + \varepsilon_t \qquad (1)$$
$$\Delta WC_t = \beta_0 + \beta_1 OCF_{t-1} + \beta_2 CFO_t + \beta_3 CFO_{t+1} + \beta_4 \Delta SALES_t + \beta_5 PPE_t + \varepsilon_t. \qquad (2)$$

Accruals quality is based on the standard deviation of the residuals estimated from firm-specific time-series regression, the equation (1). The residuals from regression reflect the accruals that are unrelated to cash flow realizations, where higher standard deviation expresses lower quality (Dechow and Dichev, 2002). This measure means the extent to which they map into past, current, and future cash flow. But, as McNichols (2002) points out, the Dechow and Dichev's (2002) model does not separate discretionary accruals from non-discretionary accruals but takes accruals as a whole. The Dechow and Dichev's (2002) model focuses on accrual estimation errors or innate firm characteristics but does not capture a bias from manager's intentional discretion.

In the Jones' (1991) model, $\Delta WC_t = \beta_0 + \beta_1 (\Delta SALES) + \beta_2 PPE + \varepsilon_t$, $\beta_0 + \beta_1 (\Delta SALES) + \beta_2 PPE + \varepsilon_t$ are assumed to be non-discretionary accruals, and ε_t, the residual from the equation is discretionary accruals. The Dechow and Dichev (2002) model focuses on the extent that accruals should be in past, current and future cash flows realization and regards accruals quality as the standard deviation of the residuals from estimated regression. McNichols (2002) asserts that economic and structural factors can cause variation in the precision of accruals estimates, regardless of the presence or absence of managerial discretion and that managerial expertise also influences the precision of estimation, even if other factors are held constant. That is, the link between accruals and cash flow realization in adjacent periods is affected by economic and structural factors, managerial expertise, and intentional managerial discretions. Based on these reasons, McNichols (2002, p. 61) asserts that the Dechow and Dichev's (2002) model has limitations related to non-separation of firm environment, managerial expertise, and managerial discretion. She also points out that the estimation errors are assumed to be independent of each other and of the cash flow realization and that the Dechow and Dichev's (2002) model does not separately consider how total accruals might be affected by the managerial discretion in accruals.

McNichols (2002) points out that the Dechow and Dichev's (2002) model assesses accruals as a whole and does not attempt to separate effects of managers' discretion from all other effects. By linking the Dechow and Dichev's (2002) model and the Jones' (1991) models, the Francis et al.'s (2008) model can measure errors associated with both the discretionary accruals from the Jones' (1991) model and the earnings quality from the Dechow and Dichev's (2002) model. Therefore, I use

Francis et al.'s (2008) model to capture a manager's intentional discretion.

5.3 Previous Studies

I show three previous studies which focus on firm characteristics as a determinants of accruals quality. Dechow and Dichev (2002) suggest that it is important to recognize the relationship between observable firm characteristics and non observable estimation error. They find that operating cycle, firm size, sales volatility, OCF volatility, and the magnitude of accruals are determinants of accruals quality.

Doyle et al. (2007a) investigate the relationship between internal controls quality and accruals quality using a sample of firms which disclose one material weakness and find that weakness firms have lower accruals quality compared to control firms. Also, the weakness firms have firm characteristics such as loss proportion, small size, young, complex, rapidly growing, and restructuring. Doyle et al. (2007b) suggest that firm characteristics affect accruals quality directly and internal control deficiency reduces accruals quality more than firm characteristics.

Ashbaugh-Skaife et al. (2008) examine what are the determinants of accruals quality; internal control deficiency, business fundamentals and operating characteristics, investment in internal controls, GAAP accounting choices, accounting conservatism, and auditor quality. They provide evidence that the determinants of accruals quality include characteristics related to inventory ratio, OCF volatility, sales volatility, rapid growth and conservative accounting choices indicate lower accruals quality.

5.4 Hypothesis Development

The objective of internal control systems is to prevent and detect accounting errors and fraud which leads to misstatement and well-organized internal control systems are effective systems for credible financial reporting. Lobo and Zhou (2006) provide evidence that firms are more conservative in their financial reporting after US-SOX through their finding of a significant reduction in discretionary accruals. Machuga and Teitel (2007) suggest that earnings quality improved after US-SOX, using a variety of earnings quality characteristics such as income smoothing and abnormal accruals. Bedard (2006) suggests that earnings quality improved in the post-US-SOX period by providing evidence that there was a decrease in the magnitude of unexpected accruals in their first internal control report. SEC-registered Japanese firms have been required to comply with US-SOX regulation since 2006. SEC-registered Japanese firms have been working on better organization of the internal controls consistent with US-SOX regulation. I predict that since the SEC-registered Japanese firms have well-organized internal control systems and there is a decrease in manager's estimation errors and earnings management, earning quality as measured by Dechow and Dichev (2002) would improve.

On the other hand, Cohen et al. (2008) and Nakashima (2011) document that accruals management decreases and real management increases in the post-US-SOX period. I predict that increases in the real management will have the effect of decreasing accruals quality. The mixed prediction led me to set up the following hypothesis:

H1: There is no difference in accruals quality in the pre-and the post-US-SOX periods.

Palepu et al. (2000) suggest that one factor for determining accruals quality is an estimation error whose accuracy depends on firm environment. Dechow and Dichev (2002, p.36) assert that accruals quality is systematically related to firm and industry characteristics even in the absence of intentional earnings management. Francis et al. (2004, p.968) document that earnings quality is determined by management's reporting and implementation decisions and by firms' innate business models and operating environments. Francis et al. (2008) suggest that earnings quality is affected by a firm characteristics factor and a discretionary (reporting) factor. Thus, since I examine what determines accruals quality, I set up the following hypothesis;

H2: There are determinants of accrual quality, such as firm characteristics and earnings management.

I test this hypothesis in the following five working hypotheses by analyzing the determinants of accruals quality.

Dechow and Dichev (2002) suggest that in a volatile operating environment there is greater use of approximations and estimations which results in larger errors of estimation and lower accruals quality. Nakashima (2011) suggests that accruals quality estimated by Dechow and Dichev (2002) is associated with sales volatility, accruals volatility, and earnings volatility. For the relation between earnings quality and volatility, Dechow and Schrand (2004) suggest that volatility is a natural part of running a business and should be reflected in earnings and that it is important to consider different types of volatility and, that if implemented properly and accruals can mitigate volatility and negative correlation in cash flows, earnings quality should be improved, but earnings quality may be reduced when accruals are used to hide value-relevant changes in cash flows.

Doyle et al. (2007b) and Ashbaugh-Skaife et al. (2008) suggest that firms with material weaknesses have common innate firm characteristics, such as a greater sales volatility and a greater OCF volatility and that internal controls deficiency is significantly positively associated with accruals quality, sales volatility and OCF volatility.

For operating cycles, Dechow (1994) suggests that firms with longer operating cycles are expected to have larger working capital requirement for a given level of operating cycle, in firms with longer operating cycles, a given change in the level of operating activity is expected to translate into a larger change in the required level of working capital. Dechow and Dichev (2002) suggest that a longer operating cycle indicates more uncertainty, more estimation and more errors of estimation, and therefore resulting in lower accruals quality. Doyle et al. (2007b) suggest that material weakness is positively associated with a longer operating cycle. Therefore, I set up the hypothesis 2a focusing on variables such as sales volatility, OCF volatility, and operating cycle as proxy to impact on accruals quality:

Working H2a: Operating characteristics such as volatility and operating cycle impact on accruals quality.

It is predictable that firm size seemed to be a determinant of accruals quality through the following arguments. Since larger firms have more stable and predictable operations, they have fewer and smaller estimation errors, are more diversified and the various portfolio effects across divisions and business division reduce the relative effect of estimation errors (Dechow and Dichev 2002). Because large firms tend to have more employees and greater resources to spend on internal auditors or consulting fees, this may aid in the generation of strong internal controls (Ge and McVay 2005). Since larger firms are able to spend greater resources on internal control systems, I take firm size as a proxy for investment in internal controls in this analysis.

Ashbaugh-Skaife et al. (2008) indicate that internal control deficiency is a factor which reduces accruals quality. Firm size affects the investment in internal controls and the investment in internal controls impacts on accrual quality. Therefore, I set up the hypothesis 2b:

Working H2b: Investment in internal control influence accruals quality.

Doyle et al. (2007b) examine the relation between internal controls deficiency and firm characteristics and suggest that internal controls deficiency is associated with loss proportion, smaller size, shorter age, more complicated structure, complexity of the operations, extreme rapid growth, and restructurings. Ge and McVay (2005) suggest that firms with younger age tend to have more material weaknesses, since younger firms are likely have less established procedures and the employees might have less experience than in older firms. For the relation between growth and accruals quality, Ashbaugh-Skaife et al. (2008) suggest that rapidly growing firms are likely to have noisier accruals caused by absorption-costing distortions to income when inventory build-ups occur in anticipation of future sales growth. Therefore, I set up the hypothesis 2c in order to examine the relation between firm characteristics and accruals quality:

Working H2c: Firm characteristics such as age and rapid growth affects accruals quality.

The objective of internal control is to prevent fraud and errors in the process of financial reporting thus internal control is expected to lead to a credible financial reporting. If there is a deficiency in internal controls, it fails to prevent and find intentional accruals management. As Bissessur (2008) mentions, if abnormal accruals reflect earnings management, the ability of abnormal accruals to predict future cash flows should be impacted by accrual quality. In other words, when managers manage earnings, accruals quality should be low. When accruals quality is low, abnormal accruals should have high incremental relevance of predicting future cash flows. In contrast, if abnormal accruals are used to reflect the firms' business activity, the predictive power of abnormal accruals for future cash flows should remain unaffected by accruals quality, since managers use abnormal accruals to reflect their private information about future performance which is not impacted by accruals quality (Bissessur 2008, p.77).

Bissessur (2008) examines the relation between accruals quality and the predictive ability of abnormal accruals for future cash flows and reports that the predictive ability of abnormal accruals for future cash flows incremental to normal accruals is not affected by accruals quality.

Chapter 4 suggests that accruals quality estimated by Dechow and Dichev (2002) and accruals quality estimated by Francis et al. (2008) are significantly associated with the mean of the absolute percentage error ($MAPE$)[1] in the pre-US-SOX period but both accruals quality measures are insignificantly negatively associated with MAPEs. Chapter four also shows that abnormal production cost is significantly associated with MAPEs in the pre-US-SOX and the post-US-SOX periods. Thus, while accounting management does not affect accruals quality, real management may affect accruals quality. Therefore, I set up hypothesis 2d and test this;

Working H2d: Earnings management impacts on accruals quality.

Previous studies use BIG 6 as a proxy for higher audit quality (Becker et al. 1998; Lobo and Zhou 2006; Ashbaugh-Skaife et al. 2008). Becker et al. (1998) suggest that discretionary accruals for firms with non-BIG6 are higher than discretionary accruals for firms with BIG 6. Lobo and Zhou (2006) suggest that firms with higher audit quality employ lower discretionary accrual in the post-US-SOX period. Ashbaugh-Skaife et al. (2008) indicate that accruals quality is associated with auditor quality. Thus, I predict that higher audit quality reduce estimation errors and earnings management and results in higher accruals quality. Therefore, I set up the hypothesis 2d below:

Working H2e: Audit quality impacts on accruals quality.

5.5 Data and Research Dedign

5.5.1 Data and Sample

This study employs data of listed Japanese firms in the U. S. market for the period 2000-2008.[2] Data is from the Nikkei Economic Electronic Databank System (NEEDS) through following the criteria: (1) SEC-registered firms, (2) not financial institutions.

Variables are from the statements of cash flows. Volatility of each variable is computed as the standard deviation of the time-series of each variable.

5.5.2 Estimation of Accruals Quality

I use the measure of accruals quality estimated by Dechow and Dichev (2002) and Francis et al. (2008) to capture accruals quality. Each of my proxies for accruals quality is the standard deviation of the residuals for 2005, 2006, 2007, and 2008 measured from 2000 to 2004, 2001-2005, 2002-2006, 2003-2007. I have four measures of accruals quality for firm-specific basis. I compare two accruals quality for 2005 and 2006; 2001-2004, 2002-2005 as pre-US-SOX accruals quality with two accruals quality for 2007 and 2008; 2003-2006, 2004-2007 as post-US-SOX accruals quality.

5.5.3 Testing Hypotheses

I test H1 using the following three ways: First, I analyze the mean differences in accruals quality in the pre-US-SOX period and post-US-SOX period. Second, the time-series plots of accruals quality in pre-US-SOX and post-US-SOX periods. Third, I look at whether an estimate of SOX is significantly less than zero from multivariate analyses. If the estimate is significantly less than zero, it means that accruals quality has been improved.

I test H2 using the following regression model:

$$AQ_{i,t} = \beta_0 + \beta_1 SOX + \beta_2 \Delta WC + \beta_3 \Delta WC*SOX + \beta_4 OCF + \beta_5 OCF*SOX +$$

$$+ \beta_6 LDEBT + \beta_7 LDEBT*SOX + \beta_8 DECAVOID + \beta_9 DECAVOID*SOX$$
$$+ \beta_{10} LOSSAVOID + \beta_{11} LOSSAVOID*SOX + \beta_{12} SALESvolatility$$
$$+ \beta_{13} OCFvolatility + \beta_{14} OC + \beta_{15} SIZE + \beta_{16} AUDIT + \beta_{17} ROA + \beta_{18} EM$$
$$+ \beta_{19} EM*SOX + \varepsilon_t,$$

Where,

AQ	= accruals quality;
SOX	= 1 in the post-SOX, that is from 2006 to 2008, and 0 otherwise, that is in the pre-US-SOX, that is 2000-2005,
ΔWC	= changes in working capitals, ΔAccountsReceivable + ΔInventory − ΔAccountsPayable − ΔTax Payment + ΔOther assets(net);
OCF	= cash flows from operating activities;[3]
LDEBT	= long-term debt, Long Debt/Average Assets;
DECAVOID	= 1 if (current year's income before discretionary accruals estimated Jones' (1991) model -last year's income) is between (0,-0.0040), and 0 otherwise;
LOSSAVOID	= 1 if (current year's income before discretionary accruals estimated Jones (1991) model-last year's income) is between (0,-0.00332), and 0 otherwise;[4]
SALESvolatility	= the standard deviation of sales, scaled by average assets;
OCFvolatility	= The standard deviation of cash flow operations, scaled by average assets;
SIZE	= log of total sales;
AUDIT	= audit quality, 1 if a firm engaged with one of BIG 4 audit firms, and 0 otherwise;[5]
OC	= operating cycle, the log of the average of {(360/Sales/ Average Account Receivable) } + (360/Costs of Goods Sold/Average Inventory)};
ROA	= Net income/Average Assets;
EM	= Earnings management measures.[6]

TABLE 5.1 Descriptive Statistics (n=256)

	Mean	Median	Standard Deviaion	Minimum	Maximum	25th Percentile	75th Percentile
OCF	0.084	0.074	0.060	-0.035	0.306	0.041	0.105
ROA	0.039	0.031	0.049	-0.102	0.229	0.010	0.058
ΔINV	-0.003	-0.003	0.017	-0.080	0.072	-0.010	0.004
ΔWC	0.002	0.002	0.029	-0.167	0.139	-0.010	0.014
ACCRUAL	-0.044	-0.042	0.048	-0.232	0.141	-0.066	-0.014
PPE	0.229	0.219	0.117	0.011	0.639	0.152	0.277
SALES	1.040	0.923	0.472	0.103	2.403	0.754	1.148
OC	4.873	4.835	0.353	4.240	6.060	4.620	5.128
$\Delta SALES$	0.048	0.042	0.107	-0.414	0.686	0.001	0.089
COG	0.789	0.647	0.523	0.036	2.214	0.495	0.854
GROWTH	6.020	4.880	13.738	-63.680	79.950	0.255	9.540
SGA	0.216	0.192	0.133	0.035	1.082	0.124	0.283
AD	0.011	0.006	0.015	0.000	0.077	0.000	0.016
RD	0.036	0.034	0.029	0.000	0.150	0.004	0.057
AGE	61.469	59.500	19.070	17.000	104.000	54.500	72.750
SEGMENT	2.055	2.079	0.316	1.609	2.833	1.792	2.250
OCF_{t-1}	0.083	0.071	0.064	-0.035	0.313	0.037	0.107
ΔWC_{t-1}	0.000	0.001	0.029	-0.167	0.139	-0.014	0.012
$ACCRUAL_{t-1}$	-0.045	-0.046	0.049	-0.232	0.141	-0.066	-0.014
$\Delta SALES_{t-1}$	0.060	0.038	0.156	-0.414	0.859	-0.003	0.088
$SALES_{t-1}$	1.011	0.908	0.492	-0.050	2.403	0.727	1.143
OCF_{t+1}	0.083	0.073	0.059	-0.035	0.306	0.041	0.105
AQ_DD	0.027	0.023	0.018	0.008	0.123	0.016	0.033
AQ_MN	0.026	0.021	0.024	0.004	0.216	0.013	0.032
DA2	0.000	0.000	0.020	-0.136	0.075	-0.009	0.009
abnOCF	0.000	0.001	0.021	-0.080	0.127	-0.009	0.009
abnPROD	0.000	0.000	0.015	-0.044	0.063	-0.007	0.006
abnDE	0.000	0.000	0.021	-0.096	0.117	-0.004	0.002
DECAVOIDDA2	0.001	0.002	0.247	-1.688	1.730	-0.013	0.023
LOSSAVOIDDA2	0.040	0.032	0.298	-2.206	2.402	0.007	0.066
adjustOCF	-0.001	-0.012	0.060	-0.119	0.222	-0.043	0.021
adjustLDEBT	0.003	-0.034	0.124	-0.116	0.370	-0.099	0.061
OCFvolatility	0.031	0.024	0.028	0.001	0.157	0.012	0.043
SALESvolatility	0.249	0.182	0.222	0.001	0.969	0.081	0.338
SIZE	-0.073	-0.086	0.504	-2.273	0.877	-0.285	0.138

Variables are defined below. all variables are deflated by average assets

OCF	cash flows from operations
ROA	net income /average assets
ΔINV	changes in inventory
ΔWC	changes in working capitals = $\Delta AR + \Delta INV - \Delta AP - \Delta TAX$ Payable + Δother assets net)
ACCRUAL	net income minus operating cash flows
PPE	property, plant, and equipment
SALES	sales
OC	operating cycles the log of the average of {·360/sales/average accounts receivable)}+ (360/cost of goods sold /average inventory)
$\Delta SALES$	changes in sales
COG	cost of goods
GROWTH	current year's sales/sales in the previous year
SGA	general administration expenses
AD	advertisement expenses
RD	R&D expenses
AGE	the log of the number of years which the firm starts operations.
ΔAR	changes in accounts receivable
ΔAP	changes in accounts payable
Nit-1	net income in the previous year
OCFt-1	cash flows from operations
OCFt+1	cash flows from operations
$\Delta SALESt-1$	changes in sales in the previous year
SALESt-1	sales in the previous year
AQ_DD	accrual quality Standard deviation of residuals from Dechow and Dichev's (2002) model
AQ_MN	accrual quality Standard deviation of residuals from Francis et al.'s (2008)model
DA2	discretionary working capital accruals by estimated Jones' (1991)model
abnOCF	the level of abnormal OCF, residuals by estimated $OCF_t = \alpha_1 SALES_t + \alpha_2 \Delta SALES_t$
abnPROD	the level of abnormal Production Costs, residuals by estimated $COG + \Delta INV = \alpha_1 SALES_t + \alpha_2 \Delta SALES_t + \alpha_3 \Delta SALES_{t-1}$
abnDE	the level of abnormal discretionary expenses, where discretionary expenses are the sum of advertising expense, R&D expenses and SG&A expenses;
DECAVOIDDA2	1 if (current year's income before discretionary total accruals by estimated by Jones models) is between (-0.03, 0) and 0 otherwise.
LOSSAVOIDDA2	1 if [(current year's income before discretionary totalaccruals by estimated by Jones models- last years' income)/average assets] is between (-0.015, 0) and 0 otherwise.
LDEBT	long-term debt
OCFvolatility	standard deviation of cash flow from operations
SALES volatility	standard deviation of SALES
SIZE	the log of SALES

5.6 Empirical Results

5.6.1 Descriptive Statistics and Correlation Results

Table 1 presents the descriptive statistics for each variable. The measures of accruals quality in this study are smaller than measures of accruals quality in Dechow and

TABLE 5.2 Spearman/Pearson Correlation Matrix n=256)

	SOX	AQ_DD	AQ_FR	OCFvolatility	SALESvolatility	OC	GROWTH	SEGMENT	AGE	SIZE	AUDIT	ROA
SOX	1.000	0.011	0.051	-0.051	0.007	-0.081	0.039	0.020	0.000	0.042	0.036	0.179
	.	0.866	0.412	0.418	0.907	0.213	0.548	0.755	1.000	0.499	0.567	0.004
												***
AQ_DD	0.016	1.000	0.721	0.326	-0.114	0.291	0.086	-0.444	-0.231	-0.209	0.085	0.333
	0.804	.	0.000	0.000	0.070	0.000	0.182	0.000	0.000	0.001	0.176	0.000
			***	***	**	***		***	***	***		***
AQ_FR	0.073	0.593	1.000	0.340	-0.149	0.317	0.158	-0.498	-0.355	-0.305	-0.049	0.434
	0.246	0.000	.	0.000	0.017	0.000	0.013	0.000	0.000	0.000	0.436	0.000
		***		***	**	***	**	***	***	***		***
OCFvolatility	-0.062	0.077	-0.044	1.000	0.220	0.097	0.076	-0.078	-0.436	-0.058	0.101	0.294
	0.324	0.220	0.487	.	0.000	0.134	0.237	0.215	0.000	0.358	0.106	0.000
					***				***			***
SALESvolatility	-0.013	-0.174	-0.225	0.417	1.000	-0.386	-0.123	0.388	-0.115	0.166	0.136	-0.189
	0.838	0.005	0.000	0.000	.	0.000	0.054	0.000	0.065	0.008	0.029	0.002
		***	***									
OC	-0.057	0.164	0.289	-0.049	-0.358	1.000	0.078	-0.177	0.084	-0.400	-0.188	0.074
	0.376	0.011	0.000	0.447	0.000	.	0.237	0.006	0.195	0.000	0.003	0.254
		**										
GROWTH	0.204	0.015	0.092	-0.068	-0.187	0.051	1.000	-0.132	-0.183	0.048	-0.120	0.542
	0.001	0.813	0.151	0.287	0.003	0.444	.	0.038	0.004	0.454	0.061	0.000
	***				***							
segment	0.013	-0.530	-0.528	0.071	0.210	-0.126	-0.102	1.000	0.206	0.371	-0.062	-0.405
	0.842	0.000	0.000	0.257	0.001	0.052	0.111	.	0.001	0.000	0.324	0.000
		***										
AGE	0.000	-0.190	-0.195	-0.250	-0.258	0.119	-0.077	0.166	1.000	0.244	0.243	-0.375
	1.000	0.002	0.002	0.000	0.000	0.065	0.228	0.008	.	0.000	0.000	0.000
		***										
SIZE	0.060	-0.309	-0.456	-0.013	-0.021	-0.339	0.115	0.488	0.287	1.000	0.037	-0.042
	0.339	0.000	0.000	0.836	0.742	0.000	0.072	0.000	0.000	.	0.560	0.508
		***	***			***	*	***	***			
AUDIT	0.036	0.029	-0.199	0.095	0.116	-0.209	-0.085	-0.110	0.313	0.054	1.000	0.005
	0.567	0.646	0.001	0.130	0.064	0.001	0.185	0.078	0.000	0.388	.	0.940
		**	***									
ROA	0.279	0.326	0.335	0.005	-0.194	0.046	0.506	-0.423	-0.270	-0.109	-0.034	1.000
	0.000	0.000	0.000	0.939	0.002	0.476	0.000	0.000	0.000	0.082	0.589	.
	***	***	***		***		***	***	***	*		

Notes: Pearson correlations are shown above the diagonal, and Spearman correlations are shown below. The bottom number in each is a two-tail p-value. See Table 5.1 for definitions .*, **, *** indicate that significnat at 10 percent, 5 percent, and 1 percent levels, respectively.

TABLE 5.3 Correlation between Accruals Quality and MAPEs (n=244)

	SOX	AQ_DD	AQ_MN	DA2	abnOCF	abnPROD	abnDE
SOX	1.000	0.011	0.051	0.142	-0.002	0.010	-0.030
	.	0.866	0.412	0.023	0.971	0.877	0.634
				**			
AQ_DD	0.016	1.000	0.721	-0.029	-0.024	0.001	-0.002
	0.804	.	0.000	0.648	0.707	0.985	0.973
			***				
AQ_MN	0.073	0.593	1.000	-0.078	0.026	-0.001	-0.023
	0.246	0.000	.	0.215	0.677	0.989	0.717
		***					
DA2	0.117	-0.001	0.007	1.000	-0.719	-0.214	-0.152
	0.062	0.993	0.905	.	0.000	0.001	0.015
	*				***	***	**
abnOCF	0.038	-0.028	-0.045	-0.619	1.000	0.020	0.039
	0.549	0.659	0.474	0.000	.	0.751	0.534
				***			
abnPROD	-0.011	-0.016	-0.026	-0.175	-0.112	1.000	-0.098
	0.865	0.797	0.680	0.005	0.074	.	0.119
				***	*		
abnDE	0.029	-0.075	-0.001	-0.071	0.009	-0.102	1.000
	0.648	0.233	0.984	0.259	0.881	0.103	.

Notes: Correlations above (below) the diagonal are Pearson (Spearman) correlations. The bottom number in each is a two-tail p-value. See Table 5.1 for definition of each variable. ** Significant at 10 percent, ** at 5 percent, and *** at 1 percent levels, respectively.

Dichev (2002) and Doyle et al. (2007a). The differences in accruals quality come from the fact that Japanese firms do not have many estimates to make and the possibility of mapping into cash flow is higher.

Table 5.2 presents a correlation matrix among the main variables, accruals quality, operating characteristics, business fundamentals, investment in internal controls, and audit quality. I find that accruals quality is significantly positively correlated with operating characteristics such as *OCFvolatility* and business fundamentals, such as operating cycle, sales growth and age and that accruals quality is negatively correlated with audit quality. This is consistent with Doyle et al. (2007a) and Ashbaugh-Skaife et al. (2008).

Table 5.3 shows a correlation among accruals quality and earnings management. This study did not find a correlation between accruals quality and earnings management.

5.6.2 Tests of H1

Figure 5.1 illustrates the time-series trend of accruals quality from Dechow and

FIGURE 5.1 Time-Series Plots of Accruals Quality

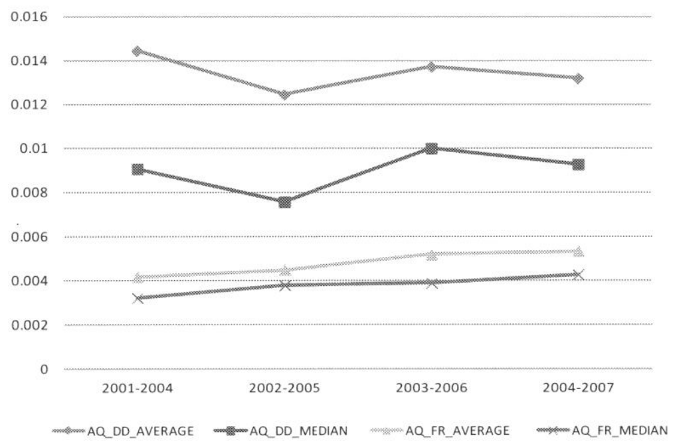

Dichev's (2002) and Francis et al.'s (2008) model. It is observed that although accruals quality from Dechow and Dichev (2002) has increase after US-SOX, accruals quality from Francis et al.'s (2008) model has remained unchanged after US-SOX.

Table 5.4 presents descriptive statistics for accruals quality in the pre-US-SOX and post-US-SOX period. While the mean (standard deviation) of accruals quality from Dechow and Dichev (2002) is 0.014 (0.023) in the pre-US-SOX period, the corresponding mean (standard deviation) is 0.013 (0.013) in the post-US-SOX period, suggesting that accruals quality insignificantly increased after US-SOX. However, the significant difference cannot be observed from this analysis, and this result does not support H1. Therefore, it appears that accruals quality has not improved.

Figure 5.1 illustrates the time-series trend of accruals quality from Dechow and Dichev's (2002) and Francis et al.'s (2008) model. It is observed that although accruals quality from Dechow and Dichev's (2002) model has increased after US-SOX, accruals quality from Francis et al.'s (2008) model remained unchanged after

TABLE 5.4 Descriptive Statistics

	Pre-US-SOX period			Post-US-SOX period			
	N	Mean	Standard Deviation	N	Mean	Standard Deviation	significance
AQ_DD	32	0.014	0.023	96	0.013	0.013	-0.401
AQ_FR	32	0.004	0.004	96	0.005	0.005	0.905

Notes: See Table 5.1 for definition .* , ** , *** indicate that significant at 10 percent, 5 percent, and 1 percent levels, respectively.

TABLE 5.5 Determinants of Accruals Management

Panel A:	Prediction	AQ_DD B	AQ_DD t	AQ_DD significance	AQ_FR B	AQ_FR t	AQ_FR significance
(Constant)		-0.032	-1.737	0.084 *	-0.016	-0.89	0.375
SOX	–	0.003	0.636	0.526	0	0.08	0.937
AWC	–	-0.174	-2.705	0.007 ***	-0.204	-3.274	0.001 ***
AWC*SOX	–	0.152	1.528	0.128	0.066	0.68	0.497
OCF	–	-0.036	-0.811	0.418	-0.079	-1.808	0.072 *
OCF*SOX	–	0.015	0.29	0.772	-0.044	-0.882	0.379
DEBT	–	-0.079	-4.41	0 ***	-0.014	-0.783	0.435
LDEBT*SOX	–	0.017	0.877	0.381	-0.004	-0.221	0.825
DECAVOIDDA2	–	0.007	1.289	0.199	0.002	0.397	0.691
DECAVOIDDA2*SOX	–	-0.004	-1.318	0.189	-0.004	-1.5	0.135
LOSSAVUIDDA2	–	-0.009	-1.052	0.294	-0.005	-0.566	0.572
LOSSAVOIDDA2*SOX	–	0.003	0.688	0.492	0.005	1.158	0.249
Operating Characteristics							
OCProfitability	+	0.192	3.436	0.001 ***	0.139	2.572	0.011 **
SALESvolatility	–	0.036	4.773	0 ***	0.014	1.857	0.065
OC	+	0.006	1.821	0.07 *	0.007	2.191	0.03 **
ROA	+	0.1	2.331	0.021 **	0.118	2.821	0.005
Investment in Internal Controls							
SEGMENT	–	-0.005	-1.212	0.227	-0.006	-1.363	0.175
SIZE	–	-0.006	-1.443	0.151	-0.016	-3.888	0 ***
Business Fundamental							
GROWTH	+	0	1.683	0.094 *	0	2.916	0.004 ***
AGE	+	0	1.364	0.174	0	0.183	0.855
Audit Quality							
AUDIT	–	0.006	1.62	0.107	-0.004	-1.214	0.226
Earnings Management							
C_EM	+	0.014	3.266	0.001 ***	0.009	2.333	0.021 **
C_EM*SOX	+	-0.005	-0.857	0.392	0	0.007	0.994
R²		0.452			0.437		
Adjust R²		0.384			0.367		
F-value (Pr>F)		6.7060 (<0.000)			6.304 (<0.000)		

Panel B:	AQ_DD B	AQ_DD t	AQ_DD significance	AQ_FR B	AQ_FR t	AQ_FR significance
(Constant)	-0.022	-1.174	0.242	-0.013	-0.734	0.464
SOX	-0.003	-1.241	0.216	-0.001	-0.197	0.844
AWC	-0.238	-3.659	0 ***	-0.251	-3.953	0 ***
AWC*SOX	0.097	0.913	0.363	0.108	1.034	0.303
OCF	-0.06	-1.304	0.194	-0.099	-2.182	0.03 **
OCF*SOX	0.08	1.456	0.147	-0.009	-0.173	0.862
DEBT	-0.074	-4.174	0 ***	-0.013	-0.725	0.469
LDEBT*SOX	0.008	0.416	0.678	-0.01	-0.538	0.591
DECAVOIDDA2	0.007	1.248	0.214	0.001	0.26	0.795
DECAVOIDDA2*SOX	-0.005	-1.666	0.097 *	-0.005	-1.694	0.092 *
LOSSAVUIDDA2	-0.008	-0.92	0.359	-0.004	-0.429	0.668
LOSSAVOIDDA2*SOX	0.004	0.967	0.335	0.005	1.173	0.242
Operating Characteristics						
OCProfitability	0.058	1.018	0.31	0.05	0.902	0.368
SALESvolatility	0.031	4.162	0 ***	0.011	1.474	0.142
OC	0.006	1.782	0.077 *	0.007	2.21	0.028 **
ROA	0.108	2.427	0.016 **	0.137	3.137	0.002 ***
Investment in Internal Controls						
SEGMENT	-0.004	-0.868	0.387	-0.004	-0.998	0.319
SIZE	-0.008	-1.848	0.066 *	-0.017	-4.129	0 ***
Business Fundamental						
GROWTH	0	2.655	0.009 ***	0	3.448	0.001 ***
AGE	0	1.176	0.241	0	0.312	0.756
Audit Quality						
AUDIT	0.008	2.114	0.036	-0.002	-0.665	0.507
Earnings Management						
N_EM	0.001	0.698	0.486	0.001	0.718	0.474
N_EM*SOX	0.009	2.709	0.007 ***	0	-0.019	0.985
R²	0.454			0.418		
Adjust R²	0.386			0.347		
F-value (Pr>F)	6.725 (<0.000)			5.823 (<0.000)		

Panel C:	AQ_DD B	AQ_DD t	AQ_DD significance	AQ_FR B	AQ_FR t	AQ_FR significance
(Constant)	-0.024	-1.234	0.219	-0.013	-0.713	0.477
SOX	-0.001	-0.252	0.817	0	-0.018	0.986
AWC	-0.25	-3.034	0.003 ***	-0.187	-2.357	0.019 **
AWC*SOX	0.049	0.314	0.754	0.062	0.415	0.679
OCF	-0.048	-1.024	0.307	-0.102	-2.242	0.026 **
OCF*SOX	0.03	0.532	0.595	-0.02	-0.367	0.714
DEBT	-0.076	-4.205	0 ***	-0.012	-0.682	0.496
LDEBT*SOX	0.016	0.82	0.414	-0.012	-0.608	0.544
DECAVOIDDA2	0.008	1.386	0.168	0.002	0.378	0.706
DECAVOIDDA2*SOX	-0.005	-1.659	0.099 *	-0.005	-1.849	0.066 *
LOSSAVUIDDA2	-0.01	-1.141	0.255	-0.004	-0.481	0.651
LOSSAVOIDDA2*SOX	0.004	0.739	0.461	0.005	1.038	0.301
Operating Characteristics						
OCProfitability	0.124	2.264	0.025 **	0.078	1.478	0.141
SALESvolatility	0.033	4.38	0 ***	0.009	1.304	0.194
OC	0.006	1.809	0.072 *	0.008	2.317	0.022 **
ROA	0.093	2.103	0.037 **	0.117	2.746	0.007 ***
Investment in Internal Controls						
SEGMENT	-0.004	-0.966	0.335	-0.004	-1.034	0.303
SIZE	-0.007	-1.637	0.103	-0.017	-3.924	0 ***
Business Fundamental						
GROWTH	0	2.584	0.011 **	0	2.911	0.004 **
AGE	0	1.485	0.139	0	0.203	0.839
Audit Quality						
AUDIT	0.006	1.603	0.111	-0.004	-1.003	0.317
Earnings Management						
DA2	0.072	0.765	0.445	-0.074	-0.814	0.417
DA2*SOX	0.232	1.009	0.315	0.05	0.225	0.823
R²	0.422			0.413		
Adjust R²	0.351			0.341		
F-value (Pr>F)	5.947 (<0.000)			5.734 (<0.000)		

Notes: See Table 5.1 for definition. *, **, *** indicate that significant at 10 percent, 5 percent, and 1 percent levels, respectively

TABLE 5.5 (continued)

Panel D:

	Prediction	AQ_DD B	t	significance	AQ_FR B	t	significance
(Constant)		-0.024	-1.266	0.207	-0.014	-0.757	0.45
SOX		0	0.059	0.969	0	-0.058	0.954
AWC	−	-0.241	-3.302	0.001 ***	-0.189	-2.676	0.008 ***
AWC*SOX		0.117	1.002	0.318	0.029	0.256	0.798
OCF		-0.027	-0.508	0.612	-0.123	-2.417	0.017 **
OCF*SOX		0.028	0.463	0.644	0.004	0.074	0.941
DEBT	−	-0.073	-3.866	0 ***	-0.017	-0.923	0.357
LDEBT*SOX		0.01	0.496	0.621	-0.066	-0.33	0.742
DECAVDDA2		0.008	1.446	0.15	0.002	0.34	0.734
DECAVDDA2*SOX		-0.004	-1.391	0.166	-0.006	-2.04	0.043 **
LOSAVDDA2		-0.008	-0.902	0.368	-0.004	-0.46	0.646
LOSAVDDA2*SOX		0.002	0.424	0.672	0.006	1.209	0.228
Operating Characteristics							
OCFvolatility	+	0.114	2.073	0.04 **	0.072	1.351	0.178
SALESvolatility	+	0.033	4.449	0 ***	0.009	1.284	0.201
OC	+	0.006	1.783	0.076 *	0.008	2.413	0.017 **
ROA	+	0.095	2.142	0.034 **	0.121	2.851	0.005 ***
Investment in Internal Controls							
SEGMENT	−	-0.004	-0.864	0.389	-0.004	-1.006	0.316
SIZE	−	-0.008	-1.705	0.09 *	-0.016	-3.752	0 ***
Business Fundamental							
GROWTH	+	0	2.404	0.017 **	0	3.032	0.003 ***
AGE	+	0	1.554	0.122	0	0.01	0.992
Audit Quality							
AUDIT	−	0.006	1.517	0.131	-0.004	-0.988	0.324
Earnings Management							
absOCF	+	-0.096	-1.041	0.299	0.105	1.175	0.241
absOCF*SOX	+	-0.125	-0.832	0.406	-0.145	-0.997	0.32
R^2		0.431			0.416		
Adjust R^2		0.361			0.344		
F-value (Pr>F)		6.165 (<0.000)			5.796 (<0.000)		

Panel E:

	Prediction	AQ_DD B	t	significance	AQ_FR B	t	significance
(Constant)		-0.034	-1.845	0.067	-0.018	-1.041	0.299
SOX		-0.001	-0.458	0.647	0.000	-0.032	0.974
AWC	−	-0.255	-3.873	0.000 ***	-0.277	-4.396	0.000 ***
AWC*SOX		0.205	2.052	0.042	0.109	1.139	0.256
OCF		-0.068	-1.521	0.130	-0.105	-2.465	0.015 **
OCF*SOX		0.032	0.626	0.532	-0.032	-0.644	0.521
DEBT	−	-0.080	-4.572	0.000 ***	-0.012	-0.717	0.475
LDEBT*SOX		0.010	0.516	0.607	-0.014	-0.812	0.418
DECAVDDA2		0.005	0.952	0.342	0.000	0.064	0.949
DECAVDDA2*SOX		-0.005	-1.762	0.080 *	-0.005	-1.814	0.071 *
LOSAVDDA2		-0.005	-0.694	0.547	-0.001	-0.094	0.925
LOSAVDDA2*SOX		0.003	0.726	0.469	0.005	1.092	0.277
Operating Characteristics							
OCFvolatility	+	0.140	2.665	0.008 ***	0.099	1.957	0.052 *
SALESvolatility	+	0.032	4.390	0.000 ***	0.009	1.288	0.199
OC	+	0.008	2.333	0.021 **	0.009	2.717	0.007 ***
ROA	+	0.115	2.652	0.009 ***	0.134	3.233	0.001 ***
Investment in Internal Controls							
SEGMENT	−	-0.003	-0.678	0.498	-0.004	-1.028	0.305
SIZE	−	-0.006	-1.404	0.162	-0.016	-3.807	0.000 ***
Business Fundamental							
GROWTH	+	0.000	2.364	0.019 **	0.000	3.477	0.001 ***
AGE	+	0.000	1.456	0.147	0.000	0.165	0.869
Audit Quality							
AUDIT	−	0.005	1.506	0.134	-0.005	-1.377	0.170
Earnings Management							
absPROD	+	-0.209	-2.743	0.007 ***	-0.202	-2.778	0.006 ***
absPROD*SOX	+	0.478	3.556	0.000 ***	0.466	3.621	0.000 ***
R^2		0.455			0.454		
Adjust R^2		0.389			0.386		
F-value (Pr>F)		6.806 (<0.000)			6.756 (<0.000)		

Panel F:

	Prediction	AQ_DD B	t	significance	AQ_FR B	t	significance
(Constant)		-0.03	-1.696	0.11	-0.027	-1.444	0.151
SOX		-0.001	-0.423	0.673	0	-0.118	0.906
AWC	−	-0.197	-3.105	0.002 ***	-0.183	-2.878	0.005 ***
AWC*SOX		0.271	2.158	0.032 **	0.026	0.205	0.838
OCF		-0.04	-0.91	0.364	-0.066	-1.474	0.142
OCF*SOX		-0.006	-0.11	0.913	-0.116	-2.041	0.043 **
DEBT	−	-0.08	-4.372	0 ***	-0.021	-1.136	0.258
LDEBT*SOX		0.042	1.192	0.235	0.001	0.022	0.982
DECAVDDA2		0.007	1.457	0.147	0.003	0.557	0.579
DECAVDDA2*SOX		-0.005	-1.915	0.057 *	-0.006	-2.141	0.034 **
LOSAVDDA2		0.002	0.166	0.869	-0.004	-0.335	0.738
LOSAVDDA2*SOX		0.006	1.242	0.216	0.006	1.184	0.238
Operating Characteristics							
OCFvolatility	+	0.078	1.433	0.154	0.046	0.843	0.401
SALESvolatility	+	0.037	4.517	0 ***	0.02	2.446	0.016 **
OC	+	0.007	2.022	0.045 **	0.01	2.909	0.004 ***
ROA	+	0.084	1.877	0.062 *	0.1	2.216	0.028 **
Investment in Internal Controls							
SEGMENT	−	-0.003	-0.589	0.557	-0.003	-0.679	0.498
SIZE	−	-0.008	-1.655	0.1	-0.016	-3.542	0.001 ***
Business Fundamental							
GROWTH	+	0	2.868	0.005 ***	0	3.085	0.002 ***
AGE	+	0	1.843	0.067 *	0	0.375	0.708
Audit Quality							
AUDIT	−	0.005	1.502	0.135	-0.004	-1.077	0.283
Earnings Management							
absDE	+	-0.056	-0.937	0.35	0.03	0.49	0.625
absDE*SOX	+	0.063	0.576	0.565	-0.108	-0.987	0.325
R^2		0.451			0.437		
Adjust R^2		0.372			0.356		
F-value (Pr>F)		5.746 (<0.000)			5.424 (<0.000)		

Notes: See Table 5.1 for definition. *, **, *** indicate that significant at 10 percent, 5 percent, and 1 percent levels, respectively

US-SOX.

Table 5.4 presents descriptive statistics for accruals quality in the pre-US-SOX and post-US-SOX period. While the mean (standard deviation) of accruals quality from Dechow and Dichev (2002) is 0.014 (0.023) in the pre-US-SOX period, the corresponding mean (standard deviation) is 0.013 (0.013) in the post-US-SOX period, suggesting that accruals quality insignificantly increased after US-SOX. However, the significant difference cannot be observed from this analyses and this result does not support H1. Therefore, it is not noted that accruals quality has been improved.

5.6.3 Tests of H2

Table 5.5 reports the regression results for equation (1) for accruals quality from Dechow and Dichev (2002) and Francis et al. (2008) respectively. The significantly positive coefficients on *OCFvolatility*, *SALESvolatility*, and operating cycle indicate that operating characteristics such as *OCFvolatility*, *SALESvolatility*, and operating cycle are determinants of accruals quality.

Larger firms are significantly negatively associated with accruals quality, suggesting that large firm spend resources into investment in internal controls and results in higher accruals quality. Rapid growth and age are positively associated with accruals quality, suggesting that growing firms have estimation errors in setting up inventories and results in lower accruals quality. Growth is a determinant of accruals quality. Sales growth is a determinant of accruals quality declined. Old firms have a complicated operating and the number of estimation and estimation errors and results in lower accruals quality. Firms with longer history have complicated operations and estimations and estimations errors and result in lower accruals quality.

The correlation between accruals quality and earnings management has not been observed. On the other hand, the results of multivariate regression analyses show that abnormal production cost is significantly negatively associated with accruals quality in the pre-US-SOX periods, while abnormal production cost is significantly positive associated with accruals quality, suggesting that abnormal production cost improves accruals quality before US-SOX, but abnormal production cost affects the decline of accruals quality.

The association between audit quality and accruals quality is not observable, suggesting that audit quality is not a determinant of accruals quality for SEC-registered Japanese firms.

5.7 Conclusion

This study investigates whether accruals quality has been changed in pre-US-SOX and post-SOX period and what determines accruals quality. I document that accruals quality based on the Dechow and Dichev's (2002) model improved but accruals quality based on the Francis et al.'s (2008) model has not been changed through the time-series plot and the mean differences analyses. Also, I document that determinants of accrual quality are operating characteristics such as OCF volatility and sales volatility, business fundamental such as growth, investment in internal controls, and real management.

Since US-SOX regulation applied to SEC-regidtered Japanese firms, there is a possibility for them to have real management. This shift to real management affects operating volatility and results in lower accruals quality. This study provides mixed results regarding SEC's assertions "SOX regulation enhances internal control system and improve accuracy and creditability and higher quality information (SEC 2003)." US-SOX increases accuracy and creditability of financial statements through enhancement of internal control system but it is doubt for them to improve quality information.

Notes:

1. Although there are several of the traditional measures of forecast accuracy: the mean absolute error, the mean square error, and the root mean square error. I use the mean of the absolute percentage error because of the most generalized measure.
2. Sample firms are as follows: Nippon Ham, Wacol, Fuji Film, Komatsu, Hitachi, Toshiba, Mitsubishi Electric, Panasonic (former Matushita), Sanyo, Sony, Omron, Murata, Makita, Kyocera, Honda, Canon, Ricoh, Itochu, Marubeni, Mitsui.
   http://pioneer.jp/corp/ir/pdf/press/announce_NYSE060124.pdf
   http://www.7andi.com/ir/pdf/fstatement/04_iy.pdf
   http://www.fsa.go.jp/news/newsj/13/kinyu/f-20020305-3.html#betu2
   http://www.fsa.go.jp/news/newsj/13/kinyu/f-20020305-3b.pdf

3   For variables *LDEBT* and *OCF*, I use variables which deduct the average in the year following to Yoshida (2005).
4   I set up the measures *DECAVOID* and *LOSSAVOID* so that the measure between current net profit and former net profit added discretionary accruals and the measure net profits added discretionary accruals fall in 10 percentage of a distribution.
5   The Japanese BIG 4 are Azusa (affiliate of KPMG). Arata (affiliate of Pricewaterhouse), Shinnihon Yugen Sekinin Kansa Hojin (affiliate of Ernst &Young), Tohmatsu (affiliate of Deloitte Touche Tohmatsu). Since Misuzu (former ChuoAoyama) finished their operating as an accounting firm in July, 2007, Arata added to Japanese BIG 4 , instead of Misuzu. However, since the Japanese BIG 4 refers the auditing contract with SEC-registered Japanese firms from 2006 through 2008, there is a possibility not to have an auditing contract before 2006 and there might be an accounting firm with a different contract in the sample, I have BIGN as *AUDIT*.
6   For earnings management, I use conservative accruals management (*C_EM*), neutral earnings management (*N_EM*), and aggressive accruals quality (*DA2*) as accruals management, abnormal operating cash flows (*abnOCF*), abnormal production costs (*abnPROD*), abnormal discretionary expenses (*abnDE*) as real management.

PART 2
EVIDENCE ON PUBLIC FIRMS IN JAPAN

CHAPTER **6**

INTERNAL CONTROL DEFICIENCIES

6.1 Introduction

This chapter investigates the type of material weaknesses and the innate characteristics for the firms that disclosed a material weakness in internal control statement after the introduction of J-SOX. The innate characteristics include business complexity, firm age, operating characteristics, financial health, and audit quality. Next, this chapter examines the determinants of material weaknesses by comparing material weakness reporting firms with control firms. Furthermore, this chapter explores the differences in accruals quality and earnings management between material weakness reporting firms and control firms. And, it provides evidence regarding accruals quality and internal controls deficiencies from Japan.

Earnings quality has been analyzed by employing various measures. It has been since the accounting scandals occurred that earnings were evaluated focusing on the quality aspect. Internal controls regulations were introduced in the world in order to improve credibility of financial reporting which was weakened by accounting scandals. Therefore, this chapter explores earnings quality which is a summary indicator of financial reporting quality by a comparison in earnings quality between material weakness reporting firms and control firms. Earnings quality is a many-sided concept which is evaluated by various measures. This study defines earnings quality as "summary indicators of financial reporting quality," and focuses on accruals quality and discretionary accruals (accruals management) as a measure of earnings quality. And, this study is conducted in the framework in which earnings quality is affected by an innate firm characteristics factor and an earnings management factor.[1]

This chapter examines whether internal control regulation impacts the innate firm characteristics factor and the earnings management factor by comparing earnings quality for materials weakness firms and control firms. A well-organized internal control system enables managers to avoid earnings management. Investigation and monitoring by external auditors and regulators also enables managers to avoid earnings management. On the other hand, there is a possibility for the approach of earnings management to be changed after the J-SOX. This is the motivation of this study - how the changes in the firm characteristics factor and the earnings management factor appear to be a result of earnings management and accruals quality as earnings quality.

This study contributes to the literature in the following ways. First, this study provides the concrete content and the types of material weakness which public firms in Japan define as the most severe internal control deficiency. Although J-SOX prescribes the definition of the terminology material weakness as the mandatory disclosure as well as US-SOX, the public firms themselves or auditors may have different thresholds or material weaknesses and the range of materiality (Doyle et al. 2007b, p.195). Second, this study provides evidence on the common innate firm characteristics of material weakness firms. The innate characteristic of material weakness firms provides a convergent concept of material weakness in Japan which does not depend on subjective judgments by firms or auditors (Doyle et al. 2007b, p.195). The evidence encourages managers to maintain good internal control systems and helps investors to recognize what innate firm characteristics are related to material weaknesses.

Third, this chapter documents accruals quality and earnings management for material weakness firms through comparing with a paired sample. Since there is such a small percentage of material weakness firms in all public firms in Japan, it is hard to clarify the general feature of internal controls (Okuda et al. 2012). To date, not much evidence regarding the effect of internal control systems for public firms in Japan has been provided.

Nakashima (2011) analyzed earnings quality and earning management by employing a sample of SEC-registered Japanese firms. If the findings in this study are different from those of Nakashima (2011), the particular behavior of public firms in Japan and the specific environment in Japan regarding internal controls and corporate governance can be identified. This is the fourth contribution. While public firms in Japan are operated under a particular business environment such as weak investor protection and lower litigation risk (Leuz et al. 2003), SEC-registered Japanese firms operate under the stricter U.S. GAAP which requires them to disclose transparent information through accepting higher disclosure levels (Coffee 1999) and under more precise investigation by SEC regulation and investors. Therefore, the U.S. Market listing itself (Machuben and Teitel 2007) works as corporate governance and this may make the attitude of SEC-registered Japanese firms (Machuga and Teitel 2007) different from public firms in Japan.

Fifth, this study provides evidence on a difference in accruals quality and earnings management between material weakness firms and control firms. This study provides evidence regarding whether earnings management of material weakness firms reflects managerial opportunism or informtiveness based on the Nakashima (2011) model. Epps and Guthrie (2010) find that material weakness allows opportunities for greater manipulation of earnings using discretionary accruals. But, managers use discretionary accruals not only to manipulate earnings but also to increase informativeness of earnings (Watt and Zimmerman 1986; Suda 2000; Leuz et al. 2003).

The remainder of this study proceeds as follows. Section two provides the concept of material weaknesses in Japan and analyzes specific types of material weaknesses. Section three develops the hypotheses. Section four shows the research design. Section five presents the empirical results. The final section summarizes and concludes this study.

6.2 Features of Material Weaknesses

J-SOX proposes the roles and responsibilities of mangers below;

> The Management has the role and responsibility to design and operate internal

controls. Out of the internal control discussed in the "basic framework of internal control," it is particularly vital for the management to assess the internal control over financial reporting in accordance with generally accepted accepted assessment standards for internal control and report its conclusion externally in order to ensure the reliability of financial reporting (BAC 2011, p.9).

Management needs to assess their internal controls from the viewpoint of materiality of the impact on the reliability of financial reporting and the materiality is focused on qualitative and quantitative points. Assessments of the effectiveness of internal controls by management should be made with two steps: they assess the effectiveness of their internal controls on a company-level basis as the first Step, and then, based on those results, they evaluate the effectiveness of internal controls on an account-specific basis as the second step.

The management must assesses the effectiveness of internal control over financial reporting to the extent necessary in light of their degree of impact on the reliability of financial reporting (BAC 2011, p.9).

J-SOX shows that material weakness must be determined along two dimensions: "probability for misstatement of financial reporting" and "significance of impact on materiality."[2] J-SOX gives each description of internal controls deficiencies and material weaknesses as:

Control deficiencies are classified into design deficiencies and deficiencies in operating effectiveness.[3] Material weakness[4] is defined in the practice standard as "a deficiency that has a reasonable possibility of resulting in a misstatement above a certain amount, or a possibility of being a qualitatively material misstatement."

Management should determine the internal control deficiencies as material weaknesses by evaluating with both quantitative[5] and qualitative[6] aspects if there is more than a possibility that a control deficiency has a significant material error (Ge and McVay 2005, p.140). Also, effectiveness of internal control over financial reporting should be assessed, in principle, on a consolidated basis."[7] While in the United States, control deficiencies are classified in three categories; namely "material weaknesses," "significant deficiencies" and "other deficiencies," in J-SOX, a deficiency in internal controls is classified into just two categories; "material weaknesses" and "deficiencies." Figure 6.1 shows the guideline for evaluating material weakness in Japan, based on Ramos's (2004) figure.

Few studies regarding material weakness have been conducted in Japan. In this chapter, I provide Japanese evidence on the specific types of material weakness, and then based on the evidence, I conduct an empirical study.

My initial sample is comprised of 88 firms taken from EDINET. In June, 2009, I identified 57 firms which disclosed at least one material weakness in the internal control statements and 9 firms which did not disclose the internal control statements. In June, 2010, I identified another 22 firms which disclosed at least one material weakness in the internal control statements.

I identify the final sample using the following criteria: (1) the month in which the fiscal year ends is March or August, (2) not financial institutions. I identify 4 firms which disclose material weaknesses in the internal control statements through EDINET both in June 2009 and June 2010. I identify 2 firms whose fiscal year ends in other than March, and 15 firms which do not have complete data from 1999 through 2010. Finally, I identify 60 firms whose fiscal year ends in March and disclose at least material weakness in June, 2009 and in June, 2010. Data used in this study is for the period 2000-2011 from the Nikkei Economic Electronic Databank System (NEEDS). The process of sample selection is shown in Table 6.1.

FIGURE 6.1 Evaluation of Material Weaknesses in Japan

		Counsik Opinion (material Misstatement)	
			Material Weakness
SIGNIFICANCE for CREDIBILITY • Based on Amount • Based on Quality	Low		High
			Deficiency
	Low	**PROBABILITY**	High

Notes: Following Ramos (2004), I prepare this figure on evaluation of "material weaknesses" from Council Opinion (2004).

TABLE 6.1   Sample Selection Procedure

Firms which disclose material weaknesses in the Internal Control Statements -EDINET in July 2009.	57
Firms which do not disclose the Internal Control Statement - EDINET in June 2009.	9
Firms which disclose material weaknesses in the Internal Control Statements -EDINET in June 2010.	22
	88
Firms which disclose material weaknesses in the Internal Control Statements -EDINET in June 2009 and June 2010.	4
Firms which delisted in April, 2012.	7
Firms in which Nikkei NEEDS shows a closing month other than March.	2
The firms which do not have complete data from 2000 through 2009.	15
Firms which have a closing month of March and disclose	60

Figure 6.2 shows a breakdown of material weakness reporting firms by their listed market. The largest numbers of material weakness firms are 22 firms (36.6%) on JASDAQ, followed by 21 firms (35.0%) on the First Section of the Tokyo Stock Exchange, 6 firms (10.0%) on the Second Section of the Tokyo Stock Exchange and 6 firms (10.0%) on the Second Section of the Osaka Stock Exchange.

Table 6.2 presents a breakdown of material weakness reporting firms by industry.[8] The largest numbers of material weakness firms are 11 firms (18.33%) in Wholesale, followed by 9 firms (13.33%) in Electric Equipment and 6 firms (10.0%) in Service.

Figure 6.3 shows the material weaknesses by type of deficiency. Following Ge and McVay's (2005) classification, I divide the 90 total material weaknesses into one of eight major deficiency types: Account-specific, Human resources, Period/End Accounting Policies, Segregation of Duties, Subsidiary Specific, Senior Management,

FIGURE 6.2   Distribution of Market

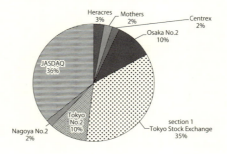

TABLE 6.2 Industrial Distribution of Material Weakness Reporting Firms

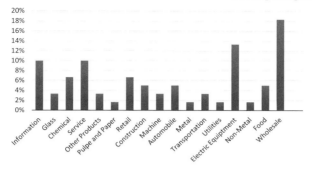

Technology and Monitoring. While the number of firms which disclose at least one material weakness is 60, the number of material weaknesses is 90, indicating that each firm has 1.5 deficiency types on average.[9]

While Period-End/Accounting Policies is the greatest number of material weaknesses (25.56%) among eight deficiency types in Japan, Ge and McVay (2005) disclose Period/End Accounting Policies is 68 (13.79%) in the U.S. Also, Account-Specific (24.14%) has the greatest number of these categories in the U.S. This indicates that there is a difference in feature on internal control deficiencies between Japan and the U.S. Internal control systems were required in the U.S. before US-SOX regulation was introduced. US-SOX required reporting of the effectiveness of the internal control systems. On the other hand, J-SOX regulation in April, 2009 required both the setting up the internal controls system itself and the disclosure of whether the internal control systems work effectively.

The public firms in Japan are obliged to set up their internal controls system and disclose whether their internal controls work well at the same time since April 2009 by the J-SOX regulation. It is likely that this is a reason why there are many material weaknesses in period/end accounting processes in Japan.

Subsidiary specific is the next greatest number of material weaknesses, 18 firms (20.0%), while as Ge and McVay (2005) show that 35 firms (7.10%) disclose subsidiary specific material weaknesses. Examples of deficiencies about subsidiaries includes the following: (1) Although consolidated subsidiaries should prepare consolidated financial statements following International Financial Reporting Standards (IFRSs), staff with insufficient knowledge about new accounting results in an unorganized procedure about inspection and approval for preparation of consolidated financial statements (Iwasaki Tsushin), and (2) Inappropriate approval procedure for money payable in subsidiaries and insufficient risk assessment for new lending result in internal control deficiencies (River Elec). The causes are insufficient accounting knowledge at subsidiaries or internal control deficiencies at subsidiaries themselves.

Senior Management is the next greatest number of material weaknesses. While there are 10 (11.11%) material weaknesses in senior management in Japan, Ge and McVay (2005) show that there are 23 (4.66%) material weaknesses in senior management in the U.S. As Ge and McVay (2005)[10] point out, in general, an ineffective control environment reflects the "tone at the top" regarding internal controls. The Treadway Commission (NCFFR 1987, p.38) states that the tone set by top management and the corporate environment or culture within which financial reporting occurs are the most important factors which contribute to the integrity of the financial reporting process. Also, Hunton et al.(2011) suggest through their unique combination study of archival and survey data that perceived tone at the top is positively related to earnings quality, after controlling for audit committee strength and firm-specific characteristics.

I identify that inventory (19%) and sales (14%) are the greatest number of the account-specific material weaknesses for the Japanese firms. On the other hand, as shown in Ge and McVay (2005), accruals (accounts receivable and accounts payable) (35 firm, 22%) and inventory (35 firms, 22%) are the greatest number of the account-specific material weaknesses, suggesting that 70 firms (44%) disclose material weakness regarding current accruals. Current accrual is the greatest number of the account-specific material weaknesses both in Japan and the U.S. However, focusing on the content of accruals except inventories, 2 firms in Japan have accounts receivable and accounts payable material weakness (4.76%), while 35 firms in the U.S. have the material weaknesses in accounts receivable and accounts payable (42%). This is a difference between the two countries. Whether a difference in the content of accruals with material weakness leads to the difference in earnings management between the two countries should be studied in the future.

FIGURE 6.3 Number of Material Weaknesses by Deficiency Type

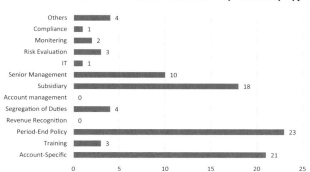

FIGURE 6.4 Number of Material Weaknesses by Account-Type

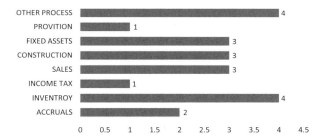

6.3 Hypothesis Development

The studies which focus on the innate characteristics of internal control deficiency firms include Krishnan (2005), Ge and McVay (2005), and Doyle et al. (2007b). Krishnan (2005) examines the association between internal control deficiencies and audit committee quality and indicates that 128 firms which report internal control deficiencies are associated with audit committee quality and financial distress.

Doyle et al. (2007b) investigate the determinants of material weakness for the 779 firms which disclose one material weakness and find that material weakness firms have firm characteristics such as smaller size, younger age, more complexity, rapidly growing, and restructuring. Doyle et al. (2007a) also suggest that while firms with company-level problems tend to be smaller, younger and weaker financially, firms with account-specific problems tend to be more complex, more diversified, and rapidly changing.

Ge and McVay (2005) examine the association between business complexity, firm experience, firm size, firm profitability and auditor, and material weakness. They find that the complexity measures are greater for the material weakness firm group and the firm size measures are smaller for the material weakness firm group. Also, they document that weakness disclosures are positively associated with complexity measures and negatively associated with firm sizes and profitability, suggesting that firms disclosing material weaknesses have more complex operations and that the firms are smaller and less profitable. The results of multi-regression analyses show that material weaknesses are positively associated with business complexity and audit quality but negatively associated with profitability.

Internal control systems are intended to prevent and find misstatements and errors in the process of financial statement preparation and reporting. Good internal control systems are expected to lead to more credible financial information disclosure. Deficiencies in internal controls such as no segregation of duties fail to prevent and find managerial intentional earnings manipulation by management and results in misstatements and errors in estimating accruals.[11]

Little evidence regarding material weakness reporting firms from Japan has been provided. I predict that material weakness reporting firms have common innate firm characteristics:

H1: Material weakness reporting firms in Japan have common innate firm characteristics.

Doyle et al. (2007b) assert "the need for internal controls is unique to each firm's particular operating environment." As a firm engages in more complex transactions and has more diverse operations, we expect the need for internal control to be higher, and thus expect the complexity of the firm to be a driver of internal control weaknesses. For example, in a multinational company the local institution and legal environment of each location might differ, and thus affect the effectiveness of internal controls." Ge and McVay (2005) point out that firms with more complicated business likely have a greater risk for a disconnect in the financial reporting process and thus lead to a material weakness. Doyle et al.(2007b) and Ge and McVay (2005) suggest that material weaknesses are likely to be positively associated with business complexity. Therefore, I set up the following working hypothesis:

Working H1a: Business complexity is significantly associated with material weaknesses in Japan.

Dolye et al. (2007b) assert that the older the firm, the more likely they are to fix the internal control system. Ge and McVay (2005) suggest that younger firms likely have less established procedure, and the employees might have less experience than in older, more established firms. I predict that younger firms focus on operating activities and thus have less established procedures in internal control system. Therefore, I set up the following working hypothesis:

Working H1b: Firm age is significantly associated with material weaknesses in Japan.

The volatility of firms' operations is systematically related to the propensity to make estimation errors in accruals (Dechow and Dichev 2002; Ashbugh-Skaife et al. 2008; Nakashima 2011) While operating characteristics such as OCF volatility and SALES volatility are significantly associated with accruals quality (Ashbaugh-Skaife et al. 2008; Nakashima 2011), there is little evidence between volatilities and material weaknesses. Nakashima (2011) suggests that there is a possibility of earnings management from the association between OCF volatility and accruals quality. Epps and Guthrie (2008) suggest that there is a significant association between operating characteristics and material weaknesses. Therefore, I set up the following working hypothesis:

Working H1c: Operating characteristics are significantly associated with material weaknesses in Japan.

The stronger the financial health of firms, the fewer internal control weaknesses in firms (Doyle et al. 2007b, pp.8-9). The ability to establish proper internal controls might vary with a firm's financial health (Ge and McVay 2005, p.151). I set up the following working hypothesis:

> **Working H1d:** Financial health is significantly associated with material weaknesses in Japan.

Larger audit firms tend to have a contract with larger clients and thus they might encounter fewer internal control problems and larger audit firms have more auditing expertise and a higher exposure to legal liability and historically imposed stronger internal control standards for their clients (Ge and McVay 2005, p.151). I predict that larger audit firms in Japan also impose strict internal control standards for their clients, I set up the following working hypothesis:

> **Working H1e:** Larger auditor (audit quality) is significantly associated with material weaknesses in Japan.

Doyle et al. (2007a)[12] predict that weaknesses in internal controls have the potential to allow both intentional error (earnings management) and unintentional error (poor estimation ability) in accruals estimation to impact the reported financial statements. Doyle et al. (2007a) set up the hypothesis that material weaknesses in internal control are negatively associated with accruals quality. They investigate the relation between accruals quality and internal control deficiency using 705 firms that disclosed at least one material weakness from August 2002 to November 2005 and document that firms with weak internal controls over financial reporting generally have lower accruals quality using an accrual quality measure by the Dechow and Dichev's (2002) model and Francis et al.'s (2008) model.

Ashbaugh-Skaife et al. (2008) examine the determinants of accruals quality; internal control deficiency, business fundamentals and operating characteristics, investment in internal controls, GAAP accounting choices, accounting conservatism, and auditor quality. They find that characteristics related to inventory ratio, OCF volatility, SALES volatility, rapid growth and conservative accounting choices are the determinants of accruals quality. Ashbaugh-Skaife et al. (2008) also document that firms reporting internal control deficiencies have lower accruals quality as measured by accrual noise and absolute accruals relative to firms not reporting internal control problems, and that firms that report internal control deficiencies have significantly larger positive and larger negative abnormal accruals relative to control firms. This suggests that internal control weaknesses are more likely to lead to unintentional errors that add noise to accruals than intentional misstatements that bias earnings upward.

Doyle et al. (2007a) suggest that material weakness firms have lower accrual quality than control firms. For a firm with weak controls, intentionally biased discretionary accruals could be greater by failing to limit management's ability to manage earning. Unintentional errors could be high if weak controls result in more estimation errors for difficult to estimate accruals Doyle et al. (2007a, p.1145). Ashbaugh-Skaife et al. (2008, p.247) find that firms that disclose internal controls deficiencies exhibit greater noise in accruals and larger abnormal accruals relative to control firms.

Dechow et al. (1996) examine the relationship between earnings manipulation and internal control deficiency for the firms subject to accounting Enforcement Actions (AAER) by the Securities and Exchange Commission. They show that accruals gradually increase as the alleged year of earnings manipulation approaches, and then experience a sharp decline. The increase in accruals is consistent with earnings manipulation. The subsequent accrual reduction is consistent with the reversal of prior accrual overstatements (Dechow et al. 1996). They find that AAER firms have greater accruals than control firms. Thus, they suggest that time-series plots of accruals of the AAER firms shows that they use earnings manipulation to overstate earnings. Dechow and Schrand (2004) point out those high accruals in absolute magnitude is a potential "opportunistically earnings management". Based on the findings of prior studies that accrual information is an important determinant of earnings management (Dechow et al. 1996; Richardson et al. 2002), we predict that accruals quality is significantly associated with positive accruals.

I predict that there is a difference in accruals quality and earnings management between material weakness firms and control firms in Japan as well as the U.S. Thus, I set up the following hypothesis:

H2: The difference in earnings quality (accruals quality and earnings management) between material weakness reporting firms and control firm in Japan is observed.

6.4 Research Design

6.4.1 Determinants of Material Weaknesses

The first objective of this study is to find the determinants of material weaknesses. I discuss the variables which might affect the disclosure of material weaknesses here. Material weakness equals to 1 if the firm discloses material weaknesses and 0 otherwise. Business complexity is measured by *SEGMENT*, the number of reported business segments. *AGE* is measured by the log of the number of the years since the firm was established. I measure *OCFvolatility*, *SALESvolatility*, and *OC* (operating cycle) as operational characteristics. I define *OCFvolatility* as the standard deviation of cash flow from operations, *SALESvolatility* as the standard deviation of the changes in sales to average assets, and *OC* as the log of the average of [(sales/360)/(average accounts receivable)+(cost of goods sold/360)/average inventory)]. I measure firm's financial health as *ROA*, return on assets and *GROWTH*, growth rate in sales as: Sales in the beginning of the year / sales in the end of the year. I measure firm size *SIZE* as the log of total sales. I measure *AUDIT*, which equal to 1 if the firm is audited by a BIG N auditor and 0 otherwise. Since many variables are significantly correlated with one another, I employ a logistic regression analysis to find the determinants of material weaknesses:

$$MW = \beta_0 + \beta_1 OCF_t + \beta_2 NI_t + \beta_3 WC_t + \beta_4 SIZE_t + \beta_5 OC_t + \beta_6 GROWTH_t \\ + \beta_7 LOSSPORTION + \beta_8 SEGMENT_t + \beta_9 OCFvolatility_t + \beta_{10} SALESvolatility_t \\ + \beta_{11} AGE_t + \beta_{12} AUDIT_t - \varepsilon_{t+1}.$$

6.4.2 Accruals Quality Measures

The measure of accruals quality is defined as the extent to which they map into past, current, and future cash flows (Doyle et al. 2007a), following Dechow and Dichev (2002) and computed as a standard deviation of the residuals estimated from firm-specific time-series regression. This study employs a measure to capture accruals quality estimated by the Francis et al.'s (2008) model[13] whose linkage of the Dechow and Dichev's (2002) and the Jones' (1991) models[14] can capture errors associated with both unintentional estimations and intentional management estimations.

Initially, the models are estimated using data beginning with year 2000 and ending with year 2004 to generate a standard deviation of residuals for the year 2005. Next, I use data beginning with year 2001 and ending with year 2005 to generate a standard deviation of residuals for the year 2006. This process is repeated and the models are sequentially re-estimated until all standard errors of residuals over the four year holdout periods are obtained (2000-2008):

$$\Delta WC_t = \beta_0 + \beta_{10} OCF_{t-1} + \beta_2 OCF_t + \beta_3 OCF_{t+1} + \beta_4 \Delta SALES_t + \beta_5 PPE_t + \varepsilon_t.$$

6.4.3 Earnings Management Measures

Earnings management which falls within GAAP can be focused on three types of earnings management: conservative accounting, neutral accounting, and aggressive accounting (Dechow and Skinner 2000).[15] I post one proxy, discretionary accruals, as aggressive accounting for accruals management measures in this study. Managers use their discretions not only in order to misstate their firms' performance for opportunistic purposes, but also to convey their inside information for informative purposes (Watt and Zimmerman, 1986; Subramanyam 1996; Suda 2000; Leuz et al. 2003, p.510). This study uses discretionary accruals estimated by the Jones' (1991) model for each year's cross sectional for all sample firms, using the following regression model:

$$\Delta WC_t = \beta_0 + \beta_1 \Delta SALES_t + \beta_2 PPE_t + \varepsilon_t.$$

Managers can take real actions which affect cash flows by delaying or accelerating sales and accelerating or postponing R&D or advertising expenses (Dechow and Skinner 2000). I follow previous studies for my proxies for real earnings management. However, it is difficult to document the extent to which managers engage in real management to manipulate earnings. Merely observing that a firm enters into a transaction that receives favorable accounting treatment is not evidence that the firm entered into the transaction just because of its accounting consequence (Dechow and Schrand 2004).

Graham et al. (2005) and Suda and Hanaeda (2007) find strong evidence that managers engage in real management such as "decrease discretionary spending on R&D, advertising, and maintenance" to meet an earnings target much more than accounting management such as "book revenue now rather than next quarter" and "alter accounting assumptions." Thus, following Roychowdhury (2006) and Cohen et al.(2008), this study focuses on production manipulation. Production costs manipulation includes reporting lower *COGS* by reducing production costs per unit through increased production. I estimate one proxy, abnormal production costs (*abnPROD*).

I compute abnormal production costs by subtracting the normal level of the sum of *COGS* and change in inventory from actual production costs. I estimate the normal level of production costs as the following equation:

$$PROD_t = COG_t + \Delta INV_t.$$
$$= \alpha_0 + \alpha_1 SALES_t + \alpha_2 \Delta SALES_t + \alpha_3 \Delta SALES_{t-1} + \varepsilon_t.$$

6.4.4 Testing Hypotheses

This study selects pair sample through the same industry and size (total assets) in order to compare the innate characteristics and earnings quality with the material weakness firms. In order to test hypothesis 1, I observe the time-series plot for both material weakness reporting firms and control firms, and thus conduct *t*-test, correlation and logistic regression analysis. In this study, I investigate firm characteristics which affect material weakness disclosure by logistic regression analysis:

$$MW = \beta_0 + \beta_1 \Delta WC_t + \beta_2 OCF_t + \beta_3 DEBT_t + \beta_4 OCFvolatility$$
$$+ \beta_5 SALESvolality_t + \beta_6 OC_t + \beta_7 ROA_t + \beta_8 SEGMENT_t + \beta_9 SIZE$$
$$+ \beta_{10} GROWTH + \beta_{11} AGE_t + \beta_{12} AUDIT_t + \beta_{13} EM_t + \varepsilon_{t+1}.$$

To test hypothesis 2, I examine the association between accruals quality and material weakness by estimating the following Francis et al.'s (2008) model. Also, I conduct analyses by separating the company-level and account-specific level material weakness:

$$AQ = \beta_0 + \beta_1 \Delta WC_t + \beta_2 OCF_t + \beta_3 DEBT_t + \beta_4 OCFvolatility$$
$$+ \beta_5 SALESvolality_t + \beta_6 OC_t + \beta_7 ROA_t + \beta_8 SEGMENT_t + \beta_9 SIZE$$
$$+ \beta_{10} GROWTH + \beta_{11} AGE_t + \beta_{12} AUDIT_t + \beta_{13} EM_t + \varepsilon_{t+1},$$

Where,
- AQ = accruals quality;
- ΔWC = accruals[16]: changes in working capital,
  = ΔaccountsReceivable + Δinventory
  $-\Delta$accountsPaylable $-\Delta$taxpayment
  $+\Delta$ Other assets (net);
- OCF = cash flows from operating activities;[17]
- $DEBT$ = long-term debt, long debt/average assets;[18]
- $SALESvolatility$ = the standard deviation of sales, deflated by average assets,
- $OCFvolatility$ = the standard deviation of cash flow operations, deflated by average assets;
- $SIZE$ = log of total sales;
- $AUDIT$ = audit quality: 1 if a firm engaged with one of the big four audit firms, and 0 otherwise;[19]
- OC = operating cycle; the log of the average of {(360/sales/ average account receivable) }+(360/costs of goods sold/ average inventory)};
- ROA = net income/average assets;
- EM = earning management measures.

Managers may follow an overall earnings management strategy and choose earnings management with lower costs. As they can choose less costly earnings management between accruals and real management, I put either earnings management into the model.

I include the variables *SIZE, AUDIT,* and *OCF/SALESvolatility* as control variables for the regression model in order not to be affected by factors other than J-SOX. The reason why I define *AUDIT* as a control variable is because there is a difference in the firms with BIG 6 and the firms with non-BIG 6 auditors. That is, discretionary accrual of the firms with non-BIG 6 is higher and audit quality of BIG 6 is higher. Also, the controlling of audit quality can make the analyses of discretionary accruals robust (Becker et al. 1998).

The reason why I define *SIZE* as a control variable is as follows; Since large firms tend to be more complex and engage in a larger number and variety of transactions (Doyle et al. 2007b), it is hard for them to implement their internal controls perfectly. Larger firms may have more opportunities to overstate earnings because of the complexity of their operations and the difficulty for external users to detect such overstatement (Lobo and Zhou, 2006). Since large firms have more assets that must be controlled, they have more financial reporting processes and procedures in place (Ge and McVay 2005), it is easy to cause errors in estimation.

On the other hand, larger firms are subject to more scrutiny from financial analysts and investors (Lobo and Zhou 2006). They have more employees and greater resources to spend on internal auditors or consulting fees, which results in helping them set up a good internal control system (Ge and McVay 2005[20]). Based on this rationale, they find a negative association between firm size and material weaknesses (Ge and McVay 2005). These recent studies provide evidence about a negative association between firm size and internal control deficiencies (Doyle et al. 2007b; Ashbaugh-Skaife et al. 2008; Okuda et al. 2012[21]).

The reason why I include *OCF/SALESvolatility* as a control variable is because accruals quality is significantly positively associated with *OCF/SALES* volatility (Doyle et al. 2007a; Ashbaugh-Skaife et al. 2008).

6.5 Empirical Results

6.5.1 Paired *t*-test

Panel A and Panel B of Table 6.3 provide descriptive statistics of firm characteristics and accruals quality. The descriptive statistics indicate that the negative sign of *OCF* of material weakness firms in Japan is the same as the sign of *OCF* of material weakness firms in the U.S. (Ge and McVay 2005) and that they have smaller segment than the segment of Ge and McVay (2005), suggesting that the material weakness firms in Japan are less complicated than the material weakness firms in the U.S. And, they show that values of *OCFvolatility* and *SALESvolatility* are similar to Ashbaugh-Skaife et al.'s (2008) *OCFvolatility* and *SALESvolatility*. Thus, the material weakness firms in Japan have similar features to the material weakness firms in the U.S.

I compare two variables using *t*-tests and Wilcoxon rank-sum tests of the difference. The *t*-test results suggest that there is a significant difference in *SEGMENT* (5.610, p<0.001), *OCFvolatility* (2.632, p<0.001) as innate characteristics, *ROA* (-3.653), *LOSSPORTION* (9.253, p<0.001) as financial health, *AUDIT* (-7.881, p<0.001) observed. The more complicated the business, the higher *OCFvolatility*, and the more material weaknesses the firm has, the lower the financial health, the lower the quality of the firm and the more the firm discloses material weaknesses. This result is consistent with the results in the U.S.

6.5.2 Correlation

I computed a correlation between innate firm characteristics and material weakness. Table 6.4 shows the results of the correlation. The result suggests that there is a significant positive correlation (Pearson, Spearman) between *SEGMENT* (0.156, 0.174), *OCFvolatility* (0.072, 0.092), *LOSSPORTION* (0.247, 0.244) and material weakness and a significant negative correlation (Pearson, Spearman) between *OCF* (-0.132, -0.112) and *AUDIT* (-0.212, -0.212) observed. The more complicated the business and the more volatile the *OCF*, the more material weaknesses the firm has. The lower the financial health, and the lower the quality of the firm, the more the firm discloses material weaknesses. This result is consistent with the results in the U.S.

6.5.3 Logistic Regression Analysis

I examine what innate firm characteristics are related to material weakness through Logistic regression. Since the innate firm characteristics might correlate with one another, I conduct a logistic regression analyses in order to identify whether there is an association with each variable. Table 6.5 reports the results of the Logistic regression analysis.

I find a positive significant association *SEGMENT* (0.232, 0.300, 0.231) with material weakness. The more complicated the business firm, the more likely it will have material weakness. On the other hand, there is no significant association with

TABLE 6.3 Descriptive Statistics of MW Reporting Firms and Control Firms (n=660)

	MW Reporting Firms			Control Firms			
Variables	Mean	S.D.	Sign	Mean	S.D.	t-value	significance
SIZE	10.048	1.794	<	10.201	1.720	-1.581	.114
OC	4.031	0.657	>	4.006	0.707	.684	.494
GROWTH	14.714	212.167	>	6.046	43.271	1.028	.304
AGE	3.757	0.633	<	3.795	0.537	-1.166	.244
SEGMENT	0.971	0.919	>	0.686	0.888	5.610	.000 ***
OCFvolatility	0.042	0.068	>	0.033	0.049	2.632	.009 ***
SALESvolatility	0.175	0.367	>	0.142	0.410	1.560	.119
OCF	-0.015	0.151	<	0.015	0.064	-4.838	.000 ***
DEBT	-0.002	0.086	<	0.009	0.097	-2.104	.036 *
ROA	-0.004	0.234	<	0.030	0.068	-3.653	.000 ***
AUDIT	0.567	0.496	<	0.767	0.423	-7.881	.000 ***
LOSSPORTION	0.323	0.245	>	0.208	0.205	9.253	.000 ***

Each variable is defined below.

OCF	OCF (cash flows from operations) minus mean of OCF
DEBT	DEBT minus mean of DEBT
ROA	return on asstes: net income /average assets
ΔWC	changes in working capitals= $\Delta AR + \Delta INV - \Delta AP - \Delta TAX$ Payable + Δother assets (net)
SIZE	log of total Sales
OC	the log of the average of [(sales/360)/(average accounts receivable) ÷ (cost of goods sold/360)/average Inventory)]
GROWTH	growth rate in sales: sales in the beginning of the year/sales in the end of the year
AGE	the years whien the firm passed since the firm was established
SEGMENT	number of reported business segments
OCFvolatility	the standard deviation of cash flow operations
SALESvolatility	the standard deviation of sthe changes in sales average assets
AQ	accruals quality (FR) =AQ_FR, The standard deviation of residuals from Francis et al.'s (2008) measure, $\Delta WC = \beta_0 + \beta_1 OCF_{t-1} + \beta_1 OCF_t + \beta_2 OCF_{t+1} + \beta_3 OCF_t + \beta_4 REV_t + \varepsilon_t$
DA	discretionary accruals: Jones' (1991)model
PROD	abnormal production cost: $COG + \Delta INV = \alpha_1 + \alpha_2 SALES_t + \alpha_3 \Delta SALES_t + \alpha_4 \Delta SALES_{t-1}$
MAPE	$= \sum_{t=1}^{n} \frac{|e_t|}{|Y_t|}$ e_t=predictive Error, Y_t=actual value in t
AUDIT	1 is the firm audited by BIG N auditor, and 0 otherwise
LOSSPORTION	number of Loss percents to total years (eleven years)

OCF/SALESvolatility, suggesting that public firms in Japan organize and manage their internal controls depending on their characteristics.

Table 6.5 shows that the coefficient of *LOSSPORTION* is (1.787, 1.801, 1.837) and has a significant positive association with material weaknesses, suggesting that the higher loss percentage the firm has, the more likely it is to have material weakness. There is no association of *AGE* and *SIZE*. Table 6.5 shows that coefficient of *AUDIT* is (-0.803, -0.766,-0.830) and has significant negative association with material weaknesses. This suggests that segment, loss portion, and auditor are the determinants of material weaknesses. It is likely that the more complicated the business, the easier it is to have material weakness. The lower the financial health, and the lower the audit quality of the firm, the easier it is to have a material weakness. This is consistent with the results of Ge and McVay (2005). Therefore, since working

Table 6.4 Correlation Matrix (n=1320)

	MW	SIZE	OC	GROWTH	AGE	SEGMENT	OCFvolatility	SALESvolatility	OCF	DEBT	AUDIT	LOSS PORTION
MW	1	-.044	.019	.028	-.033	.156**	.072**	.043	-.132**	-.065*	-.212**	.247**
		.114	.494	.304	.244	.000	.009	.119	.000	.038	.000	.000
SIZE	-.032	1	-.309**	-.136**	.552**	.276**	-.243**	-.179**	.241**	.024	.286**	-.256**
	.252		.000	.000	.000	.000	.000	.000	.000	.455	.000	.000
OC	.021	-.365**	1	-.069*	-.114**	.114**	-.047	-.148**	-.010	.274**	.046	.101**
	.436	.000		.013	.000	.000	.086	.000	.705	.000	.092	.000
GROWTH	-.036	.049	-.180**	1	-.270**	-.018	.011	.193**	-.001	.030	-.047	.032
	.193	.077	.000		.000	.531	.683	.000	.977	.345	.088	.252
AGE	-.004	.593**	-.160**	-.081**	1	.106**	-.169**	-.275**	.046	.026	.177**	-.032
	.888	.000	.000	.004		.000	.000	.000	.103	.418	.000	.254
SEGMENT	.174**	.231**	.132**	.059*	.129**	1	-.114**	-.061*	-.074**	.032	.027	.017
	.000	.000	.000	.035	.000		.000	.031	.009	.315	.343	.537
OCFvolatility	.092**	-.261**	-.078**	-.027	-.188**	-.114**	1	.196**	-.394**	-.055	-.163**	.256**
	.001	.000	.004	.323	.000	.000		.000	.000	.082	.000	.000
SALESvolatility	.041	-.145**	-.226**	.019	-.200**	-.105**	.241**	1	-.156**	-.104**	-.084**	.190**
	.140	.000	.000	.481	.000	.000	.000		.000	.001	.002	.000
OCF	-.112**	.210**	.021	.209**	.031	-.082**	-.118**	-.182**	1	.095**	.192**	-.396**
	.000	.000	.436	.000	.264	.003	.000	.000		.002	.000	.000
DEBT	-.053	.024	.158**	.066*	.054	.020	-.054	-.098**	.094**	1	.149**	-.025
	.091	.439	.000	.035	.095	.542	.089	.002	.003		.000	.435
AUDIT	-.212**	.279**	.005	.022	.182**	.026	-.160**	-.141**	.175**	.162**	1	-.188**
	.000	.000	.864	.417	.000	.361	.000	.000	.000	.000		.000
LOSS PORTION	.244**	-.195**	-.020	-.140**	.049	.028	.198**	.263**	-.364**	-.029	-.150**	1
	.000	.000	.466	.000	.084	.317	.000	.000	.000	.353	.000	

Notes: See Table 6.3 for Variable definitions; Correlations above (below) the diagonal are Pearson (Spearman) correlation. The Bottom number in each is a two-tail p-value. The second low is t-value following to White (1980). ** Significance at 10 percent, *** at 5 percent, and **** at 1 percent levels, respectively.

TABLE 6.5 Logistic Regression
Dependent Variable = MW

Independent variable	Logit Estimate (p-value)		Logit Estimate (p-value)		Logit Estimate (p-value)	
	Estimate	significance	Estimate	significance	Estimate	significance
SEGMENT	.232	.006 ***	.300	.000 ***	.231	.006 ***
OC	.004	.980	-.108	.388	.014	.918
OCFvolatility	-1.311	.388	-1.273	.385	-1.240	.412
SALESvolatility	-.010	.977	-.022	.952	.019	.957
AGE	-.088	.593	.041	.779	-.084	.609
SIZE	.106	.062 *			.108	.056 *
GROWTH	.001	.515	.001	.526	.001	.566
NI	-.511	.558	-.920	.230		
LOSS PORTION	1.787	.000 ***	1.801	.000 ***	1.837	.000 ***
OCF	-1.381	.235			-1.649	.117
DEBT	-1.010	.153	-.976	.165	-1.001	.156
AUDIT	-.827	.000 ***	-.766	.000 ***	-.830	.000 ***
Constant	-.803	.410	.132	.875	-.901	.348
Likelihood ratio X2	.129 ***		.124 ***		.129 ***	

Notes: See Table 6.3 for Variable definitions; *, ** and *** indicate that significance at 0.1 level, 0.5 level and 0.01 level respectively.

hypothesis 1, 3, 4, and 5 are supported, H1 is generally supported.

6.5.4 Earnings Quality between Material Weakness Reporting Firms and Control Firms

Figure 6.5 and Figure 6.6 show the time-series plot of accruals quality and earnings management, respectively. Figure 6.5 shows that while accruals quality of control firms improves, accruals quality of material weakness reporting firms declines. Figure 6 shows that while accruals management and real management of control firms remained unchanged, accruals management and real management of material weakness reporting firms increased slightly. The observation of Figure 6.5 and 6.6 shows that accruals quality of control firms is higher than accruals quality of material weakness reporting firms and that earnings management of control firms is lower than earnings management of material weakness reporting firms.

Table 6.6 presents the results from the *t*-test between control firms and material weakness firms. I find a significant difference on accruals quality for 01-07, 02-08, and 03-09 between material weakness reporting firms and control firms. Therefore, hypothesis 2 "The differences in earnings quality between material weakness reporting firms and control firm in Japan is observed," is supported by this result.

Table 6.7 presents the determinants of accruals quality for control firms and material weakness firms, respectively. I find a significant association on discretionary accruals for 01-07, 02-08, and 03-09 for both material weakness reporting firms and control firms. Here, let's identify whether the purpose of discretionary accruals for material weakness reporting firms and control firms respectively is opportunistic or informativeness by focusing on the coefficient and the sign of *WC*, following Nakashima (2012).[22]

The significant coefficient (*t*-value) for *WC* for the material weakness observations are of mixed sign, negative, positive, and negative, -0.026(-1.948), 0.055(2.078), 0.055(2.642), respectively. On the other hand, the significant coefficient (*t*-value) for *WC* for control firms are consistently negative, -0.143(-6.291), -0.041(-2.085), respectively. *DA* for material weakness reporting firms (2001-2007, 2002-2008, and 2003-2009) and *DA* for control firms (2001-2007, 2002-2008, and 2003-2009) are significantly negatively associated with accruals quality, suggesting that it is likely that the both firms implement accruals management through accruals. And, the sign of *WC (accruals)* is positive, suggesting that it is likely that the accruals management for material weakness reporting firms has an opportunistic purpose. On the other hand, although *DA* for control firms (2001-2007, 2002-2008, and 2003-2009) is significantly negatively associated with accruals quality, *WC (accruals)* (2003-2009) is not significantly associated with *AQ*. This suggests that it is not likely that the accruals management by using accruals for control firms reflects no opportunism following Nakashima's (2012) model.

FIGURE 6.5 Time-Series Plot of Accruals Quality

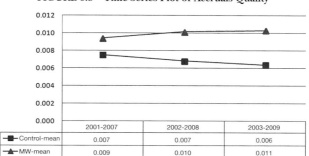

FIGURE 6.6 Accruals Management (*DA*) and Real Management (*PROD*)

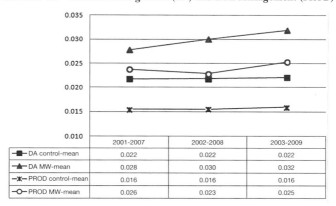

As the rationale, there are the empirical results that firms which report earnings have higher accruals before their correction (Richardson et al. 1996, p.4), and the result that the internal control deficiencies might allow a bias in accruals (Dechow et al. 1996), I suggest that it is likely that accruals quality is affected by *accruals*. Also, the association between *AQ* and real management which appeared in the pre-J-SOX period is not observed in the post-J-SOX (for 2003-2009) period for control firms.

6.6 Conclusion

I provide evidence from Japan by investigating specific types of material weaknesses,

TABLE 6.6 Paired t-test of Result for Material Weakness Reporting Firms and Control Firms

Panel A : 2001-2007

	MW Reporting Firms			Sign	Control Firms			t-value	significance	
	N	Mean	S.D.		N	Mean	S.D.			
ΔWC	420	-0.009	0.095	<	420	-0.008	0.057	-0.240	0.811	
OCF	420	0.005	0.142	>	420	-0.004	0.064	1.191	0.234	
DEBT	420	-0.001	0.098	<	420	0.000	0.105	-0.058	0.954	
OCFvolatility	420	0.040	0.066	>	420	0.032	0.048	2.130	0.033	**
SALEsvolatility	420	0.146	0.228	>	420	0.115	0.178	2.154	0.032	**
OC	420	3.986	0.693	>	420	3.902	0.946	1.462	0.144	
ROA	420	0.010	0.174	<	420	0.034	0.069	-2.581	0.010	**
SEGMENT	420	1.101	0.899	>	420	0.814	0.912	4.591	0.000	***
SIZE	420	10.060	1.733	<	420	10.176	1.721	-0.970	0.332	
GROWTH	420	22.247	264.416	>	420	6.384	26.236	1.224	0.222	
AGE	420	3.753	0.662	<	420	3.792	0.541	-0.947	0.344	
AUDIT	420	0.567	0.496	<	420	0.767	0.423	-6.284	0.000	***
MAPE	420	0.294	0.337	>	420	0.272	0.334	0.986	0.325	
AQ	420	0.009	0.016	>	420	0.007	0.017	1.715	0.087	*

Panel B : 2002-2008

	MW Reporting Firms			Sign	Control Firms			t-value	significance	
	N	Mean	S.D.		N	Mean	S.D.			
ΔWC	420	-0.003	0.084	>	420	-0.005	0.052	0.400	0.689	
OCF	420	0.005	0.141	>	420	0.000	0.064	0.600	0.549	
DEBT	420	-0.002	0.094	>	420	-0.006	0.100	0.492	0.623	
OCFvolatility	420	0.038	0.060	>	420	0.032	0.048	1.629	0.104	
SALEsvolatility	420	0.139	0.204	>	420	0.117	0.181	1.703	0.089	*
OC	420	4.022	0.676	>	420	3.888	0.972	2.323	0.020	**
ROA	420	-0.003	0.184	<	420	0.036	0.070	-4.123	0.000	***
SEGMENT	420	1.146	0.894	>	420	0.810	0.916	5.371	0.000	***
SIZE	420	10.088	1.730	<	420	10.210	1.711	-1.033	0.302	
GROWTH	420	8.131	74.732	>	420	4.938	20.059	0.846	0.398	
AGE	420	3.785	0.622	<	420	3.819	0.521	-0.853	0.394	
AUDIT	420	0.567	0.496	<	420	0.767	0.423	-6.284	0.000	***
MAPE	420	0.306	0.346	>	420	0.291	0.334	0.639	0.523	
AQ	420	0.010	0.027	>	420	0.007	0.013	2.320	0.021	**

Panel C : 2003-2009

	MW Reporting Firms			Sign	Control Firms			t-value	significance	
	N	Mean	S.D.		N	Mean	S.D.			
ΔWC	420	-0.003	0.087	>	420	-0.005	0.050	0.309	0.757	
OCF	420	0.000	0.152	<	420	0.001	0.066	-0.092	0.927	
DEBT	420	-0.003	0.092	<	420	-0.006	0.101	0.398	0.691	
OCFvolatility	420	0.038	0.061	>	420	0.033	0.050	1.408	0.159	
SALEsvolatility	420	0.143	0.216	>	420	0.118	0.199	1.746	0.081	*
OC	420	4.039	0.655	<	420	3.875	0.973	2.869	0.004	***
ROA	420	-0.017	0.209	>	420	0.037	0.067	-5.036	0.000	***
SEGMENT	420	1.190	0.888	>	420	0.818	0.921	5.965	0.000	***
SIZE	420	10.103	1.737	<	420	10.244	1.700	-1.190	0.234	
GROWTH	420	6.325	72.720	>	420	4.909	20.609	0.384	0.701	
AGE	420	3.810	0.592	<	420	3.844	0.504	-0.900	0.369	
AUDIT	420	0.567	0.496	<	420	0.767	0.423	-6.284	0.000	***
MAPE	420	0.298	0.339	>	420	0.258	0.310	1.775	0.076	*
AQ	420	0.010	0.022	>	420	0.006	0.013	3.191	0.001	***

Note: See Table 6.3 for Variable definitions. *, **, and *** indicate that significance at 0.1 level, 0.5 level, 0.01 level respectively.

the determinants of material weakness and the differences in accruals quality and earnings management between material weakness reporting firms and control firms in Japan. The following are my findings: First, period-end accounting policies and subsidiary are the most frequent types of material weaknesses, suggesting that while the most frequent deficiencies are account-specific in the U.S., this is a special feature in Japan which just starts to make firms set up internal control systems and disclose internal control reports at the same time. Account-specific deficiencies are identified for inventory and sales, suggesting that accruals and inventory are the most common problems in Japan as well as in the U.S.

Second, I find that business complexity, financial health and audit quality are the determinants of material weaknesses and that there is a significant difference in business complexity and financial health between material weakness reporting firms and control firms, suggesting that the more complex businesses the firms have, the less healthy they are. Third, I suggest that the determinant of accruals quality is discretionary accruals for both material weakness reporting firms and control firms. There is a significant difference in accruals quality and purpose of earnings management between material weakness reporting firms and control firms.

This study has limitations: although this study provided evidence from Japan regarding earnings quality and internal control by comparing material weakness reporting firms and control firms, this study did not discuss the changes of the innate firm characteristics nor the accruals quality and earnings management for material weakness reporting firms and control firms in the pre-and post-J-SOX period. Therefore, the changes of earnings quality for each sample in the pre-and post-J-SOX should be discussed. A clarification of the changes of earnings quality will provide a clue concerning the cost-benefit of internal controls regulation in Japan.

Notes:
1 Francis et al. (2008) distinguish between two determinants of earnings quality: innate sources such as business models, operating risk and operating environments, and reporting sources such as management decisions, information system, auditing, governance structure, and regulation and standards.

TABLE 6.7 Determinants of Accruals Quality

2001-2007	Panel A: Material Weakness Reporting Firms						Panel B: Control Firms					
	Accruals Manegement			Real Manegement				Accruals Manegement			Real Manegement		
	B	t-value	siginificance	B	t-value	siginificance		B	t-value	siginificance	B	t-value	siginificance
(Constant)	-0.005	-0.616		-0.005	-0.561		(Constant)	0.038	5.413	***	0.038	5.519	***
ΔWC	-0.026	-1.948	*	-0.037	-3.048	***	ΔWC	-0.143	-6.291	***	-0.140	-7.190	***
adjustOCF	0.014	1.254		0.012	1.071		adjustOCF	0.088	5.036	***	0.082	4.735	***
adjustDEB	-0.012	-1.579		-0.013	-1.633		adjustDEB	-0.012	-1.770	*	-0.012	-1.871	*
OCFvolatili	0.022	1.624		0.012	0.881		OCFvolatili	-0.017	-1.170		-0.020	-1.443	
SALESvolat	0.005	1.452		0.006	1.654	*	SALESvolat	0.028	6.610	***	0.027	6.411	***
OC	0.004	3.025	***	0.004	3.081	***	OC	0.000	-0.185		0.000	0.040	
ROA	-0.003	-0.365		-0.003	-0.375		ROA	-0.052	-3.953	***	-0.058	-4.526	***
SEGMENT	0.002	1.923	*	0.001	1.735	*	SEGMENT	0.000	-0.438		0.000	-0.559	
SIZE	0.000	-0.451		0.000	-0.360		SIZE	-0.002	-3.373	***	-0.002	-3.299	***
GROWTH	0.000	0.016		0.000	-0.083		GROWTH	0.000	-1.071		0.000	-0.902	
AGE	0.001	0.795		0.001	0.604		AGE	-0.003	-2.058	**	-0.004	-2.227	
AUDIT	-0.010	-5.522	***	-0.009	-5.422	***	AUDIT	0.001	0.746		0.001	0.715	
DA	-0.037	-2.236	**				DA	-0.044	-1.794	*			
PROD				-0.004	-0.231		PROD				-0.119	-4.649	***
Adjusted R^2	0.188				0.178			0.365				0.392		
F-value	8.450				7.973			19.514				21.795		

2002-2008	Panel A: Material Weakness Reporting Firms						Panel B : Control Firms					
	Accruals Manegement			Real Manegement				Accruals Manegement			Real Manegement		
	B	t-value	siginificance	B	t-value	siginificance		B	t-value	siginificance	B	t-value	siginificance
(Constant)	0.020	1.312		0.023	1.457		(Constant)	0.034	6.501	***	0.034	6.448	***
ΔWC	0.055	2.078	**	-0.015	-0.643		ΔWC	-0.041	-2.085	**	-0.060	-3.512	***
adjustOCF	0.014	0.699		0.002	0.103		adjustOCF	0.038	2.735	***	0.037	2.698	***
adjustDEB	-0.008	-0.524		-0.011	-0.752		adjustDEB	-0.012	-2.331	**	-0.013	-2.513	**
OCFvolatili	0.035	1.381		-0.015	-0.604		OCFvolatili	-0.008	-0.773		-0.008	-0.770	
SALESvolat	-0.001	-0.080		0.001	0.069		SALESvolat	0.028	8.480	***	0.027	8.264	***
OC	0.002	0.749		0.002	0.949		OC	-0.001	-1.376		-0.001	-1.416	
ROA	-0.023	-1.803	*	-0.019	-1.432		ROA	-0.037	-3.653	***	-0.038	-3.754	***
SEGMENT	0.002	1.230		0.002	1.109		SEGMENT	0.000	0.688		0.000	0.702	
SIZE	0.000	0.082		0.000	0.167		SIZE	-0.002	-5.280	***	-0.002	-5.298	***
GROWTH	0.000	-0.732		0.000	-0.564		GROWTH	0.000	1.286		0.000	1.079	
AGE	-0.004	-1.434		-0.005	-1.779	*	AGE	-0.001	-1.105		-0.001	-1.017	
AUDIT	-0.012	-3.885	***	-0.012	-3.850	***	AUDIT	0.001	1.178		0.001	1.225	
DA	-0.167	-5.353	***				DA	-0.040	-2.084	**			
PROD				-0.056	-1.914	*	PROD				-0.015	-0.842	
Adjusted R^2	0.138				0.085			0.408				0.402		
F-value	6.159				4.009			23.170				22.688		

2003-2009	Panel A: Material Weakness Reporting Firms						Panel B : Control Firms					
	Accruals Manegement			Real Manegement				Accruals Manegement			Real Manegement		
	B	t-value	siginificance	B	t-value	siginificance		B	t-value	siginificance	B	t-value	siginificance
(Constant)	-0.012	-0.856		-0.012	-0.894		(Constant)	0.050	7.871	***	0.050	7.753	***
ΔWC	0.055	2.642	***	0.020	1.095		ΔWC	-0.031	-1.380		-0.065	-3.346	***
adjustOCF	0.004	0.258		-0.001	-0.049		adjustOCF	0.048	3.189	***	0.048	3.161	***
adjustDEB	-0.023	-1.923	*	-0.025	-2.065	**	adjustDEB	-0.005	-0.795		-0.006	-1.037	
OCFvolatili	0.039	1.868	*	0.019	0.943		OCFvolatili	0.056	4.587	***	0.057	4.604	***
SALESvolat	0.011	2.083	**	0.013	2.271	**	SALESvolat	0.000	0.020		-0.001	-0.294	
OC	0.006	3.197	***	0.006	3.427	***	OC	-0.002	-2.735	***	-0.002	-2.620	***
ROA	-0.014	-1.504		-0.011	-1.152		ROA	-0.031	-2.585	***	-0.034	-2.852	***
SEGMENT	0.002	1.394		0.002	1.325		SEGMENT	0.001	1.333		0.001	1.340	
SIZE	0.000	0.113		0.000	0.116		SIZE	-0.002	-3.582	***	-0.002	-3.565	***
GROWTH	0.000	-0.913		0.000	-0.826		GROWTH	0.000	-1.023		0.000	-1.311	
AGE	-0.001	-0.529		-0.001	-0.612		AGE	-0.005	-3.456	***	-0.005	-3.408	***
AUDIT	-0.006	-2.554	**	-0.006	-2.533	**	AUDIT	0.000	0.049		0.000	0.185	
DA	-0.079	-3.310	*				DA	-0.076	-3.258	***			
PROD				-0.009	-0.494		PROD				-0.032	-1.512	
Adjusted R^2	0.172				0.150			0.204				0.188		
F-value	7.678				6.679			9.264				8.454		

Notes: See Table 6.3 for Variable definitions. *, **, and *** indicate significance at p<10%, p<5%, p<1%; t-value is based on White's (1980) standard error. Devendent variable is accruals quality by estimateing Francis et al.'s (2008) model.

2. Auditing Standard No.5 (AS5) also shows that material weaknesses must be determined by two dimensions; significance and probability, but AS5 follows Financial Reporting Standard (FRS) and probability is divided into the three categories: Probable, Reasonably possible, Remote. This is a difference in classifications between AS5 and J-SOX.
3. Deficiencies in design arise when a control is missing or an existing control is not properly designed and the control objective is not always met. Deficiencies in operating effectiveness arise when a properly designed control does not operate as designed, when there are many errors in operation or when the person performing the control does not properly understand the nature and objectives of the control (BAC 2006, p.35).
4. While the most severe deficiencies of internal control are prescribed "material weaknesses" in the U.S., the most severe deficiencies of internal control in Japan are literally prescribed "important deficiencies." But, since the definition in the J-SOX is almost same as the definition in US-SOX, I use "material weaknesses" for the most severe deficiencies in internal control both in Japan and the U.S. consistently.
5. Quantitative materiality can be calculated as a percentage of consolidated total assets, consolidated sales, consolidated income before income taxes and minority interests and other factors. These percentages are not defined as set amounts; rather, the percentage should be determined based on the company's situation, such as its type of business, size, and characteristics. For example, the materiality threshold using consolidated income before income taxes and minority interests may be set at approximately 5% of the consolidated income before tax. However, ultimately, the materiality amount should be considered in the context of its relationship to the quantitative materiality amount of the Financial Statement Audit (BAC 2006, p.36).
6. Qualitative materiality is determined based on the extent of impact on two dimensions; investment decisions such as information regarding a delisting criteria or financial covenants and significance on the reliability of financial reporting such as information concerning the related party transactions and big shareholders (Practice Standard, p.36).
7. Evaluation should be done on consolidated bases means that the level of material effect should be considered based on consolidated financial statements (Practice Standard p.36).
8. I have industry classification based on Nikkei Economic Electronic Databank System (NEEDS) criteria.
9. Ge and McVay (2005) investigate what type of material weaknesses for 261 firms which disclose one more than material weakness from August 2002 to November 2004. 119 of sample firms disclose account-specific, 55 firms disclose revenue recognition. They show that since the sample firms disclosed 493 deficiencies, each firm has 1.9 deficiency types on average.
10. Ge and McVay (2005) investigate what kind of deficiencies for material weakness as a sample of 261 firms that disclose at least one material weakness from August 2002 to November 2004. 55 firms among sample report revenue-recognition policies and the process for a material weakness. 23 firms disclose senior management as material weakness. One fourth is Account-Specific as a material weakness.
11. Dechow and Dichev (2002) focus on the association between firm innate characteristics and accruals quality. Dechow and Dichev (2002) suggest that it is important to recognize the relationship between observable firm characteristics and non-observable estimation

error. They find that operating cycles, firm size, SALES volatility, OCF volatility, and the magnitude of accruals are determinants of accruals quality. Accruals quality decreases for two reasons; one is because managers change accruals intentionally through earnings management and the other is unintentional errors in making assumptions and estimates at uncontrollable organizations which makes it hard to predict an uncertain future. Dechow and Dichev (2002, p.53) mention that accruals quality affected by management intentional and unintentional errors, and that while management intent is unobservable, unavoidable estimation errors by firm characteristics is observable. Dechow and Dichev (2002) report that firms with longer operating cycles, smaller size, greater SALES volatility, OCF volatility, and greater frequent negative earnings have lower accruals quality. Thus, they indicate that to assess firm characteristics is the way to evaluate accruals quality.

12 Doyle et al. (2007a) suggest that account-specific material weakness as include: (1) Inadequate internal controls for accounting for loss contingencies, including bad debts, (2) deficiencies in the documentation of a receivables securitization program, (3) No adequate internal controls over the application of new accounting principles or the application of existing accounting principle to new transactions. Also, they suggest that company-level material weaknesses include override senior management and ineffective control environment.

13 McNichols (2002) asserts that economic and structural factors can cause variation in the precision of accruals estimates, regardless of the presence or absence of managerial discretion and that managerial expertise also influences the precision of estimation, even if other factors are held constant. That is, the link between accruals and cash flow realization in adjacent periods is affected by economic and structural factors, managerial expertise, and intentional managerial discretions.

14 In the Jones' (1991) model, $\Delta WC_t = \beta_0 + \beta_1 \Delta SALES_t + \beta_2 PPE_t + \varepsilon_t$, $\beta_0 + \beta_1 \Delta SALES_t + \beta_2 PPE_t + \varepsilon_t$ are assumed to be nondiscretionary accruals, and ε_t, the residual from the equation is discretionary accruals.

15 According to Dechow and Skinner (2000), conservative accounting includes overly aggressive recognition of provision or reserve, overvaluation of acquired in-process R&D in purchase acquisitions, overstatement of restructuring charges and asset write-offs for accruals management, and delaying sales, accelerating R&D or advertising expenditure for real management. Neutral accounting includes earnings that result from a neutral operation of the process, such as income smoothing accounting (Suda 2007). Aggressive accounting includes the understatement of the provisions for bad debts and drawing down provisions or reserves in an overly aggressive manner for accruals management, and postponing R&D or advertising expenditures and accelerating sales for real management.

16 ΔWC indicates working capital accruals but in this study, I call this accruals.

17 For variables OCF, I use variables which deduct the average in the year following Yoshida (2005).

18 For variables DEBT, I use variables which deduct the average in the year following Yoshida (2005).

19 The Japanese BIG 4 are Azusa (affiliate of KPMG), Arata (affiliate of Pricewaterhouse), Shinnihon Yugen Sekinin Kansa Hojin (affiliate of Ernst &Young),Tohmatsu (affiliate of Deloitte Touche Tohmatsu). Since Misuzu (former ChuoAoyama) finished their operating

as an accounting firm in July, 2007, Arata added to Japanese BIG 4, instead of Misuzu. However, since the Japanese BIG 4 refers the auditing contract with SEC-registered Japanese firms from 2006 through 2008, there is a possibility not to have an auditing contract before 2006 and there might be an accounting firm with a different contract in the sample, I have BIGN as *AUDIT*.

20 Ge and McVay (2005) looked at two size variables, book value and market cap.
21 Okuda et al. (2012) examine the association between managers' attitudes and internal control effectiveness.
22 Nakashima's (2012) model refers to the flowchart on Figure 7.6 in Chapter seven of this book.

CHAPTER 7

INTENTION OF EARNINGS MANAGEMENT

7.1 Introduction

This chapter examines whether earnings management of material weakness reporting firms is related to managers' opportunism by analyzing the association between accruals quality and forecast errors through the Nakashima's (2012) model.

This study contributes to the literature in the following ways. First, this study contributes to the literature that examines about the relationship between material weaknesses and earnings management. This study provides evidence on whether earnings management of material weakness reporting firms reflects managerial opportunism or informativeness. Epps and Guthrie (2010) find that material weakness allows opportunities for greater manipulation of earnings using discretionary accruals. But, managers use discretionary accruals not only to manipulate earnings but also to increase informativeness of earnings (Watt and Zimmerman 1986; Suda 2000; Leuz et al. 2003). Although a number of studies regarding motives of accounting management or the way to detect earnings management have been conducted both in Japan and the U.S.,[1] this study examines whether the motives of earnings management of material weakness firms have an opportunistic purpose through focusing on the relationship between predictive errors and accruals quality based on the Nakashima's (2012) model.

Second, The findings of this study regarding the innate characteristics and accruals quality of material weakness reporting firms provides a convergent concept of material weakness in Japan which does not depend on subjective judgments by firms or auditors.

Third, this study provides empirical evidence on managerial motives for earnings management in material weakness reporting firms in Japan. To date, not much evidence regarding the effect of internal control systems for public firms in Japan has been provided. Nakashima (2011) employed a sample of SEC-registered Japanese firms. If those findings are different from this study, the particular behavior of public firms in Japan and the specific environment in Japan regarding internal controls and corporate governance will be found. While public firms in Japan are operated under particular business environment such as weak investor protection and lower litigation risk (Leuz et al. 2003), SEC-registered Japanese firms are operated under the stricter U.S. GAAP which requires them to disclose transparent information through accepting higher disclosure levels (Coffee 1999) and under more precise investigation by SEC regulation and investors. Therefore, the U.S. Market listing itself (Machuga and Teitel 2007) works as corporate governance and this may make the attitude of SEC-registered Japanese firms (Machuga and Teitel 2007) different from public firms in Japan.

The remainder of this study proceeds as follows. Section two develops the hypotheses. Section three shows the research design. Section four presents data and descriptive statistics. Section five discusses the results. The final section summarizes and concludes this study.

7.2 Hypothesis Development

The studies that focus on the innate characteristics of internal control deficiency reporting firms include Krishnan (2005), Ge and McVay (2005), and Doyle et al. (2007b). Krishnan (2005) examines the association between internal control deficiencies and audit committee quality and indicates that 128 firms which report internal control deficiencies are associated with audit committee quality and financial distress.

Doyle et al. (2007b) investigate the determinants of material weakness for the 779 firms which disclose one material weakness and find that material weakness firms have firm characteristics such as smaller size, younger age, more complex, rapidly growing, and restructuring. Doyle et al. (2007a) also suggest that while firms with company-level problems tend to be smaller, younger and weaker financially, and firms with account-specific problems tend to be more complex, more diversified, and rapidly changing.

There are mixed results about the association between firm size and internal control deficiencies. While large firms have more assets that must be controlled, they have more financial reporting processes and procedures in place (Ge and McVay 2005). On the other hand, since larger firms are subject to more scrutiny from financial analysts and investors (Lobo and Zhou 2006), larger firms tend to have a good internal control system and they have more employees and greater resources to spend on internal auditors or consulting fees, which results in helping them set up a good internal control system (Ge and McVay 2005). Based on this rationale, they find a negative association between firm size and material weaknesses (Ge and McVay 2005). These recent studies provide evidence about a negative association between firm size and internal control deficiencies (Doyle et al. 2007b; Ashbaugh-Skaife et al. 2008; Okuda et al. 2009).

Ge and McVay (2005) examine the association between business complexity, firm experience, firm size, firm profitability and auditor, and material weakness. They find that the complexity measures are greater for the material weakness firm group and the firm size measures are smaller for the material weakness firm group. Also, they document that weakness disclosure are positively associated with complexity measures and negatively associated with firm sizes and profitability, suggesting that firms disclosing material weaknesses have more complex operations, and that the firms are smaller and less profitable. The results of multi-regression analyses show that material weaknesses are positively associated with business complexity and audit quality but negatively associated with profitability.

Internal control systems are intended to prevent and find misstatements and errors in the process of financial statement preparation and reporting. Good internal control systems are expected to lead to more credible financial information disclosure. Deficiencies in internal controls such as no segregation of duties fail to prevent and find managerial intentional earnings manipulation by management and results in misstatements and errors in estimating accruals.

Doyle et al. (2007a) predict that weaknesses in internal controls have the potential to allow both intentional error (earnings management) and unintentional error (poor estimation ability) in accruals estimation to impact on the reported financial statements. Doyle et al. (2007a) set up the hypothesis that material weaknesses in internal control are negatively associated with accruals quality. They investigate the relation between accruals quality and internal control deficiency using 705 firms that disclosed at least one material weakness from August 2002 to November 2005 and document that firms with weak internal controls over financial reporting generally have lower accruals quality using an accrual quality measure by the Dechow and Dichev's (2002) model and the Francis et al.'s (2008) model.

Ashbaugh-Skaife et al. (2008) examine the determinants of accruals quality; internal control deficiency, business fundamentals and operating characteristics, investment in internal controls, GAAP accounting choices, accounting conservatism, and auditor quality. They find that characteristics related to inventory ratio, OCF volatility, sales volatility, rapid growth and conservative accounting choices are the determinants of accruals quality. Ashbaugh-Skaife et al. (2008) also document that firms reporting internal control deficiencies have lower accruals quality as measured by accrual noise and absolute accruals relative to firms not reporting internal control problems, and that firms that report internal control deficiencies have significantly larger positive and larger negative abnormal accruals relative to control firms. This suggests that internal control weaknesses are more likely to lead to unintentional errors that add noise to accruals than intentional misstatements that bias earnings upward.

Little evidence regarding material weakness reporting firms from Japan has been provided. I provide evidence from Japan and predict that material weakness reporting firms have common innate firm characteristics. I predict that internal control deficiencies affect accruals quality for material weakness reporting firms.

H1: Firm characteristics and a significant association between accruals quality and material weaknesses for material weakness reporting firms in Japan are consistent with those of material weakness reporting firms in the U.S.

H1a: Material weakness in Japan is significantly associated with innate firm characteristics.

H1b: Material weakness in Japan is significantly with accruals quality.

Nakashima (2011) finds there is a positive association between accruals quality and predictive errors by estimating with the Dechow and Dichev's (2002) model and the Francis et al.'s (2008) model in the pre-US-SOX period but no association between accruals quality and predictive errors in the post-US-SOX period. And, she finds that while discretionary accruals are not associated with predictive errors both in pre- and post-US-SOX periods, real management is significantly associated with predictive errors in pre- and post-US-SOX periods. Also, she finds that accruals quality is significantly associated with abnormal production costs in the pre-and post-US-SOX periods and that especially, abnormal production costs in the pre-US-SOX period increases accruals quality but reduces accruals quality in the post-US-SOX period. Based on these empirical analyses, she suggests that discretionary accruals do not reflect opportunistic earnings management but reflect inside information, but that abnormal production expenses reflect opportunistic earnings management.

Few studies examine the association between predictive errors and material weaknesses. I predict that since material weakness firms have weak internal control systems, they fail to have precise estimation and there is an association between predictive errors and material weaknesses.

Epps and Guthrie (2010) examine whether having material weakness allows managers to exercise earnings management through using discretionary accruals by analyzing the association between material weakness and discretionary accruals. They find that firms with material weakness generally have higher negative, income-decreasing discretionary accruals. Their finding indicates that material weakness allows for greater manipulation of earnings using discretionary accruals.

Nakashima (2011) finds that there is a positive association between accruals quality and predictive errors in the pre-US-SOX period but no association between accruals quality and predictive errors in the post-US-SOX period. Following Bissessur (2008, pp.3-4), Nakashima (2011) suggests that discretionary accruals do not reflect opportunistic earnings management but informative but abnormal production expenses reflects opportunistic management. Also, she suggests that accruals quality is significantly associated with production costs in the pre-and post-US-SOX periods. Especially, production cost in the pre-US-SOX period increases accruals quality but reduce accruals quality in the post-US-SOX period. Thus, Nakashima (2011) reports that if a significant association between accruals quality and predictive error is observed, earnings management reflects opportunism.

Thus, it is likely that the internal control systems do not work well at material weakness firms and weak internal controls fail to prevent or detect opportunistic earnings management. I predict that earnings management of material weakness firms have an opportunistic purpose and set up the following hypothesis;

H2: Material weakness reporting firms have opportunistic earnings management.

In this study, I apply the Nakashima's (2012) model which can recognize whether the intention of earnings management is opportunistic or informative. The flowchart in the figure which recognizes whether earnings management reflects opportunism or informativeness is shown as follows; As Step 1, one observes whether there is a significant association between accruals quality and predictive errors or not on a multivariate regression models whose dependent variable is predictive error. If there is no significant association between accruals quality and predictive errors, earnings management reflects informativeness but if there is a significant association between the two, the earnings management reflects an opportunistic purpose. Figure 6 shows the flowchart for one way of detecting opportunistic earnings management.

As Step 2, one observes a regression model whose dependent variable is accruals quality. If there is no significant association between accruals quality and discretionary accruals or between accruals quality and real management, the earnings management reflects informativeness. But, if there is a significant association between accruals quality and discretionary accruals or between accruals quality and real management, the earnings management has an opportunistic purpose.

As Step 3, one observes a regression model whose dependent variable is accruals quality. When it is likely that discretionary accruals reflect opportunistic earnings management, watch the sign of accruals. One evaluates that if the sign is positive, they decrease accruals quality. When it is likely that real management reflects

FIGURE 7.1 Flowchart to Recognize Whether Earnings Management Has Opportunism

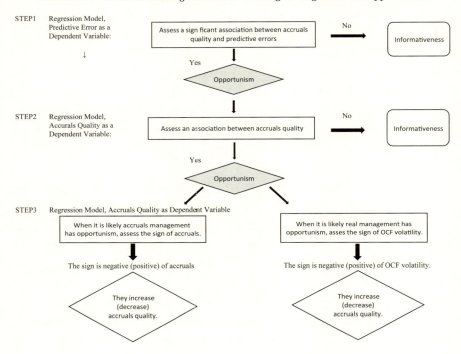

opportunistic earnings management, watch the sign of *OCFvolatility*. If the sign of accruals is negative (positive), they increase (lower) accruals quality. If the sign of *OCFvolatility* is negative (positive), they increase (lower) accruals quality.

Bissessur (2008) mentions that if abnormal accruals reflect earnings management, the ability of abnormal accruals to predict future cash flows should be affected by accruals quality. However, if abnormal accruals are used to reflect the firm's business activity, the predictive power of abnormal accruals for future cash flows should remain unaffected by accruals quality, since management uses abnormal accruals to reflect their private information about future performance, which is not affected by accruals quality. He examines the association between predictive ability of discretionary accruals and accruals quality and suggests that discretionary accruals reflect inner information for future performance.

Nakashima (2011) discusses the association between predictive errors and accruals quality in the pre-and post-US-SOX periods and the association was observed in the pre-US-SOX period but no association was observed in the post-US-SOX period.

Few studies about the predictive errors and accruals quality for material weakness firms have been analyzed. I predict that since internal control systems do not work well at material weakness firms and they are not allowed to prevent and detect opportunistic earnings management, material weakness reporting firms have an opportunistic earnings management and there is an association between predictive errors and accruals quality. Therefore, the following working hypothesis 2a should be set up.

Working Hypothesis 2a : Predictive errors of material weakness reporting firms are significantly associated with accruals quality.

Nakashima (2011) finds that predictive errors are not associated with discretionary accruals after US-SOX and are significantly associated with real management and that discretionary accruals are not associated with predictive error in the pre-and post-US-SOX periods but real management is associated with predictive error in the pre- and post-US-SOX periods. She also finds that there was a significant association between discretionary accruals and accruals quality before US-SOX but there was a significant association between real management and accruals quality after US-SOX and although accruals quality is significantly associated with production costs in the pre- and post-US-SOX periods, production cost increases accruals quality before SOX but decreases accruals quality after US-SOX. She mentions that based on the association between predictive errors and earnings management and accruals quality and earnings management, discretionary accruals reflect managers' information but production costs reflect opportunistic earnings management.

Dechow and Schrand (2004, p.7) mention that if implemented properly, accrual accounting should result in an earnings number that reflects the underlying economic variation in the company's operations. It should smooth cash flow volatility, however, that does not reflect a variation in underlying company performance and that earnings quality can be improved when accruals smooth out value-irrelevant changes in cash flows. But, earnings quality is reduced when accruals are used to hide value-relevant changes in cash flows. Following this rationale, earnings quality must be decreased if opportunistic earnings management is implemented through accruals. Richardson et al. (2002) investigate accruals for restatement firms and find that restatement firms have very large accruals in the years of alleged manipulation and accruals information is a key determinant of restatement reporting. Nakashima (2011) also finds that accruals quality is significantly associated with negative accruals and accruals increase accruals quality. Thus, I set up the following working hypothesis 2b:

Working Hypothesis 2b : Accruals quality of material weakness reporting firms is associated with discretionary accruals or abnormal production costs.

Bedard (2006) suggests that earnings quality improved in the post-US-SOX period providing evidence that there was a decrease in the magnitude of unexpected accruals in their first internal control report. SEC-registered Japanese firms have been required to comply with US-SOX regulation since 2006. SEC-registered Japanese firms have been working on better organization of the internal controls following SOX regulation.

Internal governance processes are established to maintain the credibility of firms' financial statements and safeguard against such behavior as earnings manipulation (Dechow et al. 1996, p.4). Dechow et al. (1996) examine the relationship between earnings manipulation and internal control deficiency for the firms subject to accounting Enforcement Actions (AAER) by the Securities and Exchange Commission. They show that accruals gradually increase as the alleged year of earnings manipulation approached, and then experienced a sharp decline. The increase in accruals is consistent with earnings manipulation. The subsequent accrual reduction is consistent with the reversal of prior accrual overstatements (Dechow et al. 1996). They find that AAER firms have greater accruals than control firms. Thus, they suggest that time-series plots of accruals of the AAEF firms shows that they have earnings manipulation to overstate earnings.

Managers sometimes may use accruals to produce the desired level of earnings. Dechow and Schrand (2004) point out that high accruals in absolute magnitude is a potential "opportunistically earnings management".

Based on the findings of prior studies that accrual information is an important determinant of earnings management (Dechow et al., 1996; Richardson et al. 2002), I predict that accruals quality is significantly associated with predictive errors and accruals quality is significantly associated with positive accruals. Thus, I set up the following working hypothesis 2c:

Working Hypothesis 2c : Accruals quality of material weakness reporting firms is associated with positive accruals.

7.3 Research Design

7.3.1 Accruals Quality Measures

The measure accruals quality is defined as the extent to which they map into past, current, and future cash flows (Doyle et al. 2007a), following the Dechow and Dichev (2002) and computed as a standard deviation of the residuals estimated from firm-specific time-series regression. This study employs a measure to capture accruals quality estimated by the Francis et al.'s (2008) model whose linkage of the Dechow and Dichev's (2002) model and the Jones' (1991) models can capture errors associated with both unintentional estimations and intentional management estimations.

Initially, the models are estimated using data beginning with year 2000 and ending with year 2004 to generate a standard deviation of residuals for the year 2005. Next, I use data beginning with year 2001 and ending with year 2005 to generate a standard deviation of residuals for the year 2006. This process is repeated and the models are sequentially re-estimated until all standard errors of residuals over the four year holdout period are obtained (2000-2008):

$$\Delta WC_t = \beta_0 + \beta_1 OCF_{t-1} + \beta_2 OCF_t + \beta_3 OCF_{t+1} + \beta_4 \Delta SALES_t + \beta_5 PPE_t + \varepsilon_t.$$

7.3.2 Cash Flow Prediction Models Specification

In order to compute predictive errors 1, the following regression for cash flow predictions is estimated using a sample:

$$OCF_{t+1} = \theta_0 + \theta_1 OCF_t + \theta_2 \Delta AR_t + \theta_3 \Delta INV_t + \theta_4 \Delta AP_t + \varepsilon_t.$$

OCF_{t+1} = cash flows from operations at time t+1;
NI_t = net operating income at time t;
ΔAR_t = change in accounts receivable at time t;
ΔINV_t = change in inventory at time t;
ΔAP_t = change in accounts payable at time t;
ε_t = current disturbance term.

I employ a multivariate time-series model (MULT) for one-year-ahead cash flow predictions to be estimated on a firm-specific basis, following Lorek and Willinger (1996). One-year-ahead cash flows predictions are generated in an ex ante fashion through the two cash flows prediction models above. Initially, this model is estimated using data beginning with year 2001 and ending with year 2005 to generate cash flow prediction for the year 2006. Next, I use data beginning with year 2002 and ending with year 2006 to generate a cash flow prediction for the year 2007.

This process is repeated and the models are sequentially re-estimated until all one-year-ahead cash flow predictions over the four year holdout period are obtained (2001-2009). I evaluate forecast accuracy for each model using one of the traditional measures of forecast accuracy measures which are used and accepted widely by academicians and practitioners.[2] The mean absolute percentage error (*MAPE*) is computed as follows:

$$MAPE = \sum_{t=1}^{n} \frac{|e_t|}{|Y_t|}.$$

e_t = estimation error in period t;
Y_t = actual value at time t.

7.3.3 Earnings Management Measures

Earnings management which falls within GAAP can be focused on three types of earnings management; conservative accounting, neutral accounting, and aggressive accounting (Dechow and Skinner 2000). I post one proxy, discretionary accruals as aggressive accounting for accruals management measures in this study. Managers use their discretions not only in order to misstate their firms' performance for opportunistic purposes, but also to convey their inside information for imformative purposes (Watt and Zimmaerman 1986; Subramanyam 1996; Suda 2000; Leuz et al. 2003, p.510). This study uses discretionary accruals estimated by the Jones' (1991) model each year cross-sectionaly for all sample firms, using the following regression model:

$$\Delta WC_t = \beta_0 + \beta_1 \Delta SALES_t + \beta_2 PPE_t + \varepsilon_t.$$

Managers can take real actions which affect cash flows by delaying or accelerating sales and accelerating or postponing R&D or advertising expenses (Dechow and Skinner 2000). I follow previous studies to use my proxies for real earnings management. However, it is difficult to document the extent to which managers engage in real management to manipulate earnings. Merely observing that a firm enters into a transaction that receives favorable accounting treatment is not evidence that the firm entered into the transaction just because of its accounting consequence (Dechow and Schrand 2004).

Graham et al. (2005) and Suda and Hanaeda (2007) find strong evidence that managers take real managements such as "decrease discretionary spending on R&D, advertising, and maintenance" to meet an earnings target much more than accounting management such as "book revenue now rather than next quarter" and "alter accounting assumptions." Thus, following Roychowdhury (2006) and Cohen et al.(2008), this study focuses on production manipulation. Production costs manipulation includes reporting lower *COGS* by reducing production costs per unit to increase production. I estimate one proxy, abnormal production costs (*abnPROD*).

I compute abnormal production costs by subtracting the normal level of the sum of *COGS* and change in inventory from actual production costs. I estimate the normal level of production costs as the following equation:

$$PROD_t = COG_t + \Delta INV_t.$$
$$= \alpha_0 + \alpha_1 SALES_t + \alpha_2 \Delta SALES_t + \alpha_3 \Delta SALES_{t-1} + \varepsilon_t.$$

7.3.4 Testing Hypotheses

In order to test working hypothesis 1(a), I conduct correlation and logistic regression analysis. In this study, I investigate firm characteristics which affect material weakness disclosure by logistic regression analysis and whether there is a difference in firm characteristics between the company-level material weakness reporting firms and account-specific-level material weakness reporting firms:

$$MW = \theta_0 + \theta_1 \Delta WC_t + \theta_2 OCF_t + \theta_3 LDEBT_t + \theta_4 OCFvolatility_t + \theta_5 SALESvolatiliy_t + \theta_6 OC_t + \theta_7 ROA_t + \theta_8 SEGMENT_t + \theta_9 SIZE_t + \theta_{10} GROWTH_t + \theta_{11} AGE_t + \theta_{12} AUDIT_t + \theta_{13} DA_t + \theta_{14} PROD_t + \varepsilon_{t+1}.$$

To test working hypothesis 1(b), I examine the association between accruals quality and material weakness by estimating the following the Francis et al.'s (2008) regression model. Also, I conduct analyses by separating the company-level and account-specific level material weakness:

$$AQ = \beta_0 + \beta_1 MW + \beta_2 WC_t + \beta_3 OCF_t + \beta_4 LDEBT_t + \beta_5 OCFvolatility_t + \beta_6 SALESvolatility_t + \beta_7 OC_t + \beta_8 ROA_t + \beta_9 SEGMENT_t + \beta_{10} SIZE + \beta_{11} GROWTH + \beta_{12} AGE_t + \beta_{13} AUDIT_t + \beta_{14} EM_t + \varepsilon_{t+1},$$

Where,

AQ	= accruals quality;
ΔWC	= accruals: changes in working capitals; Δaccount receivable $+\Delta$inventory$-\Delta$account payable $-\Delta$tax payment$+\Delta$other assets (net);
OCF	= cash flows from operating activities;
$LDEBT$	= long-term debt, long debt/average assets;
$SALESvolatility$	= the standard deviation of sales, deflated by average assets;
$OCFvolatility$	= the standard deviation of cash flow operations, deflated by average assets;
$SIZE$	= log of total sales;
$AUDIT$	= audit quality: 1 if a firm engaged with one of the BIG 4 audit firms, and 0 otherwise;[24]

OC	= operating cycle; the log of the average of {(360/sales/average account receivable)} +(360/costs of goods sold/average inventory)};
ROA	= net income/average assets;
EM	= earning management measures.

To test H2, I estimate the following regression equation and examine the association between predictive errors and accruals quality. Managers may follow an overall earnings management strategy and choose earnings management with lower costs. As they can choose less costly earning management between accruals and real management, I put either earnings management into the model. I include the variables *LEV, SIZE*, and *AUDIT* as control variables:

$$
\begin{aligned}
MAPE = &\ \theta_0 + \theta_1 MW + \theta_2 \Delta WC_t + \theta_3 OCF_t + \theta_4 LDBET_t + \theta_8 OCFvolatility_t \\
&+ \theta_9 SALESvolatility_t + \theta_{10} OC_t + \theta_{11} ROA_t + \theta_{12} SEGMENT_t + \theta_{13} SIZE_t \\
&+ \theta_{14} GROWTH_t + \theta_{15} AGE_t + \theta_{15} AUDIT_t + \theta_{16} AQ + \varepsilon_{t+1}.
\end{aligned}
$$

7.4 Descriptive Statistics

The sample used in this study is for the period 2000-2009 from the Nikkei Economic Electronic Databank System (NEEDS) through following the criteria; (1) SEC-registered firms, (2) the month in which the fiscal year ends is March or August, (3) not financial institutions.

Panel A and Panel B of Table 7.1 provide descriptive statistics of firm characteristics, descriptive statistics of accruals quality and mean absolute percentage errors respectively. The descriptive statistics indicate that the negative sign of *OCF* of material weakness reporting firms in Japan is the same as the sign of *OCF* of material weakness reporting firms in the U.S. (Ge and McVay 2005) and that they have smaller segment than the segment of Ge and McVay (2005), suggesting that the material weakness firms in Japan are less complicated than the material weakness firms in the U.S. And, they show that values of *OCFvolatility* and *SALESvolatility* are similar to Ashbaugh-Skaife et al.'s (2008) *OCFvolatility* and *SALESvolatility*. Thus, the material weakness reporting firms in Japan have similar features to the material weakness reporting firms in the U.S.

TABLE 7.1 Description Statistics
Panel A: Firm Characteristics

	Descriptive Statistice (n=280)						
	Mean	Median	Standard Deviation	Minimum	Maximum	25th Percentile	75th Percentile
ΔWC	0.032	0.014	0.100	-0.327	0.588	-0.009	0.056
adjustOCF	-0.019	0.024	0.198	-1.400	0.323	-0.033	0.065
adjustDEBT	-0.003	-0.043	0.091	-0.076	0.379	-0.075	0.051
OCFvolatility	0.069	0.030	0.105	-0.038	0.645	0.013	0.071
SALESvolatility	0.160	0.069	0.232	0.000	1.502	0.027	0.171
OC	4.111	3.933	0.694	2.950	6.080	3.646	4.492
ROA	1.145	0.956	0.801	0.089	5.489	0.658	1.375
SEGMENT	0.551	0.778	0.404	0.000	1.946	0.000	0.845
SIZE	9.874	9.783	1.837	5.485	14.253	8.324	11.097
GROWTH	6.723	0.800	56.700	-83.437	845.140	-8.764	10.804
AGE	1.660	1.710	0.292	0.780	2.830	1.573	1.830
AUDIT	0.500	0.500	0.501	0.000	1.000	0.000	1.000
DA	0.000	0.002	0.089	-0.533	0.497	-0.017	0.023
abnPROD	0.006	0.004	0.075	-0.587	0.378	-0.011	0.021
LOSSPORTION	0.370	0.300	0.270	0.000	1.000	0.143	0.500

Variable Definitions : *, **, and *** indicate significance at p< 10 %, p< 5%, p<1%;. t-value is based on White's (1980) standard error.
all variables are deflated by total assets in the beginning of the year.

OCF	cash flows from operating
defdertaWC	changes in working capitals = $\Delta AR + \Delta INV - \Delta AP - \Delta TAX\ Payable + \Delta other\ assets$ (net)
adjustOCF	OCF (cash flows from operations) minus mean of OCF
adjustDEBT	LDEBT (=long-term debt /average assets) minus mean of LDEBT
OCFvolatility	the standard deviation of cash flow operations .
SALESvolatility	the standard deviation of the changes in sales average assets.
OC	operating cycle=the log of the average of[(sales/360)/(average accounts receivable) + (cost of goods sold/360)average inventory)] .
ROA	return on assets: net income/average assets
SEGMENT	number of reported business segments
SIZE	log of total sales
GROWTH	growth rate in sales: sales in the beginning of the year / sales in the end of the year
AGE	the years when the firm passed since the firm was established
AUDIT	1 if the firm is audited by a BIG N auditor, and 0 otherwise
DA	discretionary working capital accruals by estimated DeAngelo (1986) model
abnPROD	abnormal production costs, resisuals by estimated $COG + \Delta INV = SALES_t + \Delta SALES_t + \Delta SALES_{t-1}$

Panel B: Accruals Quality and MAPE

	Discriptive Statistics (n=280)						
	Mean	Median	Standard Deviation	Minimum	Maximum	25th Percentile	75th Percentile
AQ	0.018	0.010	0.025	0.001	0.152	0.006	0.021
MAPE	0.416	0.265	0.355	0.003	1.000	0.119	0.709

Each variable is defined below;
Accrual Quality (FR) =AQ_FR, The standard deviation of the resicuals from Francis et al.'s (2008) measure,

$MAPE = \sum_{i=1}^{n} \frac{|e_i|}{|Y_i|}$ e_i=predictive Error in t, Y_i=actual value in t

7.5 Empirical Results

7.5.1 Empirical Results 1: Evidence from Japan

I examine what innate firm characteristics are related to material weaknesses through Logistic regression. Table 7.2 reports the results of the logistic regression analysis. Table 7.2 shows that coefficient of *SEGMENT* is 1.860 and a significant positive association with material weaknesses, suggesting that *SEGMENT* is a determinant of material weaknesses. This suggests that the greater complexity firms have, the easier it is to have a material weakness. This is consistent with the results of Ge and McVay (2005)

Table 7.3 provides descriptive statistics by a material weakness type. I compare two variables using *t*-tests and Wilcoxon rank-sum tests of the difference. Table 7.3 presents the results about whether there is a difference in firm characteristics between company-level material weakness firms and account-specific material weakness firms. The differences in accruals quality between company-level material weaknesses and account-specific material weaknesses are not observed, but there are significant differences in *OCFvolatility*, *SIZE*, *AGE*, and *AUDIT* are 3.698, -1.684,

TABLE 7.2 Logistic Regression of the Probability of Disclosing a Material Weakness

	Descriptive Statistic (n=280)					
	B	S.E.	Wald	df	Sig.	Exp(B)
ΔWC	-0.347	2.575	0.018	1.000	0.893	0.707
adjustOCF	1.122	1.243	0.815	1.000	0.367	3.070
adjustDEBT	-2.978	1.328	5.029	1.000	0.025	0.051
OCFvolatility	2.678	2.194	1.489	1.000	0.222	14.553
SALESvolatility	-5.227	0.911	32.947	1.000	0.000	0.005
OC	-0.318	0.291	1.193	1.000	0.275	0.728
ROA	0.303	0.191	2.524	1.000	0.112	1.354
SEGMENT	1.860	0.415	20.120	1.000	0.000	6.422
SIZE	0.327	0.126	6.716	1.000	0.010	1.386
GROWTH	0.001	0.003	0.077	1.000	0.781	1.001
AGE	-9.992	1.252	63.651	1.000	0.000	0.000
Audit	-2.258	0.436	26.779	1.000	0.000	0.105
DA	-0.914	2.943	0.097	1.000	0.756	0.401
PROD	0.563	2.582	0.048	1.000	0.827	1.756
Constant	17.999	2.882	38.996	1.000	0.000	65623617.110
Likelihood Ratio	358.416					
Pseudo R^2	0.447					

Notes: See Table 7.1 for Variable Definitions. Material weakness is an indicator variable that equal to 1 if the firm disclosed a material weakness in a internal control report in my sample, and 0 otherwise.

TABLE 7.3 Descriptive Statistics of Material Weakness Reporting Firms

	Company-Level				Account-Specific Level					
	N	Mean	Standard Deviation	Predicted sign	N	Mean	Standard Deviation	t-value	significance	
OCFvolatility	236	0.075	0.113	>	44	0.040	0.039	3.698	0.000	***
SALESvolatility	236	0.156	0.226	<	44	0.180	0.266	-0.626	0.532	
OC	236	4.118	0.681	<	44	4.075	0.768	0.377	0.706	
ROA	236	1.143	0.828	?	44	1.155	0.643	-0.092	0.927	
SEGMENT	236	0.558	0.375	>	44	0.514	0.541	0.515	0.609	
SIZE	236	9.812	1.916	<	44	10.204	1.304	-1.684	0.096	*
GROWTH	236	7.824	61.220	>	44	0.822	18.288	0.751	0.453	
AGE	236	1.613	0.267	<	44	1.913	0.289	-6.734	0.000	***
AUDIT	236	0.458	0.499	<	44	0.727	0.451	-3.581	0.001	***
DA	236	0.002	0.094	>	44	-0.012	0.053	0.994	0.321	
PROD	235	0.006	0.081	<	44	0.008	0.026	-0.289	0.773	
AQ	236	0.018	0.026	>	44	0.020	0.018	-0.365	0.716	
MAPE	177	0.573	11.170	>	33	0.757	4.074	-0.093	0.926	

Notes: See Table 7.1 for variable definitions. *, ** and *** indicate significance at 0.1 level, 0.5 level and 0.01 level 10 % respectively.

-6.734, -3.581 at 1%, 10%, 1%, and 1% level respectively. I find that company-level material weakness reporting firms have larger *OCFvolatility*, bigger size, younger age, and no BIG 4 auditor. While the differences in firms size and firm age are consistent with Doyle et al. (2007a) but no differences in performance such as ROA is not consistent with Doyle et al. (2007a).

Table 7.4 shows the results for the determinants of accruals quality. Panel A and Panel B show the results from the regression analyses which are put discretionary accruals and abnormal production costs into the regression equation respectively. Both panels show that there accruals quality is negatively associated with material weakness. While accruals quality has a positive association with material weaknesses in Doyle et al. (2007a) and Ashbaugh-Skaife et al. (2008), since company-level material weakness is 1 and account-specific material weakness is 0 in this study, accruals quality has a negative association with material weaknesses.

The coefficient (*t*-value) of discretionary accruals (*DA*) is -0.054(-2.385) and significant at 5% level, suggesting that accruals quality of material weakness firms is associated with accruals management. On the other hand, the coefficient (t-value) of production costs (*PROD*) is -0.012(-0.0731) and insignificant, suggesting that accruals quality of material weakness reporting firms is not associated with real management. Nakashima (2011) finds that accruals quality is not associated with discretionary accruals but is associated with real management. The result in this study shows that earnings management of material weakness reporting firms is accruals management and this is not consistent with the result from SEC-registered

TABLE 7.4　Determinants of Accruals Quality

Panel A	B	t-value	significance		Panel B	B	t-value	significance	
(Constant)	-.035	-2.036	.043	*	(Constant)	-.032	-1.803	.073	*
MW_company_account	-.011	-3.080	.002	***	MW_company_account	-.012	-3.083	.002	***
ΔWC	.082	3.984	.000	***	ΔWC	.042	3.159	.002	***
adjustOCF	-.005	-.658	.511		adjustOCF	-.007	-.863	.389	
adjustDEBT	-.069	-4.873	.000	***	adjustDEBT	-.071	-4.952	.000	***
OCFvolatility	.010	.719	.473		OCFvolatility	.010	.752	.453	
SALESvolatility	-.001	-.080	.936		SALESvolatility	.004	.578	.564	
OC	.010	4.432	.000	***	OC	.010	4.317	.000	***
ROA	.000	.023	.981		ROA	-.001	-.263	.793	
SEGMENT	.002	.596	.552		SEGMENT	.003	.864	.389	
SIZE	.003	3.304	.001	***	SIZE	.003	3.101	.002	***
GROWTH	.000	2.837	.005	***	GROWTH	.000	2.954	.003	***
AGE	-.005	-1.090	.277		AGE	-.005	-1.096	.274	
Audit	-.017	-5.291	.000	***	Audit	-.017	-5.311	.000	***
DA	-.054	-2.385	.018	**	PROD	-.012	-.731	.465	
調整R²=0.349					調整R²=0.337				
F=11.706***					F=11.075***				

Notes: See Table 7.1 for Variable Definitions ;*, **, and *** indicate significance at p< 10 %, p< 5%, p<1%;. t-value is based on White's (1980) standard error. Dependent Varialbe is accruals quality by estimating Francis et al.'s (2008).

Japanese firms in Nakashima (2011). I need to examine whether the accruals management has a manager's opportunism.

While as for company-level material weakness reporting firms, the coefficient (t-value) of *ΔWC*, *DEBT*, *OC*, *GROWTH*, *AUDIT*, and *DA* are 0.085(3.662), -0.071(4.472), 0.011(3.777), 0.000(2.617), -0.012(-3.282) and significant at 1%, for account-level material weakness reporting firms, the coefficient (t-value) of *ΔWC*, *OCFvolatility*, *SALESvolatility*, *SEGMENT*, *SIZE*, *GROWTH*, *AUDIT* and *DA* are 0.071(1.987), -0.037(-1.786), -0.008(-1.817), 0.006(2.420), 0.004(3.258), 0.000(2.076), -0.036(-11.262), -0.044(-1.828) and significant at 1% and 10% respectively.

While for company-level material weakness reporting firms sample, performance, financial position, and growth affect accruals quality, for account-level material weakness reporting firms, business complexities such as segment affects accruals quality, suggesting that this is consistent with the results of Doyle et al.(2007a) .

Table 7.8 shows the correlation. The results report that accruals quality is positively correlated with OC Fvolatility, SALES volatility, operating cycles, segment, growth, loss portion and negatively correlated with firm size, firm age, and audit and suggests that the result is the same result as the regression.

Therefore, since working hypothesis 1 and working hypothesis 2 are supported,

TABLE 7.5 Determinants of Accruals Quality

Company-level	B	t-value	significance		Account-Specific Level	B	t-value	significance	
(Constant)	-.044	-2.203	.029	**	(Constant)	.009	.350	.729	
ΔWC	.085	3.662	.000	***	ΔWC	.071	1.978	.057	*
adjustOCF	-.004	-.476	.635		adjustOCF	-.037	-1.786	.084	*
adjustDEBT	-.071	-4.472	.000	***	adjustDEBT	-.013	-.728	.472	
OCFvolatility	.010	.686	.493		OCFvolatility	-.014	-.534	.597	
SALESvolatility	.004	.526	.600		SALESvolatility	-.008	-1.817	.079	*
OC	.011	3.777	.000	***	OC	.003	1.090	.284	
ROA	-.001	-.428	.669		ROA	-.002	-.617	.542	
SEGMENT	.001	.131	.896		SEGMENT	.006	2.420	.022	**
SIZE	.003	2.436	.016		SIZE	.004	3.258	.003	***
GROWTH	.000	2.617	.009	***	GROWTH	.000	2.076	.047	**
AGE	-.006	-.968	.334		AGE	-.007	-1.442	.160	
Audit	-.012	-3.282	.001	***	Audit	-.036	-11.262	.000	***
DA	-.054	-2.118	.035	**	DA	-.044	-1.828	.078	*
Adjusted R^2=0.321					Adjusted R^2=0.916				
F=9.564***					F=37.034***				

Notes: See Table 7.1 for Variable Definitions ;*, **, and *** indicate significance at p< 10 %, p< 5%, p<1%;. t-value is based on White's (1980) standard error. Devendent variable is accrual quality by estimating Francis et al.'s (2008) model.

TABLE 7.6 Determinants of MAPE

Dependent Variable=MAPE	B	t-value	significance	
(Constant)	1.340	4.066	.000	***
MW_company_account	-.237	-3.294	.001	***
ΔWC	.124	.423	.673	
adjustOCF	.120	.757	.450	
adjustDEBT	.014	.050	.960	
OCFvolatility	-.336	-1.258	.210	
SALESvolatility	.165	1.242	.216	
OC	-.059	-1.281	.202	
ROA	-.026	-.683	.495	
SEGMENT	.077	1.215	.226	
SIZE	-.022	-1.163	.246	
GROWTH	.000	.665	.507	
AGE	-.201	-2.117	.036	**
Audit	-.020	-.309	.758	
AQ	3.271	2.930	.004	***
Adjusted R^2=0.134				
F=3.312				

Notes: See Table 7.1 for Variable Definitions ;*, **, and *** indicate significance at p< 10 %, p< 5%, p<1%;. t-value is based on White's (1980) standard error. Dependent variable is one year ahead operating cash flow by predicting accruals components model.

H1 is supported.

7.5.2 Empirical Results 2: Material Weaknesses and Predictive Errors

Table 7.6 reports that the results from multi-regression which have predictive error as a dependent variable. Table 7.6 reports that the coefficient (*t*-value) is -0.237

TABLE 7.7 Determinants of MAPE

Company-level	B	t-value	significance		Account-Specific Level	B	t-value	significance	
(Constant)	1.152	3.414	.001	***	(Constant)	-1.012	-.433	.670	
ΔWC	.120	.404	.687		ΔWC	-2.676	-.939	.359	
adjustOCF	.119	.744	.458		adjustOCF	-1.386	-.838	.413	
adjustDEBT	.230	.812	.418		adjustDEBT	-2.101	-1.442	.166	
OCFvolatility	-.402	-1.530	.128		OCFvolatility	.245	.109	.914	
SALESvolatility	.098	.695	.488		SALESvolatility	.627	.853	.404	
OC	-.081	-1.629	.105		OC	.110	.546	.591	
ROA	.001	.035	.972		ROA	.020	.067	.947	
SEGMENT	.098	1.323	.188		SEGMENT	-.578	-1.618	.122	
SIZEA	-.017	-.817	.415		SIZEA	-.141	-1.217	.238	
GROWTH	.000	.482	.630		GROWTH	.001	.146	.885	
AGE	-.212	-2.030	.044	*	AGE	.683	1.372	.186	
AUDIT	-.089	-1.312	.191		AUDIT	1.468	2.313	.032	*
AQ	3.935	3.592	.000	***	AQ	23.078	1.560	.135	
AdjustR^2=0.168					AdjustR^2=0.299				
F=3.742***					F=2.048*				

Notes: See Table 7.1 for Variable Definitions ;*, **, and *** indicate significance at p< 10 %, p< 5%, p<1%;. t-value is based on White's (1980) standard error. Dependent variable is one year ahead cash flows by predicting accrual components model.

(-3.294) and significant, suggesting that this supports H2. The results of regression suggest that predictive errors are significantly associated with accruals quality. Therefore, since predictive errors have been affected by accruals quality, it is likely that earnings management reflects opportunism.

7.5.3 Empirical Results 3: Intention of Earnings Management

H2 is to recognize whether managers of material weakness firm have earnings management with opportunism or informativeness. Table 7.6 shows the results of multivariate regression analyses for all material weakness firms. Table 7.6 shows that the coefficient (*t*-value) of accruals quality is 3.271(2.930), suggesting that this supports working hypothesis 2a. I conduct regression analyses by dividing material weakness types into company-level one and account-specific level one in Table 7.7. Table 7.8 reports that while the coefficient (*t*-value) of accruals quality for the company-level material weakness firms sample is 3.935(3.592) and significant at 1% level, suggesting that accruals quality affects predictive ability for future cash flows. It is likely that managers' estimation of material weakness reporting firms reflects errors and earnings management.

Table 7.8 Table 7.9 reports the correlation. In Step 1, I investigate whether there is a significant association between accruals quality and predictive errors. Table 7.8 and Table 7.9 show that accruals quality is correlated with predictive errors

TABLE 7.8 Spearman/Pearson Correlation Matrix (n=280)

	AQ	MAPE	ΔWC	adjustOCF	adjustDEBT	OCFvolatility	SALESvolatility	OC	ROA	SEGMENT	SIZE	GROWTH	AGE	Audit	Lossportion
AQ	1.000	.228**	.321**	-.180**	-.279**	.098	.205**	.296**	-.139*	.141*	-.242**	.197**	-.103	-.397**	.316**
		.001	.000	.003	.000	.102	.001	.000	.020	.018	.000	.001	.084	.000	.000
		***	***	***	***		***	***	**	**	***	***	*	***	***
MAPE	.307**	1.000	.160**	-.034	-.063	-.038	.156*	.102	-.076	.081	-.173*	.089	-.132	-.182**	.201**
	.000		.021	.626	.361	.588	.024	.141	.275	.242	.012	.199	.055	.008	.003
	***		**				**				**		*	***	***
ΔWC	.218**	.156*	1.000	-.095	-.095	.047	.057	.240**	-.122*	.108	-.221**	.143*	-.119*	-.201**	.227**
	.000	.024		.113	.113	.435	.339	.000	.041	.071	.000	.017	.046	.001	.000
	***	**						***	**	*	***	**	**	***	***
adjustOCF	-.310**	-.173*	.046	1.000	.164**	-.493**	-.333**	-.006	.053	-.149*	.367**	-.132*	.043	.297**	-.523**
	.000	.012	.440		.006	.000	.000	.916	.376	.012	.000	.027	.469	.000	.000
	***	**			***	***	***			**	***	**		***	***
adjustDEBT	-.323**	-.070	-.101	.117*	1.000	-.062	-.159**	.067	-.048	.065	.270**	.041	.046	.274**	-.050
	.000	.315	.092	.050		.301	.008	.261	.424	.280	.000	.497	.441	.000	.405
	***			*			***				***			***	
OCFvolatility	.245**	.175**	.071	-.284**	-.186**	1.000	.217**	-.022	.023	.149*	-.272**	.181**	-.116	-.137*	.123*
	.000	.011	.238	.000	.002		.000	.716	.708	.013	.000	.002	.053	.022	.040
	***	**		***	***		***			**	***	***		**	**
SALESvolatility	.239**	.172**	.126*	-.321**	-.090	.224**	1.000	-.063	.286**	.080	-.152*	.108	-.145*	-.329**	.264**
	.000	.013	.035	.000	.131	.000		.292	.000	.182	.011	.072	.015	.000	.000
	***	**	**	***		***			***		**	*	**	***	***
OC	.066	.039	.192**	-.109	-.057	.059	-.122*	1.000	-.559**	.293**	-.401**	-.058	-.164**	-.156**	.075
	.273	.571	.001	.068	.341	.325	.041		.000	.000	.000	.335	.006	.009	.210
	280		***				**		***	***	***		***	***	
ROA	-.156**	-.020	-.131*	.168**	.007	.007	.131*	-.668**	1.000	-.177**	.297**	.076	.065	.087	-.080
	.009	.772	.029	.005	.905	.901	.028	.000		.003	.000	.205	.279	.145	.181
	***		**	***			**	***		***	***				
SEGMENT	.147*	.010	.072	-.137*	.039	.146*	.004	.347**	-.243**	1.000	-.010	.065	.084	.027	.167**
	.014	.881	.232	.022	.520	.014	.947	.000	.000		.867	.281	.160	.652	.005
	***			**		**		***	***						***
SIZE	-.312**	-.172**	-.213**	.427**	.345**	-.369**	-.194**	-.451**	.376**	-.076	1.000	.018	.336**	.575**	-.296**
	.000	.013	.000	.000	.000	.000	.001	.000	.000	.207		.769	.000	.000	.000
	***	**	***	***	***	***	***	***	***				***	***	***
GROWTH	-.006	.068	-.264**	.215**	.131*	.010	-.063	-.185**	.257**	-.038	.162**	1.000	-.034	-.082	.048
	.919	.328	.000	.000	.028	.865	.290	.002	.000	.522	.007		.574	.172	.424
	280		***	***	**			***	***		***					
AGE	-.125*	-.032	-.149*	.086	.288**	-.234**	-.160**	-.319**	.055	.034	.486**	-.006	1.000	.248**	.060
	.036	.650	.013	.150	.000	.000	.007	.000	.355	.575	.000	.919		.000	.318
	***		**		***	***	***	***			***			***	
AUDIT	-.476**	-.186**	-.195**	.370**	.293**	-.265**	-.323**	-.161**	.203**	.030	.592**	.011	.279**	1.000	-.410**
	.000	.007	.001	.000	.000	.000	.000	.007	.001	.613	.000	.856	.000		.000
	***	***	***	***	***	***	***	***	***		***		***		***
Lossportion	.422**	.248**	.231**	-.557**	-.002	.217**	.369**	.023	-.151*	.191**	-.334**	-.162**	.051	-.403**	1
	.000	.000	.000	.000	.969	.000	.000	.699	.011	.001	.000	.007	.399	.000	
	***	***	***	***		***	***		**	***	***	***		***	

Notes: Correlations above (below) the diagonal are Pearson (Spearman) correlations. The bottom number in each is a two-tail p-value. See Table 7.1 for definitions of each variable. ** Significant at 10 percent, ** at 5 percent, and *** at 1 percent levels, respectively.

TABLE 7.9 Correlation

Company-Level		AQ	MAPE	Account-Specific Level		AQ	MAPE
	AQ	1.000	.363**		AQ	1.000	-.095
			.000				.597
			***				
			236				
	MAPE	.283**	1		MAPE	-.174	1
		.000				.334	
		***	177				

Notes: Correlations above (below) the diagonal are Pearson (Spearman) correlations. The bottom number in each is a two-tail p-value. See Table 7.1 for definition of each variable. The second row is t-value following to White (1980). ** Significant at 10 percent, ** at 5 percent, and *** at 1 percent levels, respectively.

TABLE 7.10 Determinants of Accruals Quality

Panel A:

Company-Level	B	t-value	significance		Account-Specific Level	B	t-value	significance	
(Constant)	-.044	-2.203	.029	**	(Constant)	.009	.350	.729	
ΔWC	.085	3.662	.000	***	ΔWC	.071	1.978	.057	*
adjustOCF	-.004	-.476	.635		adjustOCF	-.037	-1.786	.084	*
adjustDEBT	-.071	-4.472	.000	***	adjustDEBT	-.013	-.728	.472	
OCFvolatility	.010	.686	.493		OCFvolatility	-.014	-.534	.597	
SALESvolatility	.004	.526	.600		SALESvolatility	-.008	-1.817	.079	*
OC	.011	3.777	.000	***	OC	.003	1.090	.284	
ROA	-.001	-.428	.669		ROA	-.002	-.617	.542	
SEGMENT	.001	.131	.896		SEGMENT	.006	2.420	.022	**
SIZEA	.003	2.436	.016	**	SIZEA	.004	3.258	.003	***
GROWTH	.000	2.617	.009	***	GROWTH	.000	2.076	.047	*
AGE	-.006	-.968	.334	*	AGE	-.007	-1.442	.160	
AUDIT	-.012	-3.282	.001	***	AUDIT	-.036	-11.262	.000	***
DA	-.054	-2.118	.035	**	DA	-.044	-1.828	.078	*
AdjustR^2=0.321					AdjusteR^2=0.916				
F=9.564***					F=37.039***				

Panel B:

Company-Level	B	t-value	significance		Account-Specific Level	B	t-value	significance	
(Constant)	-.039	.020	.050	*	(Constant)	.005	.029	.851	
ΔWC	.045	.015	.003	***	ΔWC	.044	.036	.230	
adjustOCF	-.006	.009	.533		adjustOCF	-.037	.022	.111	
adjustDEBT	-.074	.016	.000	***	adjustDEBT	-.019	.019	.317	
OCFvolatility	.011	.015	.480		OCFvolatility	-.019	.027	.486	
SALESvolatility	.009	.008	.277		SALESvolatility	-.005	.004	.237	
OC	.010	.003	.000	***	OC	.003	.003	.245	
ROA	-.002	.002	.475		ROA	-.002	.003	.602	
SEGMENT	.002	.004	.650		SEGMENT	.005	.003	.045	**
SIZEA	.003	.001	.025		SIZEA	.004	.001	.005	***
GROWTH	.000	.000	.006	***	GROWTH	.000	.000	.150	
AGE	-.006	.006	.315		AGE	-.005	.005	.306	
AUDITt	-.013	.004	.001	***	AUDIT	-.037	.003	.000	***
PROD	-.013	.018	.483		PROD	-.003	.042	.937	
AdjustR^2=0.309					AdjustR^2=0.907				
F=9.053***					F=33.104***				

Notes: See Table 7.1 for Variable Definitions ;*, **, and *** indicate significance at p< 10 %, p< 5%, p<1%;. t-value is based on White's (1980) standard error. Dependent variable is accruals qualtiy by estimated Francis et al.'s (2008) model.

positively, suggesting that this supports working hypothesis 2a. Thus, both results of a multi-regression and a correlation show that there is a significant association between accruals quality and predictive errors, suggesting that it is likely that earnings management reflects managers' opportunism.

In Step 2, I examine whether earnings management reflects managers' opportunism. Table 7.10 shows results of the multi-regression. Table 7.10 shows that the coefficient (t-value) of discretionary accruals (company-level, account-specific level) are 0.054 (-2.118) and a positive significant association at 5% level, -0.044(-1.828) and a positive significant association at 10% level respectively. These results support the working hypothesis 3b. On the other hand, the coefficient (t-value) of abnormal production costs (company-level, account-specific-level) is -0.013(0.018), -0.003(0.042) and is significant. This suggests that managers seem to use discretionary accruals as their accounting management method.

As Step 3, I discuss the sign of accruals. Table 7.10 shows the regression results. Panel A of Table 7.10 shows that the coefficient (t-value) of accruals (company-level, account-specific level) are 0.085(4.663), 0.071(1.987) and significant at 10% level and significant at 1% level respectively, suggesting that this supports working hypothesis 3c. The result of this analysis supports working hypotheses 2a, 2b and 2c and thus supports Hypothesis 2.

Nakashima (2011) shows that the coefficient (t-value) of accruals is negative and significant at 1%, suggesting that SEC-registered Japanese firms have earnings management which increases accruals quality. However, through the results of this analysis, the sign of accrual is positive, suggesting that earnings management through accruals reduces accruals quality. Based on these results, it seems that material weakness reporting firm managers have accounting management through accruals and decrease accruals quality.

7.6 Conclusion

I provided evidence from Japan by investigating the determinants of material weaknesses and the association between accruals quality and material weaknesses by using a material weakness reporting Japanese firm sample. Next, I examined whether material weaknesses were associated with predictive errors. Third, I discussed whether material weakness reporting firms had managers' opportunism through earnings management.

The followings are my findings: First, I find that business complexity is a determinant of material weaknesses. Second, predictive errors are associated with material weaknesses. Third, it is likely the significant association between predictive errors and accruals quality suggests that managers of material weakness reporting firms have opportunism through accruals management. Nakashima(2011) shows that after the US-SOX period there is not observed earnings management for SEC-registered Japanese firms, suggesting that there is a difference in earnings management between SEC -registered Japanese firms and material weakness reporting firms in public firms in Japan.

My finding suggests that earnings management of material weakness reporting firms in Japan is related to accruals management, not real management, while Nakashima(2011) suggests that SEC-registered Japanese firms managers have no opportunism through accountings management in discretionary accruals. Thus, material weakness reporting firm managers in Japan seem to have opportunism through accruals management, and they have not reached to move to real management as a method of earnings management by J-SOX. The J-SOX has been just enacted in Japan and I predict that material weakness public firms in Japan have focused on organizing internal controls system and have not reached to pay attention to financial reporting quality.

This study has limitations. Since I focus on a material weakness firms sample in this study, I need to compare innate firm characteristics and earnings management of material weakness firms to control firms which do not have material weakness disclosure. Also, although I use material weakness reporting firms which disclose one more material weakness in 2009 and 2010, a comparison of the first few years of this study to future studies will be needed in order to find whether public firms in Japan are getting more familiar with internal control systems by collecting a longer span of material weakness disclosures. Furthermore, although this study applies the Nakashima's (2012) model to the material weakness reporting firm sample, future research is needed to examine whether the Nakashima's (2012) model is generalized by applying this model to various other samples.

Notes:
1. Suda (2000, pp.404-417) discusses empirical studies regarding the association between discretionary accruals and stock value changes as a way to find whether earnings management is opportunistic or informative purpose.
2. There are the mean absolute error (MAE), the mean square error (MSE), the root mean square error (RMSE), and Theil's U other than MAPE. This study employs the MAPE following Loreck and Willinger's (1996) measure of forecast accuracy.

CHAPTER 8

SURVEY ON INTERNAL CONTROLS

8.1 Introduction

The survey on "internal controls and IT" to understand the current status of accounting information systems, including awareness of internal controls for Japanese firms following publication of J-SOX was implemented in September 2012.

The subjects of the survey were public firms in Japan (those from Sections 1 and 2 of the Tokyo Stock Exchange, Sections 1 and 2 of the Osaka Stock Exchange, the Nagoya Stock Exchange, the Fukuoka Stock Exchange, and JASDAQ). The questionnaire survey regarding, was sent to the office of the president of 3,605 companies on September 1, 2012 (with a requested return date of September 28), and 212 effective responses were received.

The questions on this survey were regarding 1) management attitudes; 2) strengthening of internal controls and governance; 3) audits; 4) the environment around financial accounting systems; 5) the organization around financial accounting systems; 6) characteristics of the financial accounting systems; 7) and results from financial accounting systems. Of these, the response to the 2012 survey were able to compare responses to questions about strengthening of internal controls and governance with responses to a 2007 survey (Suda et al. 2011a: Suda et al. 2011b)

The significance of this study is as follows. First, with a decreasing number of firms disclosing deficiencies in their internal controls, it is difficult to determine from public data the current state of internal controls in actual firms as well as management awareness regarding internal controls. In this study, management awareness through this survey was seduced directly. Second, a survey on internal controls and governance was conducted prior to the enactment of the internal controls reporting system in 2007. It was possible to grasp the current state of internal controls and changes in management awareness during the past four years since the system was enacted.

This chapter is organized as follows. In Section two, the content regarding the sample of the survey on internal controls is shown. In section three, the results of the survey in regards to management attitudes of internal controls, and the strengthening of governance, and audit quality are reported. Final section summarizes the results of the survey. This study is an analysis based on survey responses. An empirical analysis using financial data will be conducted at a later date.

8.2 Survey Content and Responses

The distributions of responding firms across stock exchanges and industries are shown in Figures 8.1 and 8.2 respectively. Figure 8.1 shows us that 60% of responding firms in the 2012 survey were listed on the Tokyo Stock Exchange, while 30% were on JASDAQ. In the industry distribution in Figure 8.2, the percentages of firms in the service and trading industries in the 2007 survey were relatively high, while in the 2012 survey, tertiary industries such as retail, telecommunications, and services stand out.

FIGURE 8.1 Stock Exchange Distribution

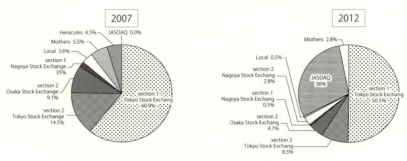

FIGURE 8.2 Industrial Distribution of Sample in 2012

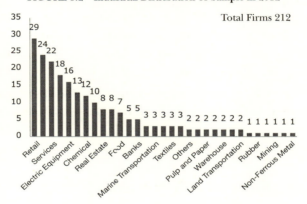

8.3 Survey on Internal Controls

8.3.1 Management Attitudes

Figure 8.3 shows the results from questions 1.1 to 1.3 regarding management attitudes, or the tone at the top (TATT).[1,2] In particular, more than half of the firms provided a response of 6 or higher in regards to question 1.1 dealing with improvements to internal controls and J-SOX compliance, and question 1.3 regarding the importance of numerical targets. I can understand from this that firms are fairly proactive in regards to internal controls, and evaluate themselves favorably. In addition, we see that they are very proactive when it comes to setting numerical management targets for sales and current net income. However, firms

FIGURE 8.3 Management Attitudes (Tone at the Top)

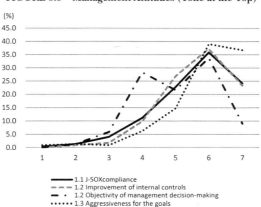

providing a response of 7 in regards to question 1.2, the objectivity of management decision-making, were particularly few in number, which tells us that firms evaluate themselves poorly in this area.

8.3.2 Internal Controls and Strengthening Governance

Next I discuss the results of the 2012 survey in regards to internal controls and strengthening governance. Figure 8.4 shows the results of questions 2.1 and 2.2. The 2007 survey was of U.S. and Japanese firms, and inquired as to the level of contribution to internal controls and strengthening of governance when a direct reporting was implemented in Japanese firms, based on the fact that differences in direct reporting between Japanese and U.S. firms received the most attention. The results of the 2007 survey were mostly the same as those in the 2012 survey. From even after four years since implementing an internal controls reporting system, about one-third of firms responded that a direct reporting corresponds with internal controls and strengthening governance, and this suggests a fairly low level of expectation. I can interpret this to mean that firms to a certain extent think positively of the Japanese system, that does not use a direct reporting. However, because more than 40% of firms answered 4 in response to this question, it may also be that firms do not yet well understand a direct reporting.

In Question 2.2 we inquired as to the function of J-SOX compliance in making

FIGURE 8.4 Effectiveness of a Direct Reporting

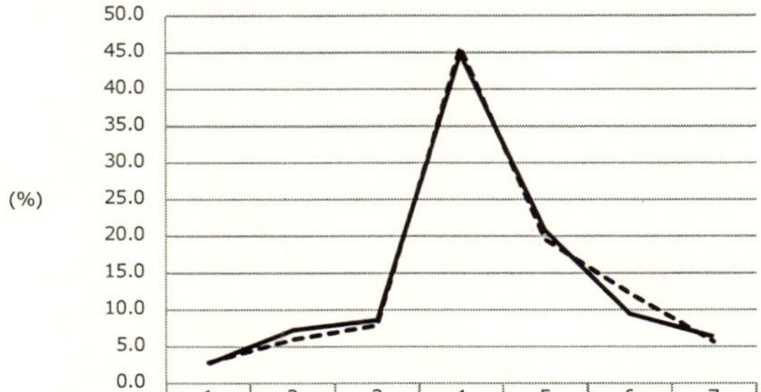

	1	2	3	4	5	6	7
---- 2007	2.8	5.0	7.9	45.7	19.6	12.3	5.7
—— 2012	2.7	7.2	8.6	44.8	20.8	9.5	6.3

internal controls and establishing governance more effective. The results are shown in Figure 8.5, which compares the results for the 2007 and 2012 surveys. More than half of respondents answered 6 or higher in both the 2007 and 2012 surveys for Question 2.2.4 in regards to the expectation of internal controls being effective for financial reporting trustworthiness. This shows that the essential purpose of J-SOX is now clearly understood. Compared with the 2007 survey results, I see from changes in the 2012 survey results an observance with laws and regulations from Question 2.2.5, and the promotion of property preservation in Question 2.2.6. In the results of the 2012 survey, more than 40% of respondents answered with 6 or higher in regards to the expectations of observance of the law. This was higher than before, while in regards to expectations for promoting property preservation, 28% of respondents answered 4, and 30% answered 5, both were somewhat lower than the 2007 survey results. I learn from this that firms expected J-SOX to be effective in protecting property.

The results of the 2012 survey also showed that many firms favorably evaluate compliance with the J-SOX laws enacted in 2008 as effective for internal controls and in strengthening governance, with more than 40% of respondents answering 5 or higher to Question 2.2.1 regarding corporate governance overall, and 2.2.5 regarding property preservation.

8.3.3 Audit Quality

The 2007 survey questionnaire inquired regarding "management views on audit

FIGURE 8.5 The Function of J-SOX in Effective Internal Controls and Governance

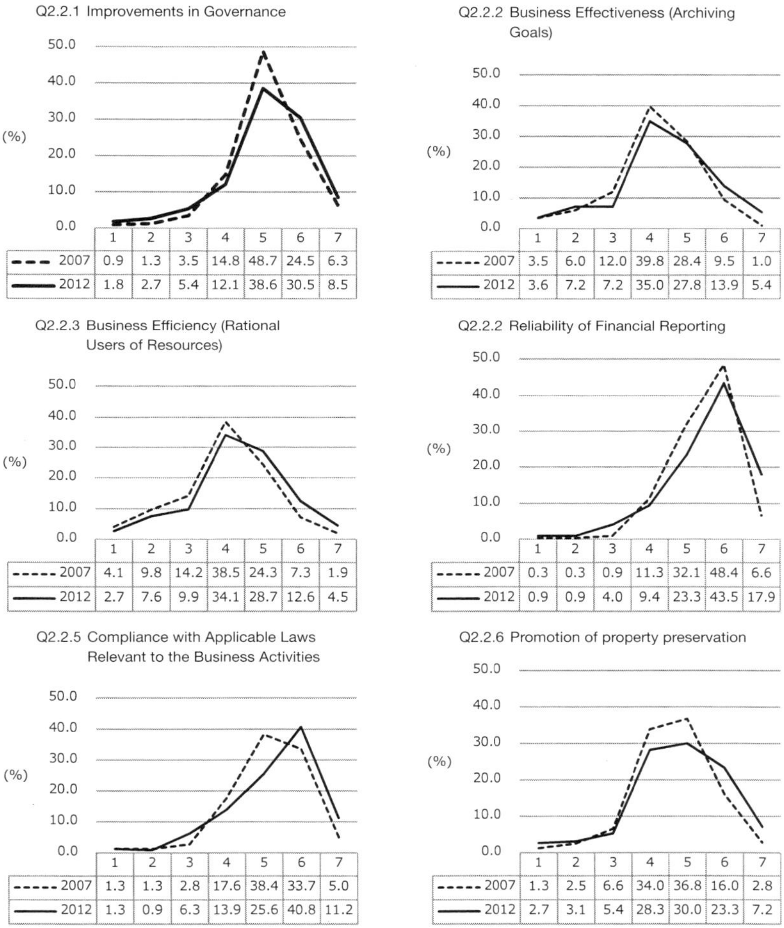

Q2.2.1 Improvements in Governance

	1	2	3	4	5	6	7
2007	0.9	1.3	3.5	14.8	48.7	24.5	6.3
2012	1.8	2.7	5.4	12.1	38.6	30.5	8.5

Q2.2.2 Business Effectiveness (Archiving Goals)

	1	2	3	4	5	6	7
2007	3.5	6.0	12.0	39.8	28.4	9.5	1.0
2012	3.6	7.2	7.2	35.0	27.8	13.9	5.4

Q2.2.3 Business Efficiency (Rational Users of Resources)

	1	2	3	4	5	6	7
2007	4.1	9.8	14.2	38.5	24.3	7.3	1.9
2012	2.7	7.6	9.9	34.1	28.7	12.6	4.5

Q2.2.2 Reliability of Financial Reporting

	1	2	3	4	5	6	7
2007	0.3	0.3	0.9	11.3	32.1	48.4	6.6
2012	0.9	0.9	4.0	9.4	23.3	43.5	17.9

Q2.2.5 Compliance with Applicable Laws Relevant to the Business Activities

	1	2	3	4	5	6	7
2007	1.3	1.3	2.8	17.6	38.4	33.7	5.0
2012	1.3	0.9	6.3	13.9	25.6	40.8	11.2

Q2.2.6 Promotion of property preservation

	1	2	3	4	5	6	7
2007	1.3	2.5	6.6	34.0	36.8	16.0	2.8
2012	2.7	3.1	5.4	28.3	30.0	23.3	7.2

quality", including "audit quality", which was a representative variable with which we could not find a consensus in archival research, and likewise queried regarding "management views on audit quality" in 2012. Figures 8.6 and 8.7 respectively show the quality of financial auditing and the quality of internal controls audits and compare survey results from 2007 and 2012. In regards to the quality of financial audits, nearly half of firms responded with 4 in the 2007 survey, though in 2012 over half of firms responded with 5 or higher. Japanese firms evaluate financial audits

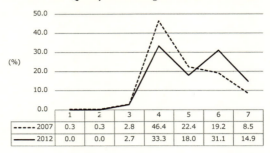

FIGURE 8.6 Quality of Auditing for Finacial Statements

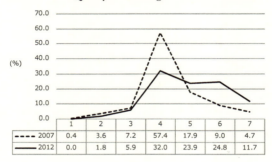

FIGURE 8.7 Quality of Auditing for Internal Controls

more highly now than in 2008.

In regards to the quality of internal controls audits, the fact that more than half of firms responded with a 4 in the results of our 2008 responses showed that evaluation standards had not been identified, thus firms could not assess internal controls audits since the internal controls reporting system had only been put in place in 2008 (Suda et al. 2011a). In the results from the 2012 survey, more than 60% of firms responded with a 5, 6, or 7, which may be seen as a high level of internal controls audits due to experience actually conducting them. This phenomenon also showed itself in Question 3.3, with nearly two-thirds of responses saying current audit times were appropriate, a positive assessment of the current status.

Figure 8.8 shows the results of questions concerning whether audit quality improves with providing audits at the same time as non-audit services. In the results of 2007, more than 30% of firms responded that they did not think quality would

FIGURE 8.8 The Effects of Non-Auditing Services on Quality of Audits and Financial Reporting

	1	2
2007	35.5	64.5
2012	49.5	50.0

FIGURE 8.9 Non-Auditing Services that Increase Quality of Audits and Financial Reporting

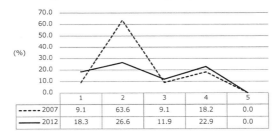

	1	2	3	4	5
2007	9.1	63.6	9.1	18.2	0.0
2012	18.3	26.6	11.9	22.9	0.0

improve, though more than 60% answered that they thought it would improve. However, even in 2012, nearly half of responding firms answered that audit quality would improve, though about half also thought quality would not improve. Thus we see that there are many firms that feel positively in regards to providing audits at the same time, as was confirmed. This is likely a trend specific to Japan.

Figure 8.9 shows the results of our question regarding non-audited services and whether firms think the quality of audits and financial reporting will improve. In regards to these services, a high percentage (26.6%) felt positive towards development of internal controls systems, followed by tax consulting, development of accounting information systems, and internal audits, in that order.

8.4 Conclusion

In this study, I queried public firms regarding attitudes toward internal control among Japanese firms, as well as management thinking regarding audit quality at the point when four years have passed since the enactment of J-SOX. And, I compared the results of the 2012 survey with the results of the 2007 survey (Suda et al. 2011a; Suda et al. 2011b). The results of our analysis brought to light several implications.

First, in regards to management attitudes, I found that management is very proactive towards internal controls, and is extremely proactive towards setting numerical business targets for things like sales and current net income. However, management is somewhat passive in regards to optimism towards their decision-making.

Second, although four years have passed since firms have implemented an internal controls reporting system, firms have low expectations regarding a direct reporting, and somewhat high assessments of the J-SOX, that does not implement a direct reporting. Third, I found a large number of firms that have positive views toward the effectiveness of J-SOX compliance in internal controls and the strengthening of governance. Fourth, in 2012, Japanese firms evaluated audits of financial statements more highly than they did in 2007. In addition, I found that firms gave high marks to the quality of internal controls audits in 2012, having gone through the experience of these audits. I can interpret this as a positive reflection on the current state of internal controls. Fifth, in regards to the relationship between the quality of audits and the simultaneous provision of audits for non-audit services, I see a trend towards a larger number of firms that feel positively towards the simultaneous provision of audits.

APPENDIX
SURVEY ON INTERNAL CONTROLS

<Managers Attitude: Tone at the Top>

1.1. How would you describe the attitude of the CEO in your company with regard to documenting and assessing the effectiveness of the internal control structure and procedures over financial reporting?

Complying with the requirements of J-SOX

Very Negative				Neutral			Highly Positive
1	2	3	4	5	6	7	

Chapter 8 Survey on Internal Controls

Improving internal controls in the company

Very Negative			Neutral			Greatly Positive
1	2	3	4	5	6	7

1.2. If independent and objective third-parties were to judge the ethics of business decisions made by the CEO at your company, what do you think they would say?

Not Objective			Moderately			Highly Objective
1	2	3	4	5	6	7

1.3. How aggressive is the CEO with regard to meeting or exceeding targets, such as sales, net income and/or earnings per share?

Not Aggressive			Moderately			Highly Aggressive
1	2	3	4	5	6	7

<Enforcement of Internal Controls and Governance>

2.1. AS5 requires the auditor to provide an independent opinion on the effectiveness of the firm's internal control over financial reporting. The direct reporting regarding the internal controls by external auditors is required in addition to the financial statements audit by external auditors. To what extent does the direct reporting contribute to improving your internal controls and corporate governance?

Seldom Effective			Neutral			Considerably Effective
1	2	3	4	5	6	7

2.2. To what extent does complying with the requirement of J-SOX contribute to the following?

   1. Improve corporate governance in your firm

Not Effective			Moderately			Highly Effective
1	2	3	4	5	6	7

   2. Improve the effectiveness of operations such as meeting the targets

Not Effective			Moderately			Highly Effective
1	2	3	4	5	6	7

   3. Improve the efficiency of operations, such as rational use of resources

Not Effective			Moderately			Highly Effective
1	2	3	4	5	6	7

   4. Improve the credibility of financial reporting

Not Effective			Moderately			Highly Effective
1	2	3	4	5	6	7

   5. Enforce compliance with the requirements of laws

Not Effective			Moderately			Highly Effective
1	2	3	4	5	6	7

6. Promote the protection of assets

Not Effective			Moderately			Highly Effective
1	2	3	4	5	6	7

<Audit by Audit Firms or CPAs>

3.1. What is the quality of *financial statements audits* by your external auditors?

Extremely Low			Standard			Extremely High
1	2	3	4	5	6	7

3.2. What is the quality of *internal controls audits* by your external auditors?

Very Negative			Standard			Extremely High
1	2	3	4	5	6	7

3.3. Though the provision of specified non-audit services by external auditors to their audit clients contemporaneously have been prohibited in accordance with the enforcement of auditors' independence in the U.S. (Section 201 of SOX-Services Outside the Scope of Practice of Auditors) and in Japan (Certified Public Accountant Act 24(2), April 2004), the SEC does not prohibit external auditors from providing non-audit services such as tax planning and consulting. When an auditor is asked to provide non-audit services in addition to the audit, do you think the quality of audit and financial reports will be enhanced? Please choose your answer 1 or 2. If you choose 2, please specify services below.

    1. The quality is not believed to be enhanced.
    2. The quality is believed to be enhanced. (Plural choices are permissible.)
        a. Development of accounting information system,
        b. Preparation of internal control system,
        c. Internal audit,
        d. Tax planning and consulting, or
        e. Other (   )

Your firm's name	Address of your firm Phone
Your name position ( )	Your email address

Would you mind writing your company name when we publish our paper?	Yes No
Would you mind co-operating with the interview based on this survey results?	Yes No

Notes:
1. Respondents to our survey were from the office of the president and corporate planning. Accordingly, we cannot confirm whether the head of the office of the president responded as a manager himself or herself in regards to "a manager's attitudes" or whether the head of the president office has an awareness of "a manager's attitudes". However, the subjects of this survey are public firms in Japan, and the responses regarding "a manager's attitudes" are viewed as the formal views of the firms.
2. The questionnaires 1.1 through 1.3 are based on those of Hunon et al. (2011).

CHAPTER 9

SUMMARY AND DISCUSSION

9.1 Summary

Chapter nine summarizes this book and shows the contributions, the future research and suggestions. This book provided evidence from Japan regarding whether internal control regulations impact on earnings quality and earnings management. This book is developed in a framework of a financial analysis that earnings quality is impacted by the innate firm characteristics, such as business models and operating environment, and the earnings management factor that affects the financial reporting process is reflected.

In the first half of the book, I examined the impacts of internal controls regulations on financial reporting quality, such as discretionary accruals, accuracy for cash flow prediction, and accruals quality for the SEC-registered Japanese firms comprehensively. In the remainder of this book, I discussed determinants of the internal controls deficiencies for public firms in Japan and analyzed whether earnings management by a manager has opportunism or informativeness. The following are the summaries of each chapter of this book.

Chapter one described the relationship between earnings management and earnings quality. In Chapter 1, why I focused on earning management and earning quality, and an approach of the study.

Chapter two reviewed the previous studies regarding the following: the actual condition of earnings management, the incentive of earnings management, the influence of the relevance of earnings management and governance, the quantitative changes in earnings management by the introduction of internal control regulations, the intention of earnings management, and the trade-off between accruals and real management.

Chapter three examined the changes in earnings management focusing on discretionary accruals as accruals management proxy, and abnormal cash flows and the changes in the incentives and the restraints behind earnings management in the pre-and post-US-SOX. The time-series plot indicated that while accruals management decreased, real management increased slightly in the post-US-SOX. I observed the increases in real management through a regression analysis. I also observed the trade-off between accruals and real management through a multivariate regression analysis. Therefore, capital market motivations were negatively associated with accruals management and positively associated with real management. In addition, I documented the significant impact of bank-oriented governance on decreases in real management after the passage of US-SOX. While stock market motivations drove the shift from accruals management to real management, leverage was likely to affect earning management as governance.

Chapter four examined whether the accuracy of cash flow predictions has been improved in the post-US-SOX period. Following Dechow and Schrand's (2004) assertion that earnings are of high quality if they are more strongly associated with future cash flow realization, I took the accuracy of cash flow predictions as financial reporting quality in chapter four. I examined whether US-SOX affected the ability of earnings to predict future cash flows and found that the predictive ability of the earnings model improved after US-SOX but the predictive ability of the accruals component model did not improve. Also, I documented determinants of the accuracy of cash flow predictions were accruals quality, earnings management.

Chapter five examines the effect of US-SOX on accruals quality as financial reporting quality. Also, I tested some determinants of accruals quality: (1) operational fundamentals, (2) investment in internal controls system, (3) earnings management, and (4) audit quality. I documented that accruals quality based on the Dechow and Dichev's (2002) model improved but accruals quality based on the

Francis et al.'s (2008) model was not been changed by the imposition of US-SOX based on a time-series plot and a mean differences analyses. Also, I documented that operating characteristics such as OCF volatility and sales volatility, business fundamental such as growth, investment in internal controls, and real management were determinants of accruals quality.

Chapter six investigated the type of internal control deficiencies for material weaknesses reporting firms , and the determinants of material weaknesses through a comparison between material weakness reporting firm and control firms. Also, chapter six discussed differences the in accruals quality and earnings management between material weakness reporting firms and control firms. In chapter six, I found that the most frequent material weaknesses were involved with Period End/Accounting Policies as a particular feature of the Japanese public firms. Also, I found that material weaknesses were significantly associated with segment, loss portion, and audit. The more segments, the more loss portion the firms had, and the more material weaknesses they disclosed. In addition, while accruals quality for material weakness reporting firms did not improve, accruals quality for control firms improved.

Chapter seven analized the determinants of material weakness for the firms that disclosed material weaknesses, and the association between material weakness and accruals quality. It also examined whether earnings management of sample firms was accomplished through accruals management. Furthermore, it discussed whether earnings management of sample firms was related to managerial opportunism. I documented that predictive errors were significantly associated with accruals quality and that accruals quality was related to discretionary accruals. It is likely that earnings management of material weakness reporting firms focused on accruals management and that earnings management reflected managerial opportunism.

Chapter eight surveys managers in the public firms in Japan in order to explore of their attitudes toward the internal control in the post of J-SOX. Through the survey results, I imply the following: while the managers are affirmative for setting up their internal controls system and a target for earnings, it seems that manegers evaluate their decision-making as low objective. Also, the public firms in Japan seem to evalate J-SOX that has not adopted a direct reporting. In addition they consider that J-SOX is effective for strengthening the internal controls system and governance.

Furthermore, they evaluate the quality of auditing for the financial statements and internal controls as high.

9.2 Contribution

9.2.1 Comprehensive Empirical Studies on Earnings Management and Earnings Quality

This book documented the impact on earnings quality, such as discretionary accruals, accuracy for cash flow prediction, and accruals quality by internal controls regulation. I documented the changes in accruals management and real management in the pre-and post-US-SOX, and the relationship between the changes in earnings management and determinants such as leverage and stock market motivation, which had not been conducted before.

I documented through evidence of the association between predictive errors and accruals quality that internal control regulations restrained only opportunistic accruals management but kept informative accruals management. I also found through evidence of an association between predictor errors and accruals quality that real management is a kind of opportunistic earnings management. This may be a new insight. In addition, the increases in abnormal productive expenses impacted on accruals quality and accuracy for cash flow predictions negatively.

9.2.2 Meanings of Internal Controls System in Japan

The System of Internal Control Regulation went into effect in Japan for financial reporting with the fiscal years on or after April 1, 2008. Public firms in Japan are required to have an internal control by management and an auditing of the internal control reports by external auditors. Chapters three through five examine whether the internal control regulation improved financial reporting quality in Japan employing SEC-registered Japanese firms' data and suggest that the results can be comparable with the U.S. results.

This book documents that there is a significant association between internal controls and accruals quality. Investors and regulators can judge which innate characteristics of a firm have lower accruals quality. I argued for the importance of organizing better internal controls focusing on accruals quality because accruals quality is one of the criteria judged for investing in a firm. Thus, this study provides evidence regarding the effect of the internal control regulation on financial reporting quality.

9.2.3 Significance of the Intention of Earnings Management

I obtained a way to judge whether a manager's earnings management has opportunism or informativeness by analyzing discretionary accruals, accuracy for cash flow prediction, and accruals quality as proxy for earnings quality in this study. This study provided a way to recognize opportunistic earnings management through the association between predictive errors and earnings management, and the association between accruals quality and earnings management.

An association between predictive errors and earnings management and an association between accruals quality and earnings management should be analyzed simultaneously. If there are both a significant association between predictive errors and earnings management and a significant association between accruals quality and earnings management, there is a great possibility of opportunism in a manager's earnings management.

9.3 Future Research

Although this book investigated financial reporting quality and earnings management impacted by internal control regulations, there are still opportunities for future research. The following items are for future study.

9.3.1 The Impacts of Internal Controls Regulation on Corporate Value

How the changes in earnings management by the introduction of the internal control regulations impacted on corporate value is another task to be discussed in the future. Especially since I found a significant association between accruals quality and real management, how real management impacts corporate value should be examined.

9.3.2 Development of Earnings Management Studies

My study employed debt leverage as a proxy of governance. The shareholding structure should be also considered as governance. The main bank system has been developed as the feature of the original governance structure in Japan, and it is said that they have played a monitoring role to management as well as having a capital relationship. The shareholding by a financial institution and the inner proprietor are effective as a governance (Osano 2005 p.102). The higher stock ratio the investors possess, the more important role they play when they monitor a manager's behavior (Ofek 1993, p.26). I should verify whether the main bank system changed in the pre-and post-internal control regulations using the main bank stock possession ratio and a firm's indebtedness to the main bank as governance.

In Chapter three, accruals management through discretionary accruals was not observed for SEC-registered Japanese firms. I found that there was a difference in earnings management between SEC-registered Japanese firms with no material weaknesses and the Japanese public firms with material weaknesses. There is a high possibility that Japanese public firms did not reach a trade-off between accruals and real management. This study applied the Nakashima's (2012) model to the sample of the firms that disclose a material weakness in order to recognize an intention of a manager's earnings management. I should apply the Nakashima's (2012) model to various samples in order to verify whether the Nakashima's (2012) model can be generalized from now on.

9.3.3 Models for Accruals Quality and Discretionary Accruals

In this book, I employed Francis et al.'s (2008) model for estimating accruals quality that combines Dechow and Dichev's (2002) model and Jones' (1991) model, and Jones' (1991) model for estimating discretionary accruals. I wanted to use the same model, Jones' (1991) model as a portion of AQ estimation model, which I used when I estimate discretionary accruals. The other models estimating discretionary accruals are modified Jones (Dechow et al. 1995) and the CFO modified Jones model (Kasznik 1999). Suda et al. (2007) found that the median of adjusted R-square of the CFO modified Jones model is the greatest among them. The estimation by using the CFO modified Jones model (Kasznik 1999) should be implemented.

Ashbaugh-Skaife et al. (2008) already used a model that a combined Dechow and Dichev's (2002) model and the CFO modified Jones model. I need to verify whether the results from the combined model of Dechow and Dichev's (2002) model and the CFO modified Jones model using data on Japanese firms are consistent with the results in the previous studies.

9.4 Implications and Suggestions

SEC-registered Japanese firms organized their internal controls system resulting in decreasing estimation errors and in restraining accruals management. This suggested that earnings quality improved slightly. On the other hand, there is a possibility that they increased opportunistic real management, such as production expenses. This suggested that earnings quality, such as accuracy of cash flow predictions and accruals quality declines.

The increases in real management affected operating volatility and resulted in lower accruals quality in practice. The quality of earnings, such as accuracy of cash flow predictions and accruals quality, remained unchanged. The SEC states that one of the main goals of the Sarbanes-Oxley Act is to enhance the quality of reporting and increase investor confidence in the financial markets (SEC 2003, V. Cost-Benefit Analysis). Although US-SOX increased accuracy and credibility of financial statements through an enhancement of the internal controls system, it is likely that the improvement of the reporting quality was questionable for SEC-registered Japanese firms.

I will close this book by proposing the following: As Roychoudhury (2006) suggests, real management would affect future performance negatively. Outside stakeholders regard real management as an actual economic activity of a firm. What we researchers can do is to encourage managers to promote self-control for restraining real management and to communicate inside information for an investor's decision-making if they intend to improve financial reporting quality. As

Suda (2007, p. 20) suggests, earnings management includes accruals management through accruals that have an intention of communicating useful information to investors, there is a risk that the strengthened penalty code may affect earnings management with informativeness. This may cause their financial reporting to decline.

A cost-benefit of internal control regulation is often discussed. Managers may avoid disclosing material weaknesses in response to market pressure in Japan. It is significant that we inform the stakeholders that internal controls system introduction is one of opportunities for them to recognize what ethics they should have through organizing their internal control systems. Ideally, we expect managers to manage their firms focusing on informative financial reporting based on their organized internal controls system.

If managers and relevant people recognize that investors and the market watch financial reporting quality, managers naturally will manage their firm through focusing on increased earnings quality improved and restraint of real management. We should enlighten the concepts of financial reporting quality for the public, aiming for a society in which managers and stakeholders focus not only on corporate value but also on financial reporting quality, and in which managers have ethics in their financial reporting and their internal control disclosures.

On the other hand, a comparison in earnings quality between material weakness reporting firms and control firms in Japan indicates that, while earnings quality for control firms improved, earnings quality for material weakness reporting firms remained unchanged. Moreover, a comparison in earnings management between material weakness reporting firms and control firms in Japan indicates that, while earnings management for control firms stayed unchanged, both accruals and real management for material weakness reporting firms increased. While the results of earnings quality are consistent with the U.S. results, the results of earnings management are inconsistent with the U.S. results. It is likely that although the internal control regulations are effective for earnings quality, the regulations may not work well for earnings management as a restraint in Japan. Therefore, in order for the internal control regulations to be more effective, a policy of strengthening governance, such as outside directors and outside internal control auditors, should be implemented.

References

Aoki, M., H.Patrick, and P. Sheard. 1994. The Japanese main bank system: an introductory overview. In M. Aoki and H. Patrick (Eds.). *The Japanese Main Bank System-Its Relevance for Developing Transforming Economics* (pp.1-50). Oxford University Press.

Arikawa, Y., and H. Miyajima. 2007. Relationship Banking in Post-Bubble Japan: Coexistence of Soft-and Hard-Budget Constraints. In Aoki, M., G. Jackson, H. Miyajima (Ed.), *Corporate Governance in Japan* (pp.51-78). Oxford University Press.

Altamuro J. and A. Beatty. 2006. Do internal control reforms improve earnings quality? Working paper.

Ashbaugh-Skaife, H., D.W. Collins, W.R. Kinney, and R. LaFond. 2008. The effect of SOX internal control deficiencies and their remediation on accrual quality. *The Accounting Review*, 83 (1) January: 217-250.

Baber, W.R., P. M. Fairfield, and J. A. Haggard. 1991. The effect of concern about reported income on discretionary spending decisions: the case of research and development. *The Accounting Review*, 66(4):818-829.

Badertscher, B.A. 2011. Overvaluation and the choice of alternative earnings management mechanism. The Accounting Review, 86 (5):1491-1518.

Balsam, S.1998.Discretionary accounting choices and CEO compensation. *Contemporary Accounting Research*, 15 (3): 229-252.

Bartov, E.1993. The timing of asset sales and earnings manipulation. The Accounting Review, 68 (4):840-855.

Basu, S. 1997. The conservatism principle and the asymmetric timeliness of earnings. Journal of Accounting Economics, 24 (1):3-37.

Beasley, M.S., J.V. Carcello, and D. R. Haemanson. 1999. Fraudulent financial reporting: 1987-1997- An Analysis of U.S. Public Companies-the Committee of Sponsoring Organization of

Treadway Commission (COSO).

Becker, C., M. DeFond, J. Jiambalvo, and K.R. Subramanyam. 1998. The effect of audit quality on earnings management.*Contemporary Accounting Research,* 15 (1):1-24.

Bedard, J. 2006. Sarbanes Oxley internal control requirements and earnings quality. Working paper.

Bedard, J. 2006. Sarbanes Oxley internal control requirements and earnings quality. Working paper.

http://www.nysscpa.org/cpajournal/2005/1105/essentials/p32.htm

Bissessur, S. 2008. *Earnings Quality and Earnings Management The Role of Accounting Accruals,* VDM Verlag Dr.Muller

Browna, N.C., C. Pottb., and A. Wompenerc. 2014. The effect of internal control and risk management regulation on earnings quality: Evidence from Germany. *Journal of Accounting and Public Policy,* 33(1): 1–31.

Burgstahler, D and I. Dichev. 1997. Earnings management to avoid earnings decreases and losses, *Journal of Accounting and Economics,* 24 (1): 99-126.

Burnett. B.M., B. M. Cripe, G.W. Martin, and B.P. McAllister. 2012. Audit quality and the trade-off between accretive stock repurchases and accruals-based earnings management. *The Accounting Review,* 87 (6): 1861-1884.

Bushee, B. 1998. The influence of institutional investors on myopic R&D investment behavior. *The Accounting Review,* 73(3): 305-333.

Business Accounting Council (BAC). 2006. *Practice Standards for Management Assessment and Audit concerning Internal Control over Financial Reporting.*

Business Accounting Council (BAC). 2007. *On the Setting of the Standards for Management Assessment and Audit concerning Internal Control over Financial Reporting (Council Opinions).*

Chen, T., Z. Gu., K. Kubota, and H. Takehara. 2014. Accruals based and real activities based earnings management behavior of family firms in Japan. *The 2014 Annual Meeting of American Accounting Association* (in Atlanta).

Chi, W., L. L. Lisic, M. Pevzner. 2011. Is enhanced auidt quality associateed with greater real earnings management? *Accounting Horizons,* 25 (2):315-335.

Coffee, J. C. 1999. The future as history: The prospects for global convergence in corporate governance and its implications. *Northwestern Law Review,* 93 (3): 641-708.

Cohen, D.A, A. Dey, and T. Z. Lys. 2008. Real and Accrual-based earnings management in the Pre- and Post-Sarbanes Oxley period. *The Accounting Review,* 83 (3): 757-787.

Cohen, D.A. and P. Zarowin. 2010. Accrual-based and real earnings management activities around seasoned equity offerings. *Journal of Accounting and Economics,* 50(1): 2-19.

Comiskey, E.E. and C.W. Mulford. 2000. *Guide to Financial Reporting and Analysis.* Wiley.

Committee of Sponsoring of the Treadway Commission (COSO). 2005. Guidance On Internal Controls for SMEs.

DeAngelo, L.1986. Accounting numbers as market valuation substitutes: A study of management buyouts of public stockholders. *The Accounting Review,* 61(3): 400-420.

Dechow, P. M.1994. Accounting earnings and cash flows as measures of firm performance The role of accounting accruals. *Journal of Accounting and Economics,* 18 (1): 3-42.

Dechow, P.M. and I. Dichev. 2002.The quality of Accruals and Earnings: The role of accrual estimation errors. *The Accounting Review,* 77:35-59.

Dechow, P.M. and W. Ge. 2006. The persistence of earnings and cash flows and the role of special items: Implications for the accruals anomaly. *The Review of Accounting Studies,* 11(2/3): 253-296.

Dechow, P. M., S. P. Kothari, and R. L. Watts. 1998. The relation between earnings and cash flows. *Journal of Accounting and Economics,* 25: 133-168.

Dechow, P. M. and C. M. Schrand. 2004. *Earnings Quality,* The Research Foundation of CFA Institute.

Dechow, P. M.and D. J.Skinner. 2000. Earnings management: reconciling the views of accounting academics, practitioners, and regulators. *Accounting Horizons.* 14(2):235-250.

Dechow, P. M. and R. G. Sloan, and A. P. Sweeney. 1995. Detecting earnings management. *The Accounting Review,* 70 (2):193-225.

Dechow, P. M., R. G. Sloan, and A. P. Sweeney. 1996. Causes and consequences of earnings manipulation: An analysis of firms subject to enforcement actions by the SEC. *Contemporary Accounting Research,* 13 (1):1-36.

Doyle, J., W. Ge, and S. McVay. 2007. Accruals quality and internal control over financial reporting. *The Accounting Review,* 82(5):1141-1170.

Doyle, J., W. Ge, and S. McVay. 2007b. Determinants of weaknesses in internal control over financial reporting. *Journal of Accounting and Economic*s, 44:193-223.

Ebihara, T. 2004. An analyses of the ability of future cash flow prediction as a measure of quality of earnings-the effect of accrual quality-, *Sango Keiri,* 36: 53-69.(in Japanese).

Ebihara,T. 2005. The effect of accruals estimation errors on the quality of earnings, *Accounting Progress,* 6: 71-85.(in Japanese).

Enomoto, M., F. Kimura, and T.Yamaguchi. 2013. Accruals-based and real earings managemnt: An international comparison for investor protection. *Discussion Paper Series Research Institute of Economics and Business Administarction.*

Epps, R.W. and C.P. Guthrie. 2010. Sa:banes-Oxley 404 material weaknesses and discretionary accruals. *Accounting Forum,* 34 (2): 67-75.

Ewert, R. and A.Wagenhofer. 2005. Economic effects of tightening accounting standards to restrict earnings management. *The Accounting Review,* 80(4): 1101-1124.

Federal Deposit Insurance Corporation (FDIC).1991. Federal Deposit Insurance Corporation Improvement Act of 1991(FDICIA).

Financial Accounting Standards Board (FASB).2010. Concepts Statement No.8-Conceptual Framework for Financial Reporting-Chapter 1, *The Objective of General Purpose Financial Reporting,* and Chapter 3, *Qualitative Characteristics of Useful Financial Information* (A Replacement of FASB Concepts Statement No.1 and No.2).

Financial Service Agency (FSA). 2007 *Provisional Translation of On the Setting of the Standards and Practice Standards for Management Assessment and Audit concerning Internal Control Over Financial Reporting (Council Opinions).* Business Accounting Council. February 15. Provisional translation.
http://www.fsa.go.jp/en/news/2007/20070420.pdf

Francis, J., R. LaFond, P. Olsson, K. Schipper. 2004. Costs of equity and accruals attributes. *The Accounting Review,* 79 (4): 967-1010.

Francis, J., R. LaFond, P. Olsson, K. Schipper. 2005. The market pricing of accruals quality. *Journal of Accounting and Economics,* 39: 295-327.

References

Francis, J., R. LaFond, P. Olsson, K. Schipper. 2008. *Earnings quality,* now Publishers, (Eds.). 2006. *Foundations and Trends in Accounting,* 1(4):259-340.

Ge, W. and S. McVay, 2005. The disclosure of material weaknesses in internal control after the Sarbanes-Oxley Act. *Accounting Horizons,* 19(3): 137-158.

Geiger, M. A. and P. L. Taylor. 2003. CEO and CFO certifications of financial information. *Accounting Horizons,* 17(4): 357-368.

Graham, J.R., C. R. Harvey, and S. Rajgopal. 2005. The economic implications of corporate financial reporting. *Journal of Accounting and Economics,* 40 (1-3): 3-73.

Gunny, K.A. 2010. The relation between earnings management using real activities manipulation and future performance: Evidence from meeting earnings benchmarks. *Contemporary Accounting Research,* 27(3): 855-888.

Hunton, J.E., R. Hoitash, and J.C. Thibodeau, 2011. The relationship between perceived tone at the top and earnings quality. *Contemporary Accounting Research,* 28(4): 1190-1224.

Ito, T., H. Patrick. and D. E. Weinstein. 2005. Reviving Japan's Economy Problems and Prescriptions. The MIT Press.

Jones, J. 1991. Earnings management during import relief investigations. *Journal of Accounting Research,* 29 (2):193-228.

Kansanin・Kansahoshu Mondai Kenkyukai. 2008. *Jojokigyo Kansanin・Kansahoshu Hakusho.* The Japanese Institute of Certified Public Accountants Publishing.

Kasznik, R. 1999. On the association between voluntary disclosure and earnings management. *Journal of Accounting Research,* 37(1):57-81.

Kimura, F., Tatsuji, Y. and Naoki, T. 2007. Kigyo no shikin chotatsu to kaikei sousa. In K.Suda, T. Yamamoto, Shota Otomasa (Eds.), *Kaikei Sosa* (pp.109-146),Diamond sha.(in Japanese).

Kimura. F. 2004. Keieisha no sairyokodo ni taisuru eikyo yoin, *Discussion Papers in Economics,* 393, Society of Economics Nagoya City University.

Krishnan, J. 2005. Audit committee quality and internal control: An empirical analysis. *The Accounting Review,* 80 (2):649-675.

Kurokawa Y. 2008. The quality of earnings and the quality of capital markets. In M. Yano (Eds.). *The Japanese Economy-A Market Quality Perspective* (pp. 195-216). Keio University Press.

Leggett, D. 2008. Earnings persistence pre-and post-Sarbanes-Oxley. Working paper, *The 2008 AAA Southeastern Regional Meeting* (in Alabama).

Leuz, C., D. Nanda, and P. D.Wysocki. 2003. Earnings management and investor protection: an international comparison. *Journal of Financial Economics,* 69 (3):505-527.

Levitt, A. 1998. *The "number game."* U.S. Securities and Exchange Commission, NYC Center for Law and Business, New York, New York City.

Levitt, A. 1999. *Quality information: the lifeblood of our markets.* U.S. Securities And Exchange Commission, The Economic Club of New York, New York City.

Li, H., P. Morton, and S. O. Rego. 2008. Market reaction to events surrounding the Sarbanes-Oxley Act of 2002 and earnings management. *Journal of Law and Economics,* 51(1): 111-134.

Lobo,G. J. and J. Zhou. 2006. Did conservatism in financial reporting increase after the Sarbanes-Oxley Act? Initial evidence. *Accounting Horizons,* 20 (1): 57-73.

Lorek, K..S. and G. L. Willinger. 1996. A multivariate time-series prediction model for cash-flow data. *The Accounting Review,* 71(1):81-101.

Machuga, S., and K. Tietel. 2007.The effects of the Mexican corporate governance code on quality of earnings and its components. *Journal of International Accounting Research*, 6 (1): 37-55.

McNichols, M. F. 2002. Discussion of the quality of accruals and earnings: The role of accruals and earnings. *The Accounting Review*, 77:61-69.

Mulford, C.W. and E. E. Comiskey. 2002. *The Financial Number*. Wiley.

Nagy, A.L. 2010. Section 404 Compliance and Financial Reporting Quality, *Accounting Horizons*, 24 (3):441-454.

Nakashima. M. 2010. Does the Sarbanes-Oxley Act Have an Impact on the Ability of Earnings to Predict Cash Flows?-An Empirical Analyses of SEC-registered Japanese firms- *Nenpo Business Analyses*, 26: 62-73. (in Japanese).

Nakashima. M. 2011. *Earnings Quality and Corporate Governance-Theory and Empirical Research*. Hakutoshobo. (in Japanese).

Nakashima. M. 2012. Do the material weakness firms have opportunistic earnings mangement?: Evidence from Japan- *Nenpo Business Analyses*, 28: 21-36. (in Japanese).

Nakashima. M. 2013. The impact of internal controls regulation on earnings quality and earnings management: Evidence from Japan, *Nenpo Business Analyses*, 29: 37-46. (in Japanese).

Nakashima. M. 2014. Earnings quality and internal controls: Evidence from Japan. In the Committee for the Internationalization of Research, Business Analysis Association (Ed.), An Analysis of Japanese Management Style, Business and Accounting for Business Researchers (pp.183-212). Maruzen Planet.

National Commission on Fraudulent Financial reporting (NCFFR), 1987. *Report of the National Commission on Fraudulent Financial Reporting* October.
http://www.coso.org/Publications/NCFFR.pdf

Netter, J. M.H. Kutner, C.J. Nachtsheim, and W.Wasserman. 1996. *Applied Linear Statistical Model*. WCB/McGraw-Hill.

Nihon Keizai Shinbun. 2006. *Shinbun, Hitach, Kubota, and NEC disclosed material* weakness, Nihon Keizai Shinbun Sha.

Ofek, E. 1993. Capital structure and firm response to poor performance: An empirical analysis, *Journal of Financial Economics*, 34(1):3-30.

Okuda, S., T. Sasaki, M.Nakashima and R.Nakamura. 2012 The determinants of internal control system and audit quality, *Kigyokaikei*, 64(10):102-108, Chuokeizaisha (in Japanese).

Osano, H. 2005. *Economics of Corporate Governance*, Nihon Keizai Shinbunsha (in Japanese).

Pan, C.K. 2009. Japanese firms' real activities earnings management to avoid losses. *The Journal of Management Accounting*, 17(1):3-28.

Palepu , K. L., P. Healy, and V. Bernard. 2000. *Business Analysis and Valuation*. New York, NY: McGraw-Hill/Irwin.

Patrick, H. 1994. The relevance of Japanese finance and its main bank system. In Aoki and Patrick (Eds.), *The Japanese Main Bank System-Its Relevance for Developing Transforming Economics* (pp. 353- 408).Oxford University Press.

Public Company Accounting Oversight Board (PCAOB).2004. Auditing Standard No.2-*An Audit of Internal Control Over Financial Reporting Performed in Conjunction with an Audit of Financial Statements*.

Public Company Accounting Oversight Board (PCAOB). 2007. Auditing Standard No.5- *Auditing Standard No.5-An Audit of Internal Control Over Financial Reporting That Is Integrated with An Audit of Financial Statements*. PCAOB Release 2007-005A.

References

Ramos, M. 2004. Section 404 compliance in the annual report. *Journal of Accountancy*, 198(4):43-48.

Richardson, S.A., A.I. Tuna, and M. Wu. 2002. Predicting earnings management: The case of earnings restatements. Working paper.

Richardson, S.A. 2003. Earnings quality and short sellers. *Accounting Horizons*, 17:49-61, Supplement.

Richardson, S.A., R.G. Sloan, M.T. Soliman, and I. Tuna. 2005. Accrual reliability, earnings persistence and stock prices. *Journal of Accounting and Economics*, 39 (3): 437-485.

Roychowdhury, S. 2006. Earnings management though real activities manipulation. *Journal of Accounting and Economics*, 42 (3):335-370.

Sasaki, T. K. Suzuki, K.Susuki and K. Suda 2006. Relation between audit quality and internal Control: evidence from Japanese companies. *Special Research Committee*, 89-119. (in Japanese)

Schipper, K. 1989. Commentary on earnings management. *Accounting Horizons*, 3(4):91-102.

Schipper. K. and L.Vincent. 2003. Commentary on earnings quality. *Accounting Horizons*, 17: 97-110.

Scott, W. 2006. *Financial Accounting Theory*. (4th ed.). Person Prentice-Hall.

Securities and Exchange Commission (SEC).2003. *Final rule: Management's Reports on Internal Control over Financial Reporting and Certification of Disclosure in Exchange Act Periodic Reports*. Release Nos.33-8238; 34-4747986. June 5 Washington, D.C.

Shuto A. 2010. *Earnings Management: Theory and Emprical Evidence from Japan*, Chuo Keizaisha. (in Japanese).

Subramanyam, K. R. 1996. The pricing of discretionary accruals. *Journal of Accounting and Economics* 22(1-3): 249-281.

Suda, K. 2000. *Positive Theory of Financial Accounting*. Hakuto Shobo (in Japanese).

Suda, K. 2007. Funshoku-kessan to Kaikeisosa no Shoso. In Suda, K.,T.Yamamoto, and S.Otomasa (Eds.), *Accounting Manipulation* (pp.2-58). Diamond Sha. (in Japanses).

Suda, K. and H.Hanaeda. 2008. Corporate financial reporting strategy: survey evidence from Japanese firms. *Securities Analyst Journal*, 46: 51-69. (in Japanese).

Suda, K. and T. Sasaki. 2008. *Kaikei Seido no Sekkei*. Hakuto Shobo. (in Japanese).

Suda, K., T. Sasaki, M. Nakashima, and S. Okuda. 2011a. *Kaikei*, 179 (6):122-138, Moriyama Shoten. (in Japanese).

Suda, K., T. Sasaki M. Nakashima and S. Okuda. 2011b. A comparison of internal control and governance systems between Japan and the U.S. (2). *Kaikei*, 180(1): 116-129, Moriyamashoten. (in Japanese).

Suda, K. and A.Shuto, 2008. Earnings management to meet earnings benchmarks: Evidence from Japan. In M. H. Neelan (Ed.) *Focus on Finance and Accounting Research*, 67-85. Nova Science Publisher, Inc., New York.

Suda, K, T. Yamamoto, and S.Otomasa (Ed.). 2007. *Accounting Manipulation* Diamond Sha (in Japanese).

Tazawa, M. 2004. The quality of accruals and the prediction of future cash flows in Japan, *Contemporary Disclosure Research*, 5:11-22.(in Japanese).

Thomas, J.K. and H.Zhang. 2002. Inventory changes and future returns, *Review of Accounting Studies*, 7(1): 63-187.

United States General Accounting Office (G.A.O). 2002. *Report to the Chairman, Committee on Banking, Housing, and Urban Affairs, U.S. Senate, Financial Statement Restatements Trends, Market Impacts, Regulatory Responses and Remaining Challenges*. October.

U.S. House of Representatives. 2002. The Sarbanes-Oxley Act of 2002. Public Law 107-204 [H.R. 3763].

  Washington D.C. Government Printing Office.
Watt, R. L. and J. L. Zimmerman.1986. *Positive Accounting Theory.* New York, NY: Prentice Hall.
White, H. 1980. A heteroskedasticity-Consistent covariance matrix estimator and a direct test for heteroskedasticity. *Econometrica,* 48 (4):817-838.
Yoshida, K. 2002. Accruals and the prediction of future cash flows in Japan? *Contemporary Disclosure Research,* 3:1-13.(in Japanese).
Yoshida, K. 2005. Do earnings drive firm-level stock returns in Japan? *Accounting Progress,* 6: 59-70. (in Japanese).
Yamaguchi T. 2009. Opportunistic real discretion and future operating performance, *Accoounting Progress,* 19(1):117-137.(in Japanese).
Yamaguchi T. 2011. Determinants of real discretionary behavior. *The Japanese Association of Management Accounting,* 19(1):57-76.(in Japanese).
Zang, A. Y. 2012. Evidence on the trade-off beween real activities manipulation and accruals-based earnings management. *The Accounting Review,* 87(2):675-703.

About the Author

Masumi Nakashima is a Professor of Accountancy in the Graduate School of Accounting and Finance at the Chiba University of Commerce, where she teaches Financial Accounting I and II, the U.S. GAAP Accounting, Case Study for Financial Accounting, and Seminar. She also teaches accounting at the undergraduate level and corporate accounting at the graduate level at the Meiji University as an adjunct lecturer. She has been teaching Japanese Culture courses at Converse Collage in South Carolina, the U.S. since 2005. She held faculty positions at Fukushima College after she received a doctoral degree in 2010. Her research interests are how internal controls, governance, and audit quality impact on earnings management and earnings quality. She has published her research in journals such as the *Journal of Business Analysis Association and Managerial Auditing Journal.* She published her book titled *Earnings Quality and Corporate Governance* in 2011. She continues to provide an empirical analysis of internal controls and governance from Japan to the world. Professor Nakashima was appointed as a board director of Asia-Pacific Management Accounting Association (APMAA) and an editor of the APMAA Newsletter, and she serves as an ad hoc reviewer and a discussant for American Accounting Association, a discussant for Asian Academic Accounting Association, and Asia Pacific Interdisciplinary Research in Accounting Conference and the APMAA. She holds a Bachelor's of English Literature degree from the Kinjo Gakuin University and an MBA and Ph.D. from Nanzan University.

■ Earnings Management and Earnings Quality
  : Evidence from Japan   〈検印省略〉

■発行日──2015年3月10日　初版発行

■著　者──中島真澄
　　　　　　なかしま ますみ

■発行者──大矢栄一郎

■発行所──株式会社　白桃書房
　　　　　　　　　　　　はくとうしょぼう
　　　　　　〒101-0021　東京都千代田区外神田5-1-15
　　　　　　☎03-3836-4781　📠03-3836-9370　振替00100-4-20192
　　　　　　http://www.hakutou.co.jp/

■印刷・製本──藤原印刷
　　　　　　Ⓒ Masumi Nakashima 2015　Printed in Japan　ISBN978-4-561-36210-4 C3034

　　　　　JCOPY 〈(社)出版者著作権管理機構　委託出版物〉
　　　　　本書の無断複写は著作権法上での例外を除き禁じられています。複写される場合は，
　　　　　そのつど事前に，(社)出版者著作権管理機構（電話03-3513-6969，FAX03-3513-6979，
　　　　　e-mail : info@jcopy.or.jp）の許諾を得てください。
　　　　　落丁本・乱丁本はおとりかえいたします。